Wave Length

by

Gary Beck

ISBN: 978-93-90202-28-7

First Edition: 2020
Rs. 1000/-

Cyberwit.net
HIG 45 Kaushambi Kunj, Kalindipuram
Allahabad - 211011 (U.P.) India
http://www.cyberwit.net
Tel: +(91) 9415091004 +(91) (532) 2552257
E-mail: info@cyberwit.net

Printed at Repro India Limited.

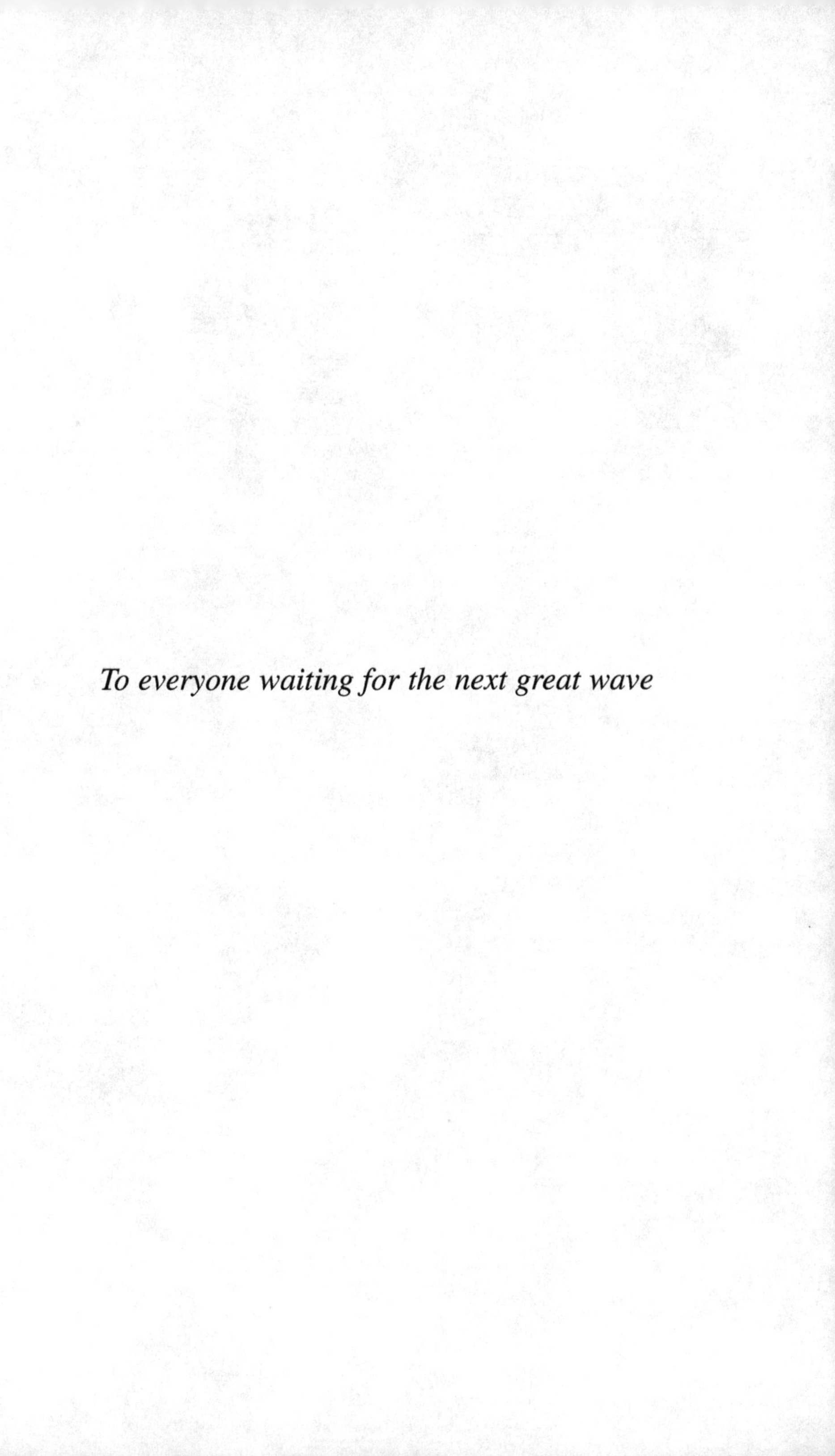

To everyone waiting for the next great wave

Chapter 1

Mike Sanchez grew up in Chula Vista, California, a coastal city between San Diego and Tijuana, Mexico. His mother, Maria Sanchez, an illegal, met his father, a gringo, in 1996. She attracted him enough to be invited to move into his dilapidated trailer on the outskirts of the city. He departed soon after, leaving her with the trailer, an embryo that he helped conceive but didn't stick around to receive, and no last name. Do Mike's became Sanchez. Various men stayed with Maria for various lengths of time and none of them cared to have a kid underfoot.

There weren't many Mexican children in the trailer camp, so despite Mike's blond hair, blue eyes and fair complexion, he was bullied and oppressed by the older boys. The same thing happened when he attended school after the kids learned his last name was Sanchez. Even the girls were cruel, calling him Miguel, instead of Michael. But he learned how to fight and the boys gradually learned to pick on easier victims, of which there was always an abundance, courtesy of the poorly managed American educational system that allowed bullying.

By the time he was 8, his third grade classmates no longer bothered him, but he made no friends. One day he found an old bicycle under the trailer and begged some money from Maria's current man, who was glad to give a couple of bucks to get rid of the kid. So Mike got the parts he needed to get it working again. He started going to Imperial Beach where he watched the surfers with fascination. Everything they did seemed cool, clean and marvelous. The thought of cutting through the waves on a surfboard began to obsess him. He thought about it during the day and dreamed about it during the night, at least when Maria and her man were quiet enough to let him sleep.

He knew that surfing cost money and his ramshackle bike wouldn't last long, so when he was 9 years old he got a job delivering newspapers,

The Chula Vista Chronicle. He had to get up at 5:00 a.m. to get to the distribution office, fold his papers, deliver them to the widespread route and get to school by 8:00 a.m. The first few weeks the older boys bullied him and messed his papers. He fought each time and they finally left him alone, but he never made friends. He was used to being alone and assumed that's the way it would be. He earned enough money to get a used but functional bike and stored the junker under the trailer, in case of emergency.

Mike had to spend most of his money on food, since there never seemed to be anything but beer in the trailer. By the time he finished the 4th grade and summer began, he had enough cash to buy a styrofoam surfboard and he headed for the beach. He couldn't afford a wetsuit, but his first launching of the board, despite his raggedy bathing suit, as well as mocking comments from other kids, was thrilling. The excitement didn't last long. No matter how hard he tried he couldn't stand up on the board without falling off. He tried every day during the summer and no one admired his perseverance, or offered help. The last day before school started a nasty older boy broke his board, then knocked him down when he objected.

The fifth grade was pretty much the same as the fourth. Nobody teased him anymore, but he made no friends. The only difference was he had grown bigger and taller during the summer and developed a little bit of self-confidence. It did bother him that he was never invited to classmate's parties and was thus unexposed to the pre-sexual explorations, gay or straight. But he accepted this as condition normal. He had his newspaper route, which earned him enough money to eat heartily, if not healthily. Some of his customers got to know him and started tipping him when he collected the weekly bill. This allowed him to save a little money each week, which he hid under the trailer.

He hung out at the beach almost every day after school and on the weekends. He kept to himself and the local surfer clique gradually got used to his presence and ignored him. They were older boys who were competent surfers. He didn't know enough to judge their skills, but he began to recognize that some surfed better than others. He studied their techniques and imitated them when no one was looking. He taught himself to swim and when he became good enough to swim out beyond where the waves broke, he would watch the surfers every move, until he got tired and returned to shore.

By the time school ended for the year, Mike realized he didn't care much for the educational system. Except computer learning. He seemed to have a natural feel for using a computer and one of his fantasies was to have his own laptop. Everything else they tried to teach him seemed meaningless in his world. The white kids seemed to belong, but they wouldn't accept him. The Mexican kids were outsiders and hated him for looking white. The black kids tried to stay invisible, because the Mexican kids took out their frustrations and hostilities on them. The teachers droned on about how all men were equal and had equal opportunity. But they never seemed to see the constant bullying that went on. Most of the white kids seemed to believe the lofty ideals, probably because they were well off.

Chapter 2

As his savings grew closer to the price of a new surfboard he started going into a small surf shop named Wave Length, a block from the beach and looking at boards. The owner was an older guy named Cliff, still tanned and fit at age 30, who used to be a champion surfer. He was friendly, but laid back and never asked Mike if he could help him. This suited Mike, because he had no idea what he was looking for. All the boards, regardless of size or color, seemed wonderful. A few days after the Fourth of July, he thought he had enough to finally buy a board. When he went under the trailer to get his savings they were gone. He rushed into the trailer and confronted Maria's latest man, a nasty, mean, ex-con drug user, Jimmy Q, who had gotten Maria hooked on heroin. When Mike accused him of stealing his money, he punched Mike in the face, knocking him down. Mike jumped up, ran at him and punched him. Jimmy Q. pulled out a knife and growled:

"Get the fuck out of here, kid, and don't come back. If you do I'll cut you good."

So Mike, 10½ years old, was suddenly on his own. Fortunately, Jimmy Q didn't break his bike so he was able to keep his paper route which gave him food money. He slept in an isolated area on the beach, got up at sunrise, delivered his papers, then went back to the beach where he studied the surfers. He began to notice the girls who hung around with the surfers, wearing tiny bikinis and thongs that amply displayed their firm looking flesh. He began to dream at night about almost naked girls, even though he didn't know what to do with them, as well as surfing.

It was almost impossible to save any money now that he was on his own. After he bought food and the few necessities, he could only put away a dollar or two a week, which he hid in a jar that he buried on the beach. Even though a surfboard was a long way off, he still went to the surf shop every day and gazed longingly at the boards. One afternoon Cliff surprised him by talking to him.

"You've been coming here for quite a while now. Are you a surfer?"

"No, sir. I want to learn."

"Do you have money for lessons? A board?"

"No, sir."

"Then how do you expect to learn?"

"I was saving for a board, but somebody stole my money."

"Where do you live, kid?"

Mike just gestured vaguely east.

"I surf at night, kid. I've seen you sleeping on the beach."

Mike started to deny it, then just shrugged.

"Are you honest?"

"Yes, sir."

"I know people who own the marina. I'll ask them if you can sleep in one of the abandoned boats. It'll be too cold to sleep on the beach soon."

"Thank you, sir. Would you give me a job?"

"Did you ever work before?"

"I've been delivering the Chula Vista Chronicle every morning for a year and a half now."

"What can you do?"

"Anything you ask. Try me."

"Well you're certainly willing. I just don't make enough money to hire someone."

"I'll work for lessons."

Cliff stared at him appraisingly.

"I don't know."

"Try me for two weeks. If you're satisfied, let me work here."

Cliff grinned. "You're sure persistent. When can you start?"

"Right now. Tonight. Tomorrow. Whenever you want."

"Alright. How about tomorrow morning? I open at eight. Come in then. I'll show you around. We'll get acquainted and find out what you can do."

"Thanks, Mr. Cliff. You won't be sorry."

"Just Cliff. See you in the morning."

Mike was so excited by the prospect of a job that he treated himself to a burger, shake and fries at the Burger Shack.

Chapter 3

Mike was waiting for Cliff who arrived at 7:45 a.m. He showed Mike how to sweep and mop, then left him alone for a while. He monitored him without being obvious and liked what he saw. The kid was diligent, thorough and extremely careful in everything he did. Later that morning he showed Mike how to dust. There was always a lot of dust drifting in from the workshop in the back. Mike watched intently as Cliff dealt with customers and he noticed that all the surfers who came in respected him. At lunchtime, Cliff ordered Thai food and asked Mike to join him. Mike bristled and said:

"Thanks. But I can get my own food."

"You just worked for four hours. You earned it. Are you too proud to eat with me?"

"No, sir," Mike replied, taken aback, not knowing how to refuse the kind invitation.

Cliff had to show him how to use chopsticks, but the food was delicious. His normal diet was McDonalds and Taco Bell. After lunch Cliff gave him other chores and by the time the shop closed at 6:00 p.m., Mike was tired.

"You did well today, kid. What's your name?"

"Mike."

"What's your last name?"

"Sanchez."

"You don't look Mexican."

"I'm not," he said stiffly. "It's my mother's name. She didn't know my father's name. If it makes any difference to you, I'll go."

"Take it easy, kid. It's cool. Let's get some dinner, then I'll take you to the marina and we'll see if we can find you a place to stay."

"Thanks, Cliff," he said shyly.

Cliff took him to the Imperial Beach Marina and introduced him to the owner, 'Big' Bill Thompson. Cliff explained Mike's situation, vouched for him. 'Big' Bill agreed to let him stay in an abandoned sailboat in exchange for a few chores from time to time and keeping an eye on the place. 'Big' Bill showed them the boat and how to run a power line from the office so Mike could have light, a refrigerator and a heater. They went aboard what 'Big' Bill called an 'old ketch', that was part of a disputed estate and had been sitting there for two years.

"The boat's still sound," 'Big' Bill explained. "The heirs won't sell it, but they're paying the yard fees, so it'll be here for a while. Just don't start a fire and burn the yard down."

"No, sir."

"I'll leave you and Cliff to look it over."

Mike and Cliff walked through the boat and Mike said:

"I've never been on a boat before. This is pretty big. What's a ketch?"

"Beats me. I've never been on a sailboat."

They looked at each other, then laughed.

"This is real nice. Thanks, Cliff."

"De nada, kid… Oops. I didn't mean to insult you."

"It's cool. I speak Spanish. I learned as a kid."

The next few days were the best in his life. Cliff taught him how to wax a board, and started introducing him to the surfers who came in. So Mike had a place to live and three jobs, though only the newspaper route paid cash. But he'd give that up in a minute if he had to choose between the route and Cliff's shop, 'Wave Length'. The day that ended his two week trial period, he spoke to Cliff.

"The two weeks is up today, Cliff. I hope I've done a good job."

"Yeah. You did well."

"I'd like to stay on, if you'll have me."

"I sort of assumed you were here to stay, but lets make it official. You're hired. Meals go with the job and I'll pay you when I can."

"You don't have to pay me."

"Don't tell me how to run my business."

"Sorry."

"I'll give you your first lesson tonight."

"Thanks, Cliff. You won't be sorry."

After they closed and had dinner, Cliff gave him a wetsuit and a board, and Mike had his first lesson. Even though he didn't get into the water for a week, he knew he looked like a surfer in his wetsuit and he began to feel like one. The summer flew by and by the time school started again, Mike felt he had been living a great life. The same kids were in his 6th grade class and they were still unfriendly, but he had become bigger and stronger during the summer and no one bothered him. He had mastered the basics of surfing and was accepted by the regulars at the beach, which gave him real confidence. Some of the surfers still teased him, but in a friendly way. They recognized the same passion for the water that drove them.

Chapter 4

Mike bitterly resented having to spend almost all day in school, when he could have been at the surf shop. The only consolation was computer class, where his teacher, Mr. Krasner was teaching him HTML and Java. Mike loved it and started writing simple code to carry out data functions. Cliff had helped him furnish his boat home, which was not only comfortable, but made him feel secure. He got up every morning, did a quick tour of the boatyard picking up trash discarded the night before, which 'Big' Bill appreciated. Then he delivered his papers. He endured school, except for computer class which he loved, until the dismiss bell sounded at 3:00 p.m. and he could race to the surf shop. Cliff, his first and only friend, really liked him and immediately cheered up when Mike arrived. He usually had a sandwich waiting for Mike, or some other snack and took him to dinner after they closed the shop.

The best time was on the weekends, when Mike was at the shop all day and he and Cliff would surf for hours at night. All summer long Cliff had him use what he called a longboard. It was ten feet long, heavy, thick and 20" wide. Cliff had explained it was the traditional way to start learning wave selection, paddling technique and turning basics. When the weather got cooler in October, Cliff switched him to a funboard that was still big, but a little smaller than the longboard. In November, Cliff thought he was making good progress and let him try a shortboard, a fish and a hybrid, a type that Cliff specialized in custom making for certain clients. Mike didn't care what board he was on, as long as he was on the water.

The Christmas holiday was great. Mike spent all day at the shop and Cliff had him waxing boards and starting to deal with simple customer requests. Then came the shocker. On Christmas morning, Cliff gave him a Christmas present. A shortboard. He never got a present before and he was embarrassed that he didn't even think of getting one for Cliff. Cliff saw how bad he felt and said kindly:

"Don't worry about it, Mike. Next year we'll be making money and you'll get me something nice."

He didn't feel too bad after that. Cliff called him Mike. It was the first time Cliff didn't call him 'kid'.

After a few months of living on the boat, Mike felt like he had a home. The boat had bunks, bedding and a galley with a propane stove and refrigerator, plates and utensils. Cliff gave him all kinds of household things, including a portable heater, which made the living space comfortable. 'Big' Bill let him go through the lost and found closet and take whatever he could use, then showed him how to fill the water tank in the boat. He even included the boat in the weekly head cleaning service. Mike had to learn boat language to know what 'Big' Bill was talking about. He found a thrift shop on his paper route and popped in regularly to pick up cheap items that he needed. He was happy for the first time in his life. He had a home. A true friend in Cliff, and 'Big' Bill was becoming a friend.

The rest of the school year couldn't go by quickly enough. He just managed passing grades, so the teachers mostly ignored him, focusing on the facile students, or the problem kids. He had become a favorite of Mr. Krasner in computer class, where he worked harder and harder to develop skills. But the best place was at the surf shop and the most satisfying was on the water. He had become skillful enough to get good rides and was totally fearless with any size wave. The other surfers noticed his determination and began to accept him. They even stopped calling him 'grom', a not entirely derogatory term for a young surfer, and called him Mike. Of course it did help that they all knew that Cliff was his mentor.

School finally ended in June and he was assigned to start middle school, the 7th grade, in September. He looked forward to not being with the same kids who ignored him for the last few years. One of his small treats was when one of the school kids came into the surf shop and he said coolly: 'Can I help you?'. Cliff had taught him an exercise routine to build strength and conditioning. He was big for his age, approaching 12, ate non-stop, and was tall and fit looking. The other surfers treated him like a person and this helped build his self-confidence.

Whenever things were slow during the day, Cliff urged him to grab a board and hit the water, just so he got used to surfing in daylight. One of the surfers, Ronnie, taught an informal karate class and Mike joined him every evening for an hour after the shop closed. Ronnie liked his work ethic and gave him special attention and Mike progressed rapidly. It was a wonderful summer. Just before he went back to school he asked Cliff to assess him as a surfer. Cliff stalled, claiming he never did anything like that before, but Mike was persistent.

"Okay. Here goes. You've progressed real well. You're building skills, you respect the ocean and you love every moment you're on it, even the wipeouts," which made them both laugh. "You may not like this. You're not talented. You work hard and learn fast, but you don't have the inborn gift that'll make you a champion…" He paused and looked at Mike to see how he was taking it.

"Go on, Cliff."

"You're going to become real good and what you don't master through skill you'll do with guts. Most surfers fear failing. Many fear the big waves. That's not you. You're driven to succeed and you'll work harder and harder to get better. If you continue to develop as I think you will, you might make the top 100 surfers, maybe even the top 50. But you'll never make the top 10. You'll look like a star, you'll have the nerve of a star, but it comes from work, not talent… I'm sorry if that sounds harsh."

"Cliff. Last year I couldn't stay on a board. Now you tell me I could be in the top 100. That's great. I don't care about competition. I just want to ride. You've said some fine things to me since I've known you, but this was the best. How many surfers are there?"

"I'm not sure. Maybe two million."

"And I could be in the top 100? That's not bad for a poor kid who had nothing a little while ago."

"That's a great attitude, Mike."

"Can I ask you a question?"

"Sure."

"You were in the top three, then you dropped out of competition. What happened?"

"My Mom and Dad died when I was a baby. There was no one else to take care of me, so I was put into foster care. My aunt found me when I was seven and I lived with her. When she died she left me her house. I was a surfer and did real well on the circuit. I was making a lot of money, but I wasted most of it. I was near the top when I got tired of the grind of competition and the way I was living. There was just enough to open this shop."

"Do you miss competition?"

"Not really. There's so much pressure to perform that you can lose sight of the joy of being on the water. I'm satisfied with my life for the time being."

"Thanks, Cliff."

"For what?"

"Talking to me. Teaching me. Being my friend. Everything."

"You're welcome, Mike."

Chapter 5

There was one big difference in middle-school. The same kids who first bullied him, then ignored him in elementary school, were just part of a much larger population. As they struggled to find their place in a new situation, Mike went about business as usual. As in each previous summer he had grown bigger and stronger and looked older than twelve. His year round tan, blond hair, blue eyes and rugged good looks definitely interested some of the girls. He went his own way and declined coach's invitations to try out for team sports. He had found his sport. He did just enough schoolwork to pass, only excelling in computer science class, where for whatever the reason, the teacher, Ms. Fallon, seemed to dislike him. He didn't let it bother him. Computer time was too precious.

Some of the surfers he knew from the beach were fourteen years old and in the 9th grade. He hung out with them and their acceptance gave him a place in the social milieu. The girls who hung out with the surfers were the best looking girls in the school. Even better looking than the cheerleaders or football groupies. Ronnie, who taught karate at the beach, had a younger brother, Davey, 13 years old, who liked Mike. Davey was small for his age, but wiry and had been practicing karate for three years. One afternoon he got into an argument after school with three neighborhood boys who didn't go to the school. They started to punch him, Mike joined in and he and Davey knocked them around, then let them go. From that day on they became close friends.

Mike was very comfortable living at the marina. He kept the ketch neat and clean, as well as rust free. He got into the habit of cleaning the yard, at least some of it each night and 'Big' Bill started asking him to clean the boats. Mike offered to do even more, as long as he could do it at night. 'Big' Bill taught him how to scrape and paint and after a while he put in two or three work hours a night, after surfing.

Somehow, Mike had come to link surfing with all the good fortune in his life, of which there had been plenty lately. If he didn't surf at least once a day, he got restless. The only time bad weather ever stopped him was during a hurricane. then he'd watch the water from a safe vantage point on the boardwalk and try to figure out how to surf in a storm. Of course he didn't tell Cliff what he was planning someday. He would have had his head examined. But he told Davey, who was also eager to try the giant waves someday.

Cliff taught him how to finish boards, with the promise of learning to cut and shape them to come. He gave Mike a surfboard design book that he read like devotees read the bible. At the same time, 'Big' Bill taught him simple boat repairs and maintenance and let him work unsupervised at night. Mike only got five or six hours of sleep a night, but he slept soundly, no longer had nightmares and woke up each morning refreshed and eager for a new day. His guidance counselor sent for him one day and wanted to know why he wasn't more motivated to learn. Mike almost laughed in his face, but managed to control himself and said:

"I'm passing my classes."

"Yes. But the only one you do well in is computer science. You need a well-rounded education, so you will get a good job someday."

Mike escaped by promising to think about it.

Mike didn't really follow the news, but Cliff and 'Big' Bill talked about the 'Great Recession', and how millions of people were losing their homes and jobs. He thought the guidance counselor was a jerk, trying to convince him to plan for a future beyond his comprehension. Though it no longer felt like it, each day was a struggle for survival. The only thing he knew for sure was that as long as he could surf, all would be well.

He had so much to do each day with his paper route, school, the surf shop, surfing and the marina that time zipped by. He never thought about the uncertainties of the future, or his terrible childhood that now seemed so long ago. Davey took him to a surfers party at Ronnie's house and they got high on pot, then kissed some of the girls, who teased them for being too young, but let them touch them. Ronnie suddenly descended angrily on them. He dragged them outside by their elbows, shook them, then growled:

"If I catch you smoking pot… No. If I even hear of you smoking pot, I'll beat you bloody and ban you from the beach. Understand?"

We were both scared by now, a new experience, and just mumbled: "Yes, Ronnie."

"As for you," he turned to me. "If I tell Cliff, he'll skin the hide off you."

"Don't tell him, Ronnie," I pleaded. "We were just doing what everyone else was doing."

"That's the dumbest excuse," he snarled. "If they start killing each other are you going to do that?"

"No, Ronnie," we echoed.

"The guys here are over eighteen. If you want to get high when you're eighteen I can't stop you. Now you're too young. Are we cool?"

"Yes, Ronnie," We echoed.

"Now get out of here."

We slunk out, hoping no one saw him lecture us. I couldn't help wondering if it would feel as good when I kissed and touched a girl if I wasn't high.

Chapter 6

The weirdest problem I had in school was my Spanish class. I had to take a language, so I figured Spanish would be easiest, since I already spoke it. Then the shocker. It wasn't anything like what I spoke. Sure. Some of the words were the same. But they sounded different. Then there were all the tenses and cases to learn. I had stayed after class the first day and I told Mr. Parish that I spoke Spanish, then asked why I had to learn all this stuff.

"You do not speak Spanish, Mr. Sanchez," he said in a snotty voice. "Mexican boys grunt low street talk. Here we learn civilized Spanish."

"I'm not Mexican," I protested.

"Your name is Sanchez."

I didn't know what he meant by civilized. I ate with a fork… Well most of the time. And I used toilet paper… All the time. But I knew when I was being insulted. When I told Cliff about it and how I'd figure out a way to get even with him, Cliff told me patiently:

"If you get into a feud with your teacher he'll fail you and you'll lose a year, or you'll have to take it in summer school. So either way you'll lose."

"But he insulted me."

"He's not the first and he won't be the last. Learn to ignore those things and you'll be better off."

I thought about sitting in a hot classroom for the summer and decided Cliff was right. So I'd forget, but not forgive, or forgive but not forget. I read it in a book but couldn't remember which was right. So I did what I had to, taught myself to ignore Mr. Parish's comments and got through the school year. I even passed Spanish. On the last day of school I had no one to say goodbye to, since my only friends were surfers and I would see them at the beach. A girl from my computer class, Jennifer something, came up to me. I had watched her out of the corner of my eye, all year. She was real pretty and had a nice body already. But I had never spoken to her before.

"I just wanted to tell you that I think you're very smart and I hope I'll see you at the beach."

"Do you surf?"

"No. But I'd like to learn."

"I could teach you, but I don't have a lot of time during the week. I have to work."

"You work at the surf shop."

"How do you know that?"

"I asked some of my friends about you."

I didn't know what to say. She wasn't the kind of girl I was used to. And she thought I was smart. I wracked my brain and finally said:

"Why don't you come by the surf shop. I'll show you around, then give you a lesson."

"That'll be cool. When?"

"How about Monday? About ten o'clock."

"See you then, Mike."

I stared at her as she walked away and couldn't believe my luck. A nice girl like that was interested in me. I guess it was time to ask Cliff about girls.

It took me until Sunday to work up my nerve to ask Cliff about girls. But I had to do it, since I would be seeing Jennifer on Monday. I had been fantasizing about being with her, kissing, touching, holding her on a surfboard, so I finally had to speak.

"I met this real nice girl at school and I think she likes me. She's coming here tomorrow. If you can spare me for a while I'm going to give her a surfing lesson."

"Do you like her?"

"A lot."

"Then I'm sure we can let you go for a while."

"Thanks, Cliff... Cliff?"

"Yeah?"

"How do I act with her? I don't know what to do."

"Then keep it simple. Be polite. Be nice. Don't grab. And listen to what she says."

"I can do that."

"Good. One very important thing. Don't ever take her to your boat."

"Why not?"

"It could cause all sorts of trouble for 'Big' Bill if it became known that you brought a girl there. He'd have to have you arrested for trespassing, or he could lose the marina."

"I wouldn't want that. What if she asks me where I live?"

"Say you're crashing with some surfers and you wouldn't bring anyone nice there."

"Sounds good."

"Don't spend any money on her. You can't afford it. If she doesn't understand that, you shouldn't be with her... And don't try to do much sexually. You're too young."

"I'll be thirteen next month."

"That's what I mean. How old is she?"

"I guess 12 or 13, but her body is developed."

"You're both too young to do anything more than kiss and touch a little. Make sure you respect her."

"Yes, Cliff. Thanks."

By the time Jennifer came into the shop on Monday morning, I had been worrying for hours that she wouldn't come. When I saw her come in the door I couldn't believe that she actually showed up. Her long, blonde hair was in a pony tail and she wore a snug t-shirt that said 'Close Sea World', tight jeans and sandals. I was tall for my age, about 5'8" and she was just a little shorter. Her big smile warmed me and I felt a surge of confidence go through me. This beautiful girl liked me. She wouldn't be here if she didn't. With her looks and body she could get a dozen guys on the beach to teach her to surf. Cliff was real cool when I introduced her.

"Nice to meet you, Jennifer. Why don't you show her around, Mike. Then if she's interested, give her a lesson."

"Sure, Cliff."

There really wasn't that much to see, a bunch of boards and other equipment, so we left for the beach.

"Aren't you bringing any boards?"

"Not for the first lesson."

I guess I babbled on about Cliff as we walked, cause she finally said:

"You really like him."

"He's my best friend."

When we got to the beach she took off her t-shirt and jeans. She was wearing a dark blue bikini that matched the color of her eyes and showed off her shapely body.

"What's first," she asked and I could hardly tear my eyes away from her soft, red lips.

She knew I was looking at her and posed, just like the older girls did. I forced myself to stay cool, and said:

"It's up to you. If you just want to have fun on a board, I'll show you the basics and you can start tomorrow. If you want to learn to surf well, it'll take longer."

"What do you suggest?"

"That's up to you. One way is quick fun. The other is hard work."

"I like hard work," she replied with a dazzling smile that had me saying 'thank you. Thank you. Thank you.'

I taught her the way Cliff taught me, though I touched her much more. She was bright, strong, smart and learned fast. By the third day she was ready to go out. We made a list of what she'd need and Wednesday morning she bought a wet suit. She asked about buying a board, but Cliff gave her a loaner, until she decided how seriously she'd take surfing. She was a good athlete and caught on quickly. Friday morning after she caught her first ride, she did a triumphant dance, followed by cartwheels. Then she kissed me. It went on and on and when she moved away it felt like we had been cut apart.

"My first ride and my first kiss. Thanks, Mike."

She was thanking me? I couldn't believe my luck.

Chapter 7

It was hard to believe that things could get better and better, but each day was extra special because of Jennifer. She recognized that I had work commitments, yet she hung out in the surf shop for hours, hoping I'd free up and take her to the beach. Somehow, almost every day, Cliff let me go for a few wonderful hours. We spent more time in the water pressing against each other, then on our surfboards. It was way better then the high on pot. She didn't seem to have any other obligations, since she went surfing at night with Cliff and me. Then I'd ride home with her on our bikes. We'd stand in her doorway, a big house in the richest neighborhood of Chula Vista, Jamul, kissing and rubbing against each other, until it got late. I slept less, but it was worth it.

One night we were locked together and the door suddenly opened. We almost tumbled inside, but moved apart and Jennifer introduced me to her mother. Mrs. Winslow was tall, blond, maybe even older than Cliff, and drunk.

"Come inside, Miss. You're too young to be doing things with boys."

Jennifer turned red, yelled: "I'll be 13 next month," and rushed inside. Mrs. Winslow glared at me.

"Goodnight," and she closed the door in my face.

The next day Jennifer apologized for what happened and told me I was invited to dinner that night. When the shop closed I grabbed a clean shirt and we rode to her house. I had only seen houses like this in the movies. They actually had a butler, cook and a maid. There were a lot of other guests. The men were wearing white jackets and black bow ties. The women were in short, black sleeveless dresses, and lots of jewels. They all ignored me, which was good, since I had no idea what to say to them. I watched how they ate and imitated them, though I didn't know what I was eating. Just after dessert, something like ice cream in a tall glass with fruit in it, Mrs. Winslow spoke to me.

"Jennifer tells me you work in a surf shop."

"Yes, Ma'am."

"You may call me Mrs. Winslow."

"Yes, Ma'am."

"He also delivers newspapers," Jennifer contributed.

"A paper boy?" Mr. Winslow asked.

"Yes, sir."

"I thought people read online," one of the men said.

"Some people still read newspapers, sir," I answered.

When the ordeal was finally over, I knew what the poor boys in the orphanage felt like. Jennifer escorted me to the door with tears in her eyes. I tried to reassure her.

"It's cool. Everything's alright."

"No. It's not. Tomorrow morning we're flying to Paris. When we come back I'll be going to a private school in San Francisco."

My head started pounding. I could barely breathe.

"When will I see you?" I asked despairingly.

"I don't know. If I can ever get away I'll phone you at the surf shop."

We clung to each other desperately, until Mrs. Winslow ordered:

"Say goodnight, Jennifer."

I rode home saying over and over 'I'll see her again'. But one part of me was afraid it was over. I moped and brooded throughout July and ran to answer the phone in the shop whenever it rang. It was never Jennifer.

I was still depressed at the loss of Jennifer at the end of July and Cliff finally had enough. He took me aside after work and said:

"Mike. It's time to get on with your life. I know Jennifer was very special for you. But she's gone. I hope she comes back. Not as much as you do, but I know how you feel. It was first love and unusual for two kids your age, so it was even deeper than normal. But you have obligations to yourself and your friends to get on with your life."

How could I tell him I cried inside myself every day. I started to speak, but couldn't find the words. Cliff put his arm around me and said softly:

"You've been really lucky. You loved a beautiful girl who loved you. Like it or not, it's over. You should be grateful for what you had. Most kids never have someone like that."

"I hear you, but I think about her night and day. What should I do?"

"Appreciate what you have. Get your ass out on the ocean, let the water heal you. Try it. Let's go now."

"Yes, Cliff. I'll try."

Of course I knew nothing could make me forget Jennifer, or feel better. But Cliff turned out to be right. My love for the water reawakened me and I gradually began to lose the dark mood that spoiled enjoyment of what I had. Cliff noticed the change, but didn't say anything, glad to have me feeling good again. Then something funny happened the last week in August. Some of Jennifer's friends came into the shop. After looking around, one of them spoke to me.

"Hi. I'm Zoey. This is Vicki and Carrie."

"I'm Mike, not Mikey, so I don't rhyme with you."

They thought that was funny and Zoey said:

"We know who you are. Jennie told us all about you. We want to know if you'll give us surfing lessons."

I looked them over. They were blonde, though different shades, tan, shapely, wearing bikini tops, cut off shorts, flip flops and what I was beginning to recognize as expensive jewelry. Their fingernails and toenails glistened with different shades of red gloss They may not have been Jennifer, but they looked pretty good.

"Sure. $10 an hour each."

"Is that what you charged Jennie?" Vicki asked.

"Until she became my girlfriend."

"She told us about what you did together," Carrie said.

"Everything?" I replied, which made them giggle.

"What if only one of us wants lesson?" Zoey asked, posing provocatively.

"Then it's $30 an hour."

"Do you think you can handle all of us?" Vicki asked in a husky voice, that made me eager to teach.

"It'll be fun to try," which really made them giggle.

"When can we start?" Carrie asked.

I turned to Cliff. "Can I give some lessons tomorrow?"

"Sure. What time?"

I turned to the girls. "10 a.m.?"

"How about the afternoon?" Zoey said.

"Two o'clock?"

"That's good," Vicki said.

"You'll need to get wetsuits and a few other things," I told them. "Come in around one o'clock and we'll get you fitted," which made them giggle again.

They left and I realized I had been sniffing their perfume, which was a little different, but smelled great. Part of me couldn't help wondering if these were rich girls playing with the kid from across the tracks. But they looked even better than they smelled.

"Looks like you got some customers," Cliff said.

"Yeah. I'm charging them $10 each an hour. How much is your share?"

"Keep it all, Mike."

"Thanks. They'll be buying wetsuits."

"Good. I'll give you a commission."

"What's that?"

"A percentage of the sale."

"You don't have to do that."

"I want to. Besides. If your popularity keeps growing, we'll have every girl in the school shopping here."

He laughed when I threw my dust rag at him."

Chapter 8

The girls showed up Saturday, only 15 minutes late. It took a while for them to try on wetsuits and they didn't want black suits. We finally compromised with them just buying jackets. After we arranged to order emerald green suits for them that they paid for with an American Express card. I picked out some old boards, showed them how to carry them and we headed for the beach. I turned towards an isolated area, but they wanted the main drag. They were paying, so I wasn't going to argue. They had good bodies and we got a lot of attention as we sat up near the water. Then I asked the standard question:

"Do you want to learn to be good surfers, or just have fun?"

"What's the difference?" Zoey asked.

"Good surfing requires a lot of preparation. If you want to have fun, I'll show you some basics today, including paddling, and you'll ride tomorrow."

"Let's try that," Vicki said, and the others nodded.

I showed them how to lie on the board and paddle, then I showed them how to stand. I had them practice getting up for a while, until they assured me they got the basic idea. By this time we had attracted a crowd, including some of the 15 year old surfers who the girls slyly posed for. It was a bit distracting, but I didn't get annoyed. It was obvious they wanted the attention. When I thought they were ready, I said:

"Grab your boards, girls. It's time to get into the water."

I led them to the water, showed them how to attach the leash to their ankles, and they waded in with squeals about the cold. I didn't bother telling them that it was almost bathtub warm and they had neoprene jackets. I monitored their paddling, showed them how to duck under the wave when it was breaking over them…

"We'll get our hair wet," Carrie protested.

I didn't respond. They had temporary bathing caps and if they wanted to surf, their hair would get wet. The waves were ankle slop, which made it easy to go out and get them used to the water. They shrieked at the tiny waves as if they were giant rollers. I was tempted for a moment to tell them about sharks, but I wanted the next paid lessons. I let them paddle around for a while, but they didn't get quieter. I demonstrated how to turn and get ready for the ride and how to stand up. When they seemed to get the basics, I told them they did well and we headed for the shore. As we went in I admired their shapely legs and tight butts.

The girls basked in the attention as they came out of the water, three young hotties, who just conquered the ocean. Some of my surfer buddies demanded introductions and I made them. After the girls socialized for a while, I led them to the public showers to rinse the salt off their jackets and boards. They removed their jackets and looked sexy with the water running down their tanned bodies. We went back to the shop, where they put on pants, asked if they could leave the jackets, then wanted to pay me with a credit card. I requested cash and Zoey gave me $60 for two hours of lessons. We arranged to meet tomorrow at the same time and they left, three decorative birds chirping away about their adventure.

By this time I knew I wasn't going to get anywhere personally with them. I had seen enough beach bunnies to know they were looking for boys older than me. But I didn't mind. It was fun handling their bodies. If they came back I'd have another treat.

"So how did it go, Mike?"

"Alright. I got paid $60 for two hours."

"Are you interested in one of them?"

"They're interested in older guys. Besides, I'm not ready for another girl friend yet."

"Well if it's any consolation, they spent over $800. Your commission comes to more than $80."

"Thanks, Cliff. If they come back tomorrow I'll sell them boards. Then they'll be equipped for hunting."

"Don't be cynical, kid. There aren't a lot of girls like Jennifer."

"Do you think that I'll ever meet anyone like her again?"

"You'll change as you grow up. You'll be different and so will the girls you meet."

"I guess so."

The girls did come back the next day and they bought boards. They were much quieter on the way to the beach and went into the water without a fuss. I reviewed paddling techniques, then showed them again how to turn. The waves weren't much bigger from yesterday, so the conditions were good for beginners. I demonstrated how to stand until they all said they got it. Then, one at time, talked them through standing up on the board. I kept them at it until they all had their first ride. They were thrilled and babbled a mile a minute. I started to tease them and remembered my first ride, so I let them enjoy their accomplishment.

When we came out of the water, some of the guys from yesterday were waiting for us. The girls greeted them and Zoey said:

"We're going to hang out, Mike. We'll come by the shop later and pay you."

"That's cool."

I turned and Vicki touched my arm, then said softly:

"I know you like us, but girls want boys two years older."

I nodded and kept going, trying to figure out what she meant. Was I supposed to have an 11 year old girlfriend? That was whack. And what about Jennifer? She was my age. I guess I had a lot to learn about girls. They came to the shop later and paid me, but after that I only saw them on the beach at a distance, surrounded by boys.

Chapter 9

So summer ended and school started and my feelings for Jennifer began to fade away. Zoey, Vicki and Carrie were part of the surfer clique now, so I saw them every day, but they just said hello, then clung to the older boys. Davey and I were still tight and he kept asking me to introduce him to the girls. I finally told him Vicki's explanation that girls wanted boys to be two years older. He thought it was as whack as I did. Davey kept talking about how horny he was and how badly he wanted a girl. I was starting to feel the same way, but I didn't tell him I jerked off at night. Each day he told me about some girl at school who put out, but he never approached any of them.

I began to wonder if Cliff got horny and one day I asked him. He laughed.

"I live with a woman. Her name's Lucille Fairchild. We're pretty close, but we don't have a lot of time together."

"How come?"

"She's working on her doctorate at the university in San Francisco. If she doesn't finish this year her fellowship runs out and she'll have to get a job before she gets her PhD."

"What's that?"

"It's a doctor's degree."

"Cool. Will she work in a hospital?"

"Not that kind of doctor. It's an advanced college degree in different subjects, like history or literature."

I didn't understand, but I let it go.

"How come she never comes to the shop?"

"She's too busy."

"Does she surf?"

"No. She doesn't like the ocean."

"That's weird."

"Some people are like that. Maybe that's why we get along so well. We live in two different worlds and meet in the middle."

"I'd like to meet her."

"Sure. When her schedule allows."

There was a nice change in school. I had a new Spanish teacher, Miss Alvarez. She was fat, nice and friendly. She had dark hair, dark skin and always wore bright colored blouses and skirts. She didn't insult me when she corrected my pronunciation. I liked her. I still had Miss Fallon for computer science, but she seemed to like me better this year. When she'd stop at my table to see what I was working on, she'd rest her hand on my shoulder. It was always very warm. One day she noticed I was playing 'Call of Duty', and asked me to stay after class. I didn't know what she was going to do, send me to the principal, flunk me, kick me out of her class, but I was worried. I really wanted to build my computer skills.

"Why were you playing a game instead of doing your assignment?"

"I finished my assignment. It was only for a few minutes. I don't have a computer and this is the only chance I get to play."

"I see. What were you playing?"

"'Call of Duty'. It's a shooter game."

"I assume it's violent."

"Yes, Miss Fallon."

"Are you violent?"

"No, Miss Fallon."

"You never fight?"

"Only to defend myself."

"Why don't you have a computer?

I was getting uncomfortable and part of me wanted to walk out, but I answered.

"I can't afford one."

"I see. I have an extra laptop at home that I no longer use. If I give it to you, will you promise not to play games in class?"

"Oh, yes, Miss Fallon."

"I can't give it to you at school, or it'll cause problems. Can you come to my house on the weekend?"

"Tell me where and I'll take time off from work."

"Where do you work?"

"At the Wave Length surf shop during the day."

"Are you a surfer?

"Yes."

"You said during the day. You have another job?"

"Yes. I deliver papers in the early morning and I do chores at the marina at night."

"I see. Can you come to my house Saturday after work?"

"Yes."

"I live in Eastlake Greens. Do you know where that is?"

"Yes."

"I'll give you my address," which she wrote on a piece of paper. "What time does your store close?"

"6:00 p.m."

"I'll expect you at seven. Don't tell anyone."

"I won't."

"Good. We'll talk then."

Chapter 10

I wanted to tell Cliff about my going to Miss Fallon's house on Saturday, but I couldn't, since I promised her. I wouldn't do anything to jeopardize getting a computer. I really didn't make promises, so it was important to keep my word. I guess in a different way I gave my word to Cliff and 'Big' Bill, who trusted me. I wouldn't want to break that trust. It turned out to be a strange week. Cliff was quieter than usual, barely responding to questions or comments, with a 'yes' or 'no'. 'Big' Bill was angry about something, so I avoided him, even though I knew it wasn't me. Then there was Miss Fallon. I watched her out of the corner of my eye in computer class and maybe looked at her closely for the first time.

Miss Fallon wasn't as old as Cliff, but she wasn't a kid. She had long blonde hair in a pony tail, bright green eyes, a very pretty face, full red lips and what looked like a shapely body on a tall frame. It was hard to tell, since she always wore loose fitting, long-sleeved shirts and slacks. But the more I studied her, the more I thought she would have made a great beach bunny. She didn't pay anymore attention to me than usual, but somehow I knew she was very aware of me.

Cliff's girlfriend came to the shop on Saturday just before we closed. He introduced us and Lucille said:

"Cliff's told me all about you. He thinks you're special."

"He told me you were very smart. He didn't tell me you were beautiful."

She laughed. "How old are you?"

"Thirteen."

"Where did you learn to talk to a woman like that?"

I was confused. "Did I insult you?"

"No, silly. You were very sweet. You're going to break a lot of hearts soon."

I didn't know what she was talking about, but I didn't care, as long as I could keep staring at her. She was tall, with long dark hair, dark eyes, a face like a movie star and a body to match. From the little Cliff told me about her I expected a fat, old librarian. She looked like an athlete. She was wearing a warm-up suit and sneakers and she may have been old, but she looked great.

"Cliff and I are going for a run. Do you want to come with us?"

"Thanks, Miss Lucille. I have to meet a friend."

"Call me Lucy. No surfing tonight?"

"No, Miss… Lucy."

"Cliff tells me you're very good."

"Thanks," I mumbled shyly.

"Another time then."

"Sure."

"Everything's shut down," Cliff said. "You lock up."

"Sure."

I watched them jog off, admiring her well-formed ass. I put out the last light, rolled out my bike, locked the door and headed for Miss Fallon's house. It was in a nice section of town that I passed many times, but I never knew anyone who lived there. A lot of well-dressed, good-looking people were outside and nobody paid attention to me as I peddled by. I pulled up in front of her building, one of four identical four story apartment houses with balconies. I rang her bell and she buzzed me in. I took the elevator to the top floor and she was waiting at her door.

"Leave your bike in the hall."

I started to lock it and she said:

"Nobody'll bother it," so I left it.

I followed her into the apartment and couldn't take my eyes off her body. She was wearing a green bikini top that matched her eyes and short white shorts that revealed the curve of her tight butt. She had broad shoulders and a small waist and she looked great. She turned and I could see the swell of her breasts and I started to get an erection.

"I can't offer you a beer. How about lemonade?"

"Sure."

She went to the kitchen and I looked around. The living room was pretty big, with a black leather couch and chair, white coffee tables and a grey rug. There were bright colored pictures on the wall with funny shapes. She came out carrying a tray with a pitcher of lemonade and glasses. I sat on the edge of a chair and shifted my legs, so my erection wouldn't show. I found it hard not to look at her body, especially when she leaned forward and poured. We sat there for a minute sipping our drinks, then she said:

"I try to identify gifted computer students and follow them to be sure they have true potential. I watched you last year and saw some possibilities. It takes time to be certain of real talent, but promising students should be encouraged. Unfortunately they're few and far between."

She looked at me expectantly and I didn't know what to say, so I just nodded. She stared at me intently, then got up and walked out of the room. I couldn't figure out why she was dressed that way, showing her body to a student. But part of me didn't care. It was a great body. She came back with a laptop, a carrying case and a tote bag.

"There's a manual, a charger and a mouse in the bag. Get used to using the internet." She handed me the items. "We'll discuss your progress in a few months. Don't spend all your computer time playing games."

"Yes, Miss Fallon."

"Do not tell anyone that I gave you this and that you were at my house. Can I rely on you?"

"Yes, Miss Fallon."

She led me to the door, her breast rubbing against my shoulder and I wondered how I was going to cover my erection. She didn't seem to notice, said: "Goodbye," and closed the door. I held the bag in front of me in case I met anyone, rolled the bike into the street, and headed for the marina. The first thing I did when I got there was open the case and inspect the laptop. It was a shiny, new-looking Lenovo, which I thought was made in China or Japan. It was cool. Now I had to get an internet connection. I'd ask Cliff in the morning. I ate a bologna and cheese sandwich, went to bed, opened the laptop and started reading the manual. The last thing I remember before I fell into a dreamless sleep, was Miss Fallon leaning against me, as she showed me how to plug in the charger.

Chapter 11

I must have overslept, because Cliff woke me Sunday morning and as I emerged from unconsciousness, I realized I went to sleep holding the laptop on my chest.

"What's that?"

"My new computer."

"When did you get it?"

"Last night. My teacher gave it to me."

"That's where you went?"

"Yeah."

"That was nice of him."

"Her. Miss Fallon. You should see her. When I got there she was wearing a bikini top and shorts. What a body!"

"You didn't come on to her?"

"No, Cliff. She's my teacher."

"Did she come on to you?"

"No. She said she wants to help promising computer students and she'd check my progress in a few months."

"That sounds okay. Are you any good at that?"

"Yeah. And I really like it. I want to learn all kinds of programming."

"Good. Just don't be a troll."

"What's that?"

"Jerks who send nasty things to people on the social networks."

"I wouldn't do that. Well maybe to Jennifer's mother," which we both laughed at.

"Get dressed. We'll grab some breakfast, then catch some waves."

"Great."

The beach was crowded and Cliff drew the usual attention, lots of people saying hello, some following us, a few asking for autographs. It was only when we got out past the breakers that things settled down. The other surfers were in awe of him, so they all tried to be cool, but they watched his every move. He had been working with me on improving my stance to better control the board, which really helped my ride. We took a break and just lay on our boards, occasionally paddling to stay in place. I loved the peaceful contrast to the thrill of the ride.

"I've been meaning to ask you something," I said

"What?"

"A lot of the guys do these tricks on their boards, like handstands and flips and stuff..."

"And?"

"What do you think of it?"

"I prefer the pure ride. What they do is athletic and even difficult, but it's not the way I want to surf."

"Thanks."

"Do you want to try stunts?"

"No. I just want to get better rides."

"Me too."

Cliff was the best there was.

More and more of the high school kids were coming into the surf shop, asking for me. I assumed Zoey, Vicki and Carrie mentioned me to their friends. Some of the girls wanted lessons and Cliff was very obliging letting me have the time. Some of the kids bought equipment or wetsuits and Cliff gave me a commission on the sales. Some of the girls were great looking, but it was obvious they were interested in older boys. This didn't bother me and my popularity with my fellow surfers soared when I introduced them to the girls. I started saving money for a new bike and Cliff took me to the bank and showed me how to open a savings account. Jennifer had just about faded away and I started looking more closely at the girls who came into the shop. I was ready for another girlfriend.

One ongoing frustration was the lack of an internet connection at the marina. After much thought and careful preparation I spoke to 'Big' Bill about getting a website and advertising on the internet. His idea of communication was to run signal flags up the mast, or radio the Coast Guard for storm warnings.

"I don't know anything about computers or the internet. What's this web you're talking about?"

"It's your place of business on the internet. It'll advertise the marina, the boat yard, sales, repairs, every part of you business."

"How do you get one of those web things?"

"You make them."

"I can't do that."

"I can make it for you."

"And you really think it's useful?"

"Sure, Bill. Boaters looking for a marina can find you online. Boat buyers can see the boats for sale. It'll get you new business."

"How much will it cost?"

"I'll do the website for free. You'll have to pay a monthly fee for a service provider."

"What does that cost?"

"Thirty or forty dollars a month. I'll find out."

He still looked unsure, so I said:

"If it brings in one new sale it pays for itself. I'll make a sample website and you can decide if you like it or not."

"What do you get out of it?"

"If it works, I can use your internet connection."

"That sounds fair. Show me the web thing when you're ready."

I used the computer at school to go to an app that offered free downloads of basic websites and selected a banner and format that looked good. The banner read:

Imperial Beach Marina

Chula Vista, California

William Thompson, Proprietor

I found stock footage of a marina, a boatyard, repair shop and boats, and posted them with different colored headers. I set up sections for Home, About Us, Services, Contact us, and added Big Bill Productions.

Miss Fallon stopped by my desk while I was fine-tuning the website sample and watched for a minute.

"Why are you doing that? she asked softly.

It took a moment for me to figure out what to say. I couldn't tell her I lived in the boatyard.

"This is for a friend who will let me use his internet connection in exchange for the website."

"Very clever, Mike. Keep up the good work."

I guess she didn't dislike me after all.

Chapter 12

'Big' Bill was thrilled with the website when I showed it to him on my laptop, and impressed that I did it so well. He was an instant convert to the internet. I looked up the local service providers, picked the best one and had 'Big' Bill phone and order service, with me at his side to answer any questions. Ten days later we were up and running, with an extra router that ran to my boat, so I had an internet connection. Within a week I was staying up later and later online, playing 'Tour of Duty' with other shooters. Cliff noticed I was getting dark circles under my eyes and asked what I was doing. When I explained what I had done for 'Big Bill', he asked if we should have a website for the shop, and I said:

"Definitely." Then he ordered me to get to sleep earlier, which I promised to do.

I took much more care preparing the 'Wave Length' website, taking pictures of surfboards, colorful wetsuits, equipment, lesson rates, the exterior of the shop and Cliff. He loved it. Then I had a great idea.

"We could have a mail-order component that could be transacted online."

"We can try it," Cliff mumbled, "but I don't want to be a shipping clerk."

"If it's successful, you can hire someone to take care of all mail order business."

"What about you?"

"No, thanks. I don't want to be a shipping clerk," which cracked us up with laughter.

I had saved some money, so at Christmas time I got a present for Cliff, a slick diver's watch I bought on E-bay, real cheap. He was really touched by the gift. He gave me a beautiful hybrid surfboard that he made for me. I had admired it while he was working on it and assumed it was for a special customer, judging by the care and effort he put into it. I impulsively hugged him, which embarrassed both of us. At Cliff's suggestion, I got a box of cigars for 'Big' Bill, who was delighted, but confessed he didn't get me anything.

"You got me a home and an internet connection. I owe you for years to come."

He mumbled something and it was the first time I ever saw him at loss for words. I got Miss Fallon a tiny but expensive bottle of perfume, but I wasn't sure how to give it to her. I couldn't go to her house and it seemed stupid to mail it, so I decided to give it to her after the holidays, when school started again. It was weird having people in my life to give gifts to, but it felt good. It reminded me I was no longer alone.

Sales were up at the surf shop and online sales requests were growing, so Cliff started thinking about hiring someone after the summer. I was still getting a commission for sales I made and I actually had pocket money. 'Big' Bill made two equipment sales online and practically crushed me in a bear hug. He also started getting inquiries for berths at the marina for the summer. He insisted on giving me a commission, which I suspected was at Cliff's urging. Word spread among the surfers that I designed websites and several of my friends asked me to do it for them. I charged $50 for a basic site that satisfied them. I made websites for free for my friend Davey and his brother Ronnie.

I was still giving surfing lessons and one of Zoey's friends, Tammie, who wasn't quite ready for the sexual demands of older boys, started hanging out with me. She was just as pretty as her friends, as rich, as well-dressed, but shy. As she gained confidence surfing, she spent more time at the beach in the evenings when Cliff and I surfed. One night

Cliff left early and she asked to go out with me. She was scared of night surfing, but she didn't let fear stop her and she did alright. When I praised her, she got self-conscious, then suddenly kissed me. I kissed her back and she tasted good. After that we spent more and more time together.

I experienced my first earthquake the morning of February 1st, at around 6:15. I wasn't even halfway through my newspaper delivery route when the earth began to shake and I tumbled off my bike. I didn't get hurt, but it was a scary feeling. It took a few minutes before the ground felt solid again and I could continue my deliveries. Everybody I met that day talked about where they were and what happened to them in the big quake of 2010.

So I had a girlfriend, good friends, a computer and lots of things were going well. Then one of the anchors that held my little world together shattered. The Chula Vista Chronicle, for which I had been delivering newspapers for almost three years, that paid for my food, abruptly ceased print publication in March. Their explanation was subscriptions had dropped so much that they were now going to only publish online. The delivery boys and dispatcher were outraged and yelled and cursed at the staffer who announced the change. I was upset, less about the money, than the secure routine of getting up early each morning and riding through the still sleeping town, delivering papers. I looked at the boys, who still weren't friends after all this time and the dispatcher, who was always nasty to me, and suddenly felt free. I got my bike, went to the door, turned and yelled:

"Call me if you need delivery boys online," then peddled away, laughing to myself at the silly looks they gave me.

Chapter 13

At first it was very strange getting up at 5:30 a.m. and not delivering newspapers. The day after delivery ended I actually went through my usual morning routine. I started for the district office, then remembered it was over. I went back to the boat, put on my wetsuit, went to the beach, ran two miles, surfed for an hour, then went to school. It was a great morning, despite the drastic change. It turned out that Cliff really understood the difference it made to me, not having that part-time job.

"It's time you went on salary. I should have done it a year ago. You're a valuable employee."

I started to protest, but he cut me off.

"This isn't open for discussion. Five dollars an hour starting today. You'll have to get

working papers, so it'll be official."

"I got them for my delivery job and they're still good."

"Good. Then you're on salary starting today."

"Thanks, Cliff."

When Tammie found out I was running and surfing in the morning before school, she joined me. She could only run half a mile at first, but as the weeks went by she ran farther and farther. Her surfing improved almost daily, as she lost her fear, and she fell in love with the ocean. On Sundays we occasionally hung out with my surfer friends, that now included Zoey, Vicki and Carrie, who seeing that the older boys respected me, didn't look down at Tammie for having a younger boyfriend.

Tammie even started taking Ronnie's evening karate class. There were six or seven of us who worked out with him at least three or four times a week. I suggested to them that we give Ronnie $10 a week, or whatever we could afford. He objected, until I insisted he was a teaching pro and should be paid. Tammie and I gave him $10 each week and most of the others gave him something. I never asked how much.

As the school year began winding down, Miss Fallon questioned me about my computer progress and gave me manuals for C# and .Net that I should learn during the summer. She suggested I get familiar with hacking, though she didn't explain why. She also told me that I should improve my other grades next year, since with my brain and talent I could get a college scholarship in computer science. College seemed a million years away, if ever. But she was very concerned and I didn't want to hurt her feelings, so I said:

"Sure, Miss Fallon. I'll do that. Computers are almost as cool as surfing."

She laughed. "They're a lot more important, but I know what you mean."

"Did you ever surf?"

"No. Why?"

"You look like a surfer with that great body… Excuse me. Sorry. I shouldn't have said that."

"It's alright. No harm done."

"If you ever want to learn, I'll be glad to teach you. I teach regularly."

"How much is a lesson?"

"Always free for you, Miss Fallon. Come to the surf shop anytime. I'll be available."

"That's very sweet, Mike. We'll see."

School ended June 15th and I was free for almost three months to do what I loved best, surfing, the shop, the marina, the beach and Tammie. Not only all those good things, but I was a valuable employee and I had brains and talent. Cool.

It had taken me a while to get used to not delivering newspapers anymore. I didn't

admit it to anyone else, but I guess it caused a twinge of insecurity, losing something that had been a fixture for so long. But I was over it now. The first week after school ended it felt great working in the shop all day. I gave a lesson or two a day, made sales and between salary and commission I was putting money in the bank regularly. I could afford to buy a bike from someone leaving town. It looked brand new, was made of titanium and only weighed about 10 pounds. It was a cool ride.

My fourteenth birthday was coming soon and I found myself thinking about getting a motorcycle. I don't know where the idea came from, but I kept visualizing one of those sleek, bright green Japanese cycles that the heroes rode in action movies. It was a real downer when Cliff told me you had to be 16 to get a license. I felt a little better when he said I could get a learner's permit at 15 ½. But everything was just about perfect right now, so I could wait.

Chapter 14

While I was at the shop during the day, Tammie hung out on the beach with the surfers, riding until she was exhausted. Some of the boys came on to her, offering sex, drugs and rap, but she told them she was my girlfriend and they respected that. Of course it didn't hurt that Davey and Ronnie were there and at my request looked out for her. Zoey, Vicki and Carrie kept inviting her to go to parties with the older boys, but Tammie wouldn't go. Yet the other girls still liked her and remained good friends. I never bothered thinking about the complications of friendship or relationships. I was too busy. Either you were a friend, or I didn't care what happened to you. There wasn't any loyalty where I came from and I only learned it from Cliff.

By the end of June I had brushed up on Java and was starting .Net, which was fascinating. I started thinking about what I could do with it and out of the blue, I got an entirely different idea. Why not make money designing websites? I had been casually doing them for my friends. Why not do it professionally? All I needed was a dynamite website and a payment method. I went to the internet and found Pay Pal. It would be simple to open an account, if I could use the shop for a credit reference. Then all I needed was a price range for small businesses and personal sites and exposure on as many search engines as possible.

Cliff thought it was a great idea and let me use the shop for my account, when I assured him there was no way anyone could fault him. I looked up business practices on the internet and found some good suggestions; get 50% in advance before starting the job, show a rough cut and get the other 50% before going to final. Also get an email approving the rough cut, so there would be no disputes about the final version. I had no idea how much to charge, so I started with $100 for personal sites, $250 for small businesses, additional cost to be determined if anything more than basic format was required. It would be up to the buyer to get a domain name and site. I started having fantasies about money rolling in and having an assistant, who looked remarkably like Miss Fallon.

Tammie thought it was a good idea. I didn't tell her my Miss Fallon fantasies, but she cautioned me that unless you're well known, it could take a while to get customers. That was very thoughtful of her and I was appreciating how smart she was more and more, as well as her nerve on the ocean. She was 14 on July 2nd, and I bought a gold ankle bracelet on E-Bay for her birthday. She wasn't as shy as she used to be. Many nights after we finished surfing we'd lie on the beach, cover ourselves with a blanket and kiss and rub against each other. One night I was so excited my penis popped out of my bathing suit and I ejaculated. The next night she took off her bikini top and I caressed her breasts. She got so excited that I slipped my hand between her legs and touched her and she came with a loud cry.

Within a few days we were getting naked and rubbing against each other until we came. I screwed up my courage and asked Cliff how to touch a girl. He told me how and where to use my hands, mouth and penis. Then he instructed me not to penetrate her unless I was wearing a condom.

"If you think you're coming close to having sex, go to the drugstore, buy a box of condoms and you can practice putting it on a cucumber or banana. That's how they do it in sex-ed workshops.

"Thanks, Cliff."

"Mike."

"Yeah?"

"Don't get her pregnant."

"No, Cliff."

I wasn't sure how to tell if we were close to doing it, but one night I licked her between her legs and she went wild and came like a racehorse. After her panting subsided, she took my penis in her mouth and licked and sucked until I came in a geyser. We lay there holding each other and I confided I never licked a girl before. She said she never even touched another boy's penis, let alone put it in her mouth. I informed her I was no authority, but she had natural talent, which made her giggle. Then she told me I did too.

The next day I bought condoms. It was a funny experience. They had different color boxes, different sizes and so much information about lubricants, thinness, and special features, that I just picked what looked like regulars. That night, after we licked and sucked each other, I was still hard and Tammie asked if I wanted to do it. I took out a condom, put it on easily, wondering what all the fuss was about, moved between her legs and she guided me inside her. She was tight and it hurt her at first, so I moved slowly. Then she suddenly opened up and we moved faster and faster together until we came with a rush. We clung together, breathing hard, our bodies sweaty and slippery, but holding each other tightly. We talked quietly and she asked about my family. I couldn't bring myself to say that I never knew my father and my mother was a junkie living in a trailer.

"My folks are dead."

"Oh. I'm so sorry."

"That's okay. It happened when I was a kid."

"I've been meaning to ask you for weeks. Where do you live?"

"I crash with some of the surfers. They party and use drugs, so I get there late and leave early."

"I wish I could ask you to my house, but my parents won't allow boys there."

"What do they think you do at night?"

"That I'm with my friends, surfing and hanging out at the beach."

"Well that's true."

She grinned impishly. "They think it's very innocent. I'm still a child to them… After tonight I'm a woman."

I didn't know how to respond to that and just said:

"I guess so."

I biked home with her, as I did every night we were together, and my lightweight bike seemed to almost float along. We kissed goodnight and I got hard. She smacked me playfully.

"Wait till tomorrow," and went in.

She wasn't shy anymore. As I rode home to the boatyard I wished I could tell the world about what we did tonight, but one part of me had enough common sense to know I had to keep my big mouth shut and not ruin a good thing.

Chapter 15

My birthday was on July 14th, which some of my smartass teachers had proudly told me was 'Bastille Day' in France. As if they were the only ones who knew that. Tempting as it was, I never responded: 'off with your head, dumbass'. Tammie gave me a sold gold I.D. bracelet, with my name engraved. It was heavy. On the underside it said: 'From T with love'. She made me promise not to ever give it to anyone else. I thought that was weird. Who would I give it to? But she was my girlfriend and I didn't want anyone else, so it was easy to promise. Cliff gave me a hi-tech sports watch with lots of functions. It was big, heavy sleek and elegant. Now I'd have to strengthen my arms to wear bracelet and watch. Just kidding.

Cliff and Lucille took Tammie and me to dinner at a French restaurant. The surprise was that 'Big' Bill came to the restaurant. He gave me an envelope, said: 'Happy birthday', and turned to leave. Then he turned back.

"Mike persuaded me to get this web thing and I didn't expect much, but I was wrong. I got lots of reservations for the rest of July and August, a lot of new repair jobs and I sold a boat this morning that was sitting for a year, with the owner calling me every day asking why I didn't sell it yet. So thanks, Mike."

He hugged me clumsily, declined Cliff's invitation to join us for dinner and left. Cliff insisted I open the envelope and it contained $500. I said:

"That's too much."

I started to get up and go after him and Cliff said:

"You don't have to do that. It's his gift to you and his way of telling you that you earned it."

I thought about that, then said:

"I guess I did. Thanks, Cliff."

"De nada, amigo… Oh. Sorry I didn't mean…"

"Cliff!"

"What, Mike?" he asked in a concerned voice, afraid he offended me.

"You're supposed to speak French here."

He burst out laughing and we all joined in.

Riding our bikes later to Tammie's house, she said:

"You think a lot of Cliff, don't you?"

"Yes. He's my best friend and he looks out for me."

"You know he's famous."

"Sure. How do you know?"

"The guys and girls always talk about him… Some of them think you're his son."

I almost fell off my bike.

"Where did they get that idea?"

"They say he never made friends or taught anyone before and they know neither of you are gay, and you do look alike."

"I better make sure not to call him dad when I'm with the guys or girls."

She swatted me playfully.

"You're such a tease."

I was still laughing to myself when I kissed her goodnight and left. It got me thinking how lucky I was to have Cliff, who was like a big brother. I had to tell him the rumor. He'd get a kick out of it.

The next day at the shop I was putting away some wetsuits and I started thinking about what Tammie told me, the rumor that I was Cliff's son. I laughed, then thought that no one was ever jealous of the attention Cliff gave me, at least that I had noticed. I know that Davey and Ronnie liked me for myself and the others seemed to. Could Cliff have arranged that? No. But I guess his reputation didn't hurt. I quickly reviewed my beach life and concluded that I treated everyone fairly and didn't have to worry if I belonged there. One thing for sure. If I wasn't the right kind of person, Cliff wouldn't be interested in me.

I started working on my website and I took a lot of time trying to decide what it would look like. Between the shop, the boat yard and Tammie, I hadn't spent much time with Davey, so the next time I went surfing I asked him to go out with me. As we were paddling out I told him how busy I'd been and I missed our time together. But he was cool.

"Don't worry, dude. I know you're into a lot of stuff. I'm glad for you."

"Thanks, Davey. You're a good friend."

"Then I need a favor, friend."

"Sure. What?"

"You brought all those great girls to the beach. Can you find one for me?"

"I can try. I don't know if I can do anything until school starts again. But I can talk to

Tammie and ask her if she can introduce you to one of her friends."

"Will she think I'm a dork because you're asking for me?"

"No. She thinks you're cool."

"Yeah?"

"Yeah. I won't tell her you're a dork until after she gets a girl for you."

"Thanks a lot," and he splashed me.

We stayed out for about an hour, doing more talking than riding. It was fun. Just as we

were about to head in Tammie paddled out to us, so we stayed and watched her ride for a while. She was doing pretty good. She came back from a nice ride and asked:

"How'm I doing?"

"Good," I replied. "I want to ask you something."

"What?"

"Do you have a girl friend you can introduce to Davey?"

"Maybe. Is he nice?"

"I can talk," Davey blurted. "Ask me."

"Alright. Are you nice?"

"I think so. What do you say, Mike?"

"He's a nice guy, Tammie. He's my age, so he needs a girl who isn't just looking for an

older guy."

"I understand. I'll talk to some of my friends and ask if they want to meet a nice, good looking guy who surfs."

Davey glowed. "Thanks, Tammie," and he babbled to her all the way to shore.

Chapter 16

Tammie and I tried to be cool about what we were doing together, but all the regulars knew, including Cliff. I found out from Davey that some of them actually looked out for us, from a distance, to be sure no hoods or weirdoes bothered us. It was a good feeling that they had my back and I began to understand how vulnerable we were, making out on the beach at night. It got me thinking about Tammie, a rich, privileged girl, being with a guy like me, doing it in public. Then I realized I wasn't a raggedy, half breed, poor kid anymore. I was making money, well maybe not a lot, but enough to feel independent. I was learning how to deal with different kinds of people and building self-confidence as I discovered my talents. Maybe it wasn't strange that Tammie wanted to be with me.

Then the unexpected once again reared its ugly head. Tammie came to the beach on a beautiful day a week after my birthday, in tears. I thought someone hurt her and rage raced through me.

"What's wrong? What happened? Are you alright?"

She cried even harder, put her arms around me and pressed her head in my neck.

"Oh, Mike. My parents just told me we're moving."

"What? When?"

"In two weeks. We're moving to Tucson, Arizona."

I didn't know what to say. We had become close in many ways, so the thought of losing her was a shock. I just stood there holding her, at a complete loss what to say or do. Davey came up to us a minute later.

"Hey. You guys shouldn't make out during the day. You're beach night owls."

She turned and he saw the tears running down her cheeks.

"Are you guys having a fight? Sorry. I'll take off."

I still couldn't speak, so Tammie said:

"My family is moving. I have to leave Mike."

He patted my shoulder. "Sorry, dude. That's bad. I'll see you guys later," and he walked off without asking Tammie if she found him a girl friend. That was cool, cause I know it was important to him.

We sat in an isolated spot on the beach, holding hands, not talking, already feeling lost to each other. It got darker and darker and we didn't notice the millions of glistening stars on a beautiful summer night, in what had been briefly paradise for us. We rode our bikes to her house and stood on the porch, holding each other tightly, until she started crying and went in. I went back to the boatyard and sat on the foredeck of the ketch, staring at nothing, until I fell asleep.

I got to the shop a little late in the morning and Cliff told me Tammie phoned and her folks were taking her to Tucson to see the new house, her school and the country club. I looked at Cliff as if the earth had been yanked from under me. He just clasped my shoulder and let me know he was there for me. There wasn't anything he could say and nothing I could do, so I tried to control myself and got to work.

Tammie never came back to Chula Vista. She phoned me at the shop and told me they were staying at a resort hotel until their new house was ready and her dad hired a moving company to pack and bring everything to Tucson. She told me to get a cell phone so we could talk regularly and said how much she missed me already. But I was starting to shut down to her. I knew she was gone from my life. I had lost so many important things that there was a coldness that took over, to preserve whatever good feelings I still had. I couldn't run away with her, or bring her to live on my boat. We were kids. There wasn't much point in visiting her in Tucson. It was too far to ride on my bike. And what would we do? There wasn't a beach where we could make out. Even if her parents let me in, they wouldn't leave us alone. So it was over.

I did get a cell phone, but I didn't call Tammie and give her the number. She called the shop and the first time Cliff told her I was giving a lesson. After that he insisted I talk to her.

"She didn't do anything wrong. It's not her fault her parents moved. She was good for you. She deserves to hear the truth. It was special, but there's no way you can be together. It'll keep hurting both of you if you don't end it cleanly, say goodbye and get on with your lives."

He was right. I couldn't climb into a hole because she was taken away. And it wasn't fair to avoid her, so I called her. We spoke for a long time and she cried a lot, swore she'd love me forever and didn't understand why I didn't want to talk to her on the phone anymore. I tried to explain, but I either did a lousy job, or it didn't mean anything to her. When I finally disconnected she was crying like a baby. Part of me was remote, but I remembered how I felt when I lost Jennifer and guessed Tammie was feeling the same way. She was a surfing pal, a sex partner, a friend, and I liked her a lot, but I didn't love her. That made it easier to accept her departure. The one lesson I never forgot – nothing lasts.

I think Cliff and Bill got together and planned extra work for me, because they kept me very busy. It was only at odd times that I got a sudden pang of missing Tammie and oddly it wasn't so much sex on the beach, as her warm, eager presence, especially surfing. I hung out more with Davey, who had started surfing with me and Cliff at night. One night, after a good ride, we hit the beach and Davey said:

"I'm not going to your blanket with you, dude."

The nights with Tammie flashed through my mind and it seemed long ago, even if it was only a few days. I must have been feeling better, because it struck me funny.

"I'll manage without you," I replied.

Then he got a serious expression.

"If I get a girl, can I use your spot?"

"Sure, Davey. Unless I need it again."

"Cool."

Chapter 17

Now that I had real sex, actually did it, I looked at girls differently, trying to assess how willing they might be. My favorite viewing was still the beach bunnies with their tan, shapely bodies bursting out of their bikinis. The more daring girls were wearing thongs, which displayed almost everything to lustful guys who could look, but not touch. I found myself coming on to plainer girls, not crudely, I learned that from Tammie, but letting them know I was interested and available. One afternoon a woman came into the shop with her ten year old son asking about lessons for him. I told her the rate and she said she'd like to book ten lessons over two weeks. While we were talking I looked her up and down. She was even older than Cliff, but still looked pretty good. She caught me checking her out and gave me the once over.

"I'd like to pay you in advance… What is your name?"

"Mike."

"Can you come to my house in one hour and I'll give you the entire amount?"

For three hundred dollars? "Sure."

"We live in Jamal. Do you know where that is?"

"Yes."

She gave me her street address and walked out. I did a little more work, then told Cliff I had to run an errand. I peddled fast to her house, an erection growing as I fantasized about her. There was a noticeable swelling in my pants when I got there. A maid answered the door and took me through all kinds of rooms filled with expensive looking stuff, outside to the pool. The lady was wearing a thong and a tiny top. She was hot. She led me into a small building she called a cabana, closed the door and said:

"Take off your pants."

I could only guess what was coming, but I took them off quickly. I was wearing jockey shorts and I was just about bulging out of them. She came to me, reached down and squeezed my penis.

"How old are you?"

"Sixteen," I lied.

"Nice cock for a boy your age. Take off your shorts."

I did and she nodded approvingly.

"I don't know whether to suck it or fuck it."

She slipped off her top and ordered:

"Lick my nipples."

While I did, she dropped her thong, then squeezed my balls hard. I jumped and she laughed. I tried to kiss her, but she shoved me away.

"Don't do that! Bite my nipples." I did and she said: "Harder," then moaned as I obeyed.

She knelt down, licked the tip of my penis and I almost came. She sucked my penis. "Don't come." Then she pushed me down on a couch, stood over me, then slowly squatted down onto my penis without touching it and began to move up and down.

"Pinch my ass hard. Scratch it." She moaned as I hurt her, and moved faster and faster, then yelled. "Now." She flowed hot and juicy on me and I shot my come into her. She sort of hovered over me for a minute, then hopped off, put a towel between her legs, slipped on a terrycloth robe and said:

"The maid will give you your check," then walked out.

Part of me wanted to go after her and punch her in the face, but I was covered with both our juices, so I took a towel, wiped myself and got dressed. The woman was gone, the maid was waiting, handed me the check and led me out. I pedaled a few blocks, stopped and looked at the check. It was for $300, signed, Darlene Sheridan. I was mixed up. She treated me like a hired boy. Angry thoughts raced through me. I started thinking about what I could do to her. Then I admitted she didn't force me. And it was a new experience. But I didn't feel good, so even if she asked me, I wouldn't do it again.

Chapter 18

A few days later I was on the beach giving the Sheridan boy a lesson and I saw this dynamite blond in a skimpy bikini watching us. I looked closer and it was Miss Fallon. She was built. I continued the lesson, occasionally checking her out from the corner of my eye. She looked better at every glance. I finished the lesson, sent the boy to the shop to buy the most expensive wetsuit and surfboard, and walked to Miss Fallon.

"Hello, Miss Fallon. Nice to see you here. You're sure looking good."

"Why thank you, Mike."

"Ready for a lesson?"

"I don't think so. Let's talk."

"Sure."

"How are you doing with C# and .Net?"

"They're coming along. Do you want to test me?"

She laughed. "No. I just want you to keep learning. Did you look up hacking yet?"

"No. But I'll do it this week."

"Good. It's important to know what goes on on the internet. I have something to show you."

Fantasies of a quick glimpse of her hidden parts flashed through my mind, but she reached into her backpack and took out what looked like a little computer that was all screen. I never saw one like it.

"What is that?"

"It's an IPad, a tablet that connects to the internet, and does a lot of other functions. She powered it up, swiped it, and the screen filled with apps and functions. She went over them with me, showed me how email works, then a search engine.

"Touch the safari button, then when the keyboard comes up, touch type in hacking."

I did and a menu came up and she pointed to Wikipedia:

"Go there."

She explained that it was a free access, free content encyclopedia that almost anyone could edit. Cool. I daringly said:

"I could come to you house tonight and you can teach me how to use it."

She smiled sweetly. "You're a very nice boy, Mike, but I'm not interested in what you may be thinking."

Holy shit! Did she know what I was thinking? I blushed and changed my stance so my penis didn't bulge prominently. What did she want from me and why was she showing me that hot body?

"Can I talk frankly to you?"

"Sure."

"I've been watching you for a reason..." Yeah. But not for the one I was thinking... "You're smart, talented and very mature for your age. I'm considering asking your help in a special project."

"What kind of project?"

She looked around to make sure she wasn't overheard.

"Can you keep a secret?"

"Sure."

"Can I trust you to keep one of mine?"

I thought about it for a moment. She had been very good to me, so I could promise.

"Sure."

She studied me intently, then said:

"I came to Chula Vista two years ago, after I left the school I had been working at for three years. There was a terrible incident. A group of boys and girls cyberbullied one of my students, a bright, shy girl, who was overly sensitive. They spread nasty rumors about her doing vile sex acts, insulted her, called her filthy names, threatened her, until she couldn't take it anymore and committed suicide."

"Why didn't she tell someone? Ask for help?"

"I don't know. She didn't. And a very nice person died because of some evil-minded kids. She left a note on her computer describing what they did to her, but the school dismissed her Mother's complaints. I only found out about it accidentally. I went to the principal and demanded justice, but she denied the school had any responsibility. I went to the police and they said there was nothing they could do. I talked to elected officials and they didn't care. My principal called me a troublemaker and an agitator and warned me my job was at risk. I quit and came here. But I didn't forget about the kids who drove that poor girl to her death."

I began to get a feeling for what was coming.

"What do you want from me?"

"Will you help me punish those kids?"

"I won't kill anyone for you."

She didn't laugh so I knew how serious she was.

"Do you believe in right and wrong?"

I thought about that for a moment and said:

"Yes."

"I don't want those kids to get away with murder. So if I can plant evidence they were cheating or stealing and make it public, they'll get what they deserve."

"Why don't you do it?"

"I don't have those computer skills. I'm hoping you can learn them."

She sounded sincere and it might not be a bad thing to get those kids, but what if she had another reason?

"I have to learn a lot more before I say yes. But I can start learning hacking and we can talk more about this. No promises for anything but to keep your secret."

"That's fair. Thank you, Mike. You'll make a great white hat."

"What's that?"

"A righteous hacker."

"We'll see. In the meantime I shouldn't come to your house again. Unless you come up with a better idea, you should take surfing lessons, so we can talk."

"Alright. But I'll pay you."

"No. This isn't for money.".

Chapter 19

I didn't see Miss Fallon for several days, then she came to the shop to book a series of lessons. I introduced her to Cliff, who checked her out thoroughly. I thought it was funny, because he usually was very discreet and didn't eyeball women customers.

"So you're his computer teacher. Mike talks about you a lot. He thinks you're special."

"That's nice to hear. He's my best student."

"So what got you interested in surfing?"

"Mike talks about it a lot and it sounds exciting. I thought I'd give it a try."

"Mike's a good teacher. You can rely on him."

"I will."

Miss Fallon may have looked great in a bikini, but she wasn't much of an athlete. When I showed her how to do something she seemed to get the idea, but had a difficult time doing it because she was poorly coordinated. On the other hand, surfing lessons weren't the real reason she was seeing me. This way we could talk. It became very clear after a few lessons that she was obsessed with punishing the kids who drove her student to suicide. The more she told me about it, the more it seemed to go beyond a student-teacher relationship. According to her I was her best student and she treated me nicely, but she was completely impersonal. I didn't want to hurt her feelings, or lose her help, so I told her:

"I understand how angry you are at those kids, but I have to decide if it's right for me to do anything to them."

She got very upset at that.

"Don't you see how evil they are?"

"Sure. But I've had to deal with kids like that all my life."

"Than you should understand they can't be allowed to get away with it... Oh. How can I persuade you?"

'You can have sex with me', flashed through my mind, but I replied:

"I looked up hacking and it's way beyond me right now. I'd have to know unix, Linux, Perl, Lisp, C++, and learn how to write open source software..."

"That much?"

"Yeah. It's complicated. I'll start and keep you informed of my progress, but you'll have to be patient."

A crazy look passed over her face and suddenly she didn't look so pretty.

"You don't know how this eats at me."

"I'm sorry about that. This girl must have been very important to you."

"She was..." Then she got a suspicious expression. "Why do you ask?"

"Well you want revenge on those kids."

She took a deep breath and her usual cheerful disposition returned.

"I don't want revenge. I want justice."

I'd have to learn a lot more about what happened before I got involved. Part of me guessed I could play her and persuade her to have sex with me. But another part saw her differently now. So I said:

"I'll get started learning stuff."

"Thanks, Mike. I knew I could rely on you."

August was half over and I was enjoying the water more and more each day. Everything was going well at the shop and the boat yard. I was actually saving money and had almost $500 in my savings account. Then I got my first professional web design request. I got an email from Wally Custerback, who owned a bar/restaurant facing the beach. He sponsored the volleyball tournaments and wanted to branch out to surfing tournaments. He invited me and Cliff to dinner to discuss a website and tournament sponsorship.

Wally was big, loud, bald and going to flab, like an ex-athlete who no longer bothers to work out. We had dinner at an expensive seafood restaurant. He explained if we had dinner at his restaurant we'd never have a chance to talk, because people would keep interrupting us. The first thing he talked about, almost as loudly as if he was on the playing field, was a website.

"Everybody keeps telling me I need a website, but I don't know much about it. You look awful young to be an expert. How old are you?"

"Fourteen."

"Well convince me you know what you're doing."

It was weird. I got this flash of understanding that Wally was so loud, because he was insecure. I knew about insecure and knew just how to handle him.

"I'm a web designer, Wally. I've been doing it for two years without a complaint."

"Who are your customers?"

"Individuals and businesses."

"What businesses?"

"A few you'd know are the Imperial Beach Marina and the Wave Length Surf Shop."

He asked Cliff'

"You like what he did?"

"He did a great job."

"That's it? You're not going to sell me on him?"

"No. It's between you and him."

"But you recommend him?"

"Definitely. Talk to 'Big' Bill, if you like."

"Nah. Your word's good." Then he turned to me. "How much'll it cost me?"

Without a second's hesitation, I said:

"My basic fee is $1,000. Any other charges will be discussed."

Out of the corner of my eye I could see Cliff trying not to laugh. Wally shrugged, nodded, then said:

"That sounds o.k. What do I get for it?"

"Your site designed to your satisfaction, with the information and visuals you give me. I get half in advance, the remainder when I show you the rough cut and you approve it."

"That sounds simple enough."

"I try to make it simple, because computer stuff is complicated."

"Yeah. I know. Well we've got a deal. Do we need a contract?"

"No. I'm a designer, not a corporation."

"Yeah. I understand. How do we start? Do you want $500 now?"

"No. Let's get together and I'll show you some samples and we'll get an idea what you want the site to look like. If you're happy with that, we'll go ahead."

"Sounds good to me," he mumbled in relief. "Now lets talk about a surfing tournament."

"Well it's too late to do anything big this summer," Cliff said. "But if you're really serious about this, we could have a 16 and under tournament at the end of September, with a few prizes and trophies. Mike and I will plan, help organize and recruit competitors. The Sponsor will have to pay for the prizes, trophies and promotion, as well as the surfer magazine ad, the local newspapers and the tv station. If it works out to your satisfaction, we can plan a bigger event in the Spring."

"How much'll it cost?"

"Well prizes and trophies between $750 and $1,000. You'll have to figure out promotional costs."

"Sounds good. Let's do it. Are you going to enter, Mike?"

"No."

"Why not? You're the right age."

"We sell to these kids. I don't want to compete with my customers."

"That's pretty mature for a kid your age."

"I'm pretty mature for a kid my age."

"He's a smart kid," Wally said to Cliff. "How do we start?"

"We pick dates for the event. If we have enough entrants, we could do it over two weekends, Saturdays and Sundays. The first weekend will be the qualifying events. The next weekend the actual competition. If there's time, you could get a nice banner made and posters and flyers."

"I can do that. Will you be the judge?"

"No. I'll get three judges the kids will respect. I'll be the tournament director." Cliff looked at the calendar. "How about September 17th and 18th, and the 24th and 25th? Does that give you enough time to organize everything?"

"Yeah. That's more than a month. I'll get flyers and posters right away and we can start distributing them. What's next?"

"You give me a check for $1,000. I'll give you receipts and return any extra. If we need more money is it available?"

"Yeah. This is exciting. We are going to have a lot of fun… What about the website, Mike?"

"Do you have time tomorrow night?"

"I'll be at the restaurant. How long will it take?"

"If you know what you like, half an hour."

"Good. Come about seven and have dinner with me. Then we'll talk."

"Sure."

"Alright, guys. I gotta run. Have whatever you want. Dinners on me and the manager will bill me." He wrote a check, handed it to Cliff and left.

"Thanks, Wally," Cliff and I called after him.

We both ordered shrimp cocktails and lobster. I asked Cliff what he thought of Wally.

"He wants to be a big operator and be admired. He seems to be a nice guy, but we'll know more about him in the next few weeks."

"What do we do next?"

"We spread the word in the surfing community. I'll order the trophies, you pick the prizes. I suggest first place a board, second a wet-suit, you figure out third."

"Sure. Do we have time to make t-shirts?"

"Great idea, Mike. We can sell them on the beach. You sure you don't want to compete?"

"I had to compete all my life, until I came here. And there was nothing to win, only survival. Is there something wrong with me now that I don't want to beat the other guy?"

"No, Mike. I think it's a sign that you're feeling secure enough so you don't have to prove anything."

Chapter 20

Cliff got a notepad and began outlining the tournament rules. As he was writing I designed the t shirt 'Wally's' and Wave Length 16 and under surfing tournament and the dates, on the back. A surfer riding a tube on the front. I showed it to Cliff, who sent me to the t shirt place nearby to order 100, billed to Wally. On the way there I got a great idea for the tournament and celled him.

"Cliff. It's Mike. We should have the tournament in sections, 16 and under, 14 and under, 12 and under, 10 and under, separate sections for boys and girls, and a novice class in each section." There was a long silence. "What do you think?"

"Forget the t shirts for now. Come back here and design a flyer we can put up everywhere. And Wally can use the info for newspaper ads."

"I'm on my way."

"Mike."

"Yeah?"

"Right on!"

We made up a flyer, got Wally's approval over the phone and ordered a thousand copies. They were ready the next afternoon and I hired one of the beach kids to take them to all the stores within a few blocks of the beach and ask to post them. I tacked them up on the boardwalk and posted them near the stairs to the beach. I set up a website meeting with Wally and brought 100 flyers along. He phoned the local newspaper and placed ads for the next few weeks. He told me how impressed he was with how quickly we got things done. He loved the t shirts and was completely won over when I got an idea:

"Can you go on the local radio and tv stations and promote the tournament?"

"Wow! Great idea. I'll call my buddies there… What do I say?"

"Give the tournament info, dates, age groups, then talk about how good surfing is for boys and girls, and the community at large."

"You're one smart kid. How would you like to work for me? I'll double what Cliff pays you."

"Thanks, Wally. I appreciate that, but I'm committed to Cliff."

"Well it's an open offer."

After that, I could do no wrong with Wally. I showed him the Imperial Beach Marina website, then Wave Length's and he loved them. I didn't bother telling him that was because he hadn't seen professionally designed sites. We picked photos of the restaurant, happy diners, some customer reviews, the volleyball tournaments and a page for the surfing tournament. While we sat there I made a banner, 'Wally's , feeding the health and appetite of the community', He went wild for it and said he'd buy the idea from me to use it on all his advertising.

"Consider it a gift for sponsoring the surfing tournament."

"That's very generous of you, Mike. I tell you what. Consider yourself a guest of the restaurant any time you like."

"Thanks, Wally. That's real nice of you."

He gave me a check for $500, shook my hand and I left with the fee from my first paying customer. It was a good feeling. I made a note to get Davey to enter the 14 and under, and help him prepare. Then I got another flash. Could we get a wet suit maker to donate a jacket for each section winner, in exchange for sponsorship publicity? I'd have to talk to Cliff.

Chapter 21

I kept getting more ideas about what we could do for the tournament and Cliff and Wally approved almost all of them. Actually the only one Cliff vetoed was for him to do a celebrity demonstration. I wasn't overly convincing because I knew he'd refuse, but it was worth the effort.

"Your demo would be a real draw, and good for business."

"Nice try, Mike. But no thanks. I only ride for pleasure these days."

I couldn't argue with that. I finished the rough cut of Wally's website and he loved it. He showed it to customers and his manager and they all responded enthusiastically. He gave me the other $500 and wanted to know if it would be ready for the tournament. I told him how to get an internet service and the domain site and said It'd be ready before the tournament.

"If you get it up sooner I'll give you a bonus."

"I'll see what I can do."

I had been getting so many good ideas lately that I couldn't believe I had forgotten 'Big' Bill. I went to his office, waited until he got off the phone, then told him about the tournament. He was eager to participate, wanted to be a sponsor and agreed to give money for prizes and lend a jet ski boat for water rescue. I suggested he publicize the event to his friends and customers and I'd add a notice on his website. I added the marina to the t-shirt, ordered another thousand flyers and made a note to add the event to the Wave Length website. Bill wanted to pay me, but I refused, reminding him I lived there rent free. Cliff was delighted that I included Bill and a little embarrassed that he didn't think of it.

I was busy during the day, but I went surfing with Cliff and Davey almost every evening. I worked with Davey with Cliff observing. and later he'd advise me how to improve Davey's technique. It was typical of Cliff that he never corrected me in front of someone else. It's funny about how feelings change. At first I was in awe of him as a surfer. I took that for granted now and he was world class as a person to me.

The only real problem I had with August just about over and school ahead, was Miss Fallon. As her surfing lessons wound down, she became increasingly urgent to involve me in punishing the bullies. She told me how the football team spread stories of the girl giving them blowjobs, how she was mocked for her appearance, for being smart, then threats to hurt her, which resulted in her leaving a twitter message: 'I can't go on anymore. I'm ending it.' And she jumped off a crosswalk into highway traffic and was killed instantly.

I had tried to assure Miss Fallon that I would think about it, but she was becoming increasingly urgent in demanding a commitment. One afternoon she got very agitated when I wouldn't promise to help her, and stormed off. She had yelled loudly enough to attract attention and Zoey, Vicki and Carrie walked over and asked what happened. I tried to downplay the incident.

"She's just frustrated that she isn't doing better with her surfing lessons."

"Maybe she's frustrated because you won't give her other lessons," Zoey teased.

"She's my computer teacher."

"We know that. But she's hot," Vicki said.

"That's whack. She's old."

"Not with a body like that,:" Zoey replied.

"What's with you girls? Did I come on to you when I was giving you lessons?"

"You looked us over all the time," Carrie said.

"Sure. You're great looking girls. But I didn't do anything."

"That's because you were getting it on with Jennifer, then Tammie. Who are you with now, Miss Fallon?" Zoey asked.

"You gotta be kidding. I wouldn't come on to a teacher."

"What if one of us was available?" Vicki asked.

"I could never choose between you. Besides, you want older guys."

"What if we changed our minds?" Carrie muttered.

I was running out of excuses and said jokingly:

"It would have to be all three, or none."

They looked at me appraisingly, then each other, and Zoey said huskily:

"What would we do?"

"Hey. I was kidding. I couldn't keep up with you. You're the hottest girls on the beach. You don't need me. You can get any guys you want."

"What if we want to try you? We heard a lot about you from Jennifer and Tammie."

"Alright. I'll tell you the truth. I have a girlfriend."

"We haven't seen you with anyone," Carrie accused.

"That's cause she isn't a surfer."

"Where does she live?" Vickie demanded.

"In Jacar."

"We live there," Zoey declared. "Maybe we know her. What's her name/"

"I can't tell you."

"Why not?" Vicki said.

"Because she's older and doesn't want her folks to know."

"Where does Miss Fallon live?" Vicki snapped.

"How should I know?"

"Is your girl Miss Fallon's age?"

"No. She's seventeen. Why do you keep asking about Miss Fallon?"

"Because we think that you're getting it on with her," Vicki answered.

"Well I'm not and don't talk about it, or you'll get her into trouble."

"We'll see how things go," Vicki said and they ambled off, looking great from the rear, but I saw them in a different way now.

Chapter 22

School started and it took a while for me to get adjusted. It was a shock not being at the shop or beach all day. I finished Wally's website a week before the tournament. He loved it and gave me a $500 bonus. The t-shirts were selling at the shop and the restaurant and began to be seen all over the city. But by the weekend of the surfing trials I was back in the routine of running and surfing early, going to school, then the shop.

A lot of kids pre-registered at the shop for the tournament. Most of them came with their parents, who were interested in lessons and equipment for their kids, which was great for business. But a lot more kids showed up Saturday morning, so by the time trials started we had over a hundred and fifty boys and girls. In order to handle that many kids, Cliff assigned three to ride at the same time from each section. Most of them were eliminated on the first ride, but they all received a chit to get a free t-shirt at the shop. My brilliant idea.

The local newspaper sent a reporter and photographer, the tv station sent a crew and they interviewed everyone. Cliff had me do the interview representing the tournament and I praised everyone, especially the kids, and thanked the sponsors for giving such a healthy, fun experience to the community. The tv girl, a plastic looking blonde who didn't look like she'd get to a bigger station, asked why I wasn't competing.

"I'm the assistant tournament director and I give lessons to many of the kids. I'm not here to compete with them. This is their day."

"But don't you want to be out there showing how good you are?"

"I ride for the beauty of being on the water, not to prove anything."

She wasn't happy with my answer, but Cliff was.

"I just hope you know how proud of you I am."

"Thanks, Dad," which gave us a laugh.

Zoey, Vicki and Carrie had been hovering nearby during my interview and heard me call Cliff, Dad.

"So it's true," Zoey gushed. "He's your father."

"No. It's a joke between us."

"We don't believe you," Vicki accused

"Why would I lie about that? I'd be lucky if he was my Dad."

They stalked off, great looking girls who were becoming a pain in the ass.

By the end of the day about 60 kids were eliminated. No accidents, no injuries, no arguments, no complaints. A very nice day. Sunday was just as nice, except we had a big audience due to the tv report, which included my interview. I was suddenly a celebrity and people asked for my autograph.

Another 40 kids were eliminated, so we had 50 entrants for the next weekend. We sold a lot of t-shirts and ordered another 200. Again a very nice day. Wally was ecstatic. Bill was delighted and Cliff was happy. I saw them huddling together looking in my direction, but I was too busy talking to parents and a writer/photographer from a junior surfing magazine to wonder what they were up to.

The following Saturday we drew a big crowd. Now that the number of entrants was more manageable, each competitor had three rides. The newspaper and tv people were here again, as well as the junior surfer's magazine. It was a long, fun day and by the end there were 24 kids left. 3 boys and 3 girls in each section. Davey had made it to the finals and Zoey, Vicki and Carrie were flirting with him. He'd never believe me if I told him how nasty they were, so I didn't say anything and let him enjoy himself. We had our first complaints that there were no 18 and unders, and no bodyboards. Cliff explained that the sponsors put the tournament together almost overnight, apologized for the oversights and promised to include them in the next tournament. Wally was walking on air because everybody was talking about him and business was booming at his restaurant.

Sunday was a beautiful beach day and every inch was packed with spectators. The tournament had become a big event for the city and newspaper and tv coverage was extensive. Plastic blonde interviewed me again and asked who my favorite competitors were.

"I hope everyone does well, but I'd really like the girls to get more attention. I'm pulling for my friend Davey, in the 14's and under."

Plastic blonde was suddenly more pleasant, maybe because I mentioned the girls?

"Why do you want the girls to get more attention?"

"There are way more boy surfers. The girls should be encouraged to enjoy the water, instead of just being beach bunnies."

"Wow! What have you got against beach bunnies?"

"Nothing. I just want to see girls surfing, not just watching."

"Thank you, Mike Sanchez, assistant tournament director of the Imperial Beach Surfing Tournament, and a voice for female equality. Any last words for our viewers?"

"I'd like to thank our sponsors, Wally's Restaurant, Wave Length Surf Shop and the Imperial Beach Marina for making this event possible. Also all the competitors and the fine crowd that enjoyed their skills."

The tournament ended with 1st place winners getting a diver's watch, 2nd place a wet suit jacket, 3rd place wet suit pants. Everyone seemed happy with their prizes. Davey won the 14's and under and was thrilled when he was on tv with the other winners. The girl who placed 2nd in the 14's and under introduced herself after just about everyone went home.

"I didn't want to speak to you before, in case you thought I wanted favoritism. I'm Abby."

'Hi. You did pretty well. How long have you been surfing?"

"Almost a year."

"The girl who beat you, Donna, has been surfing for three or four years."

"She's good."

"Yeah. You can be good."

"Should I get lessons?"

"It never hurts. But practice is more important."

"Don't you want a student?"

"Sure. But I'd rather date you."

"Could we do both?"

"Sure. Come to the shop after school and we'll get acquainted."

"See you then."

I watched her walk away. She had a great body. This was definitely an unexpected treat. But my surprises weren't over. After we oversaw the clean-up of the beach, I couldn't believe how many people just dumped their trash on the sand, Cliff called me to join him, Wally and Bill.

"You tell him, Cliff," Wally urged.

"No. It's your idea."

"Alright. Mike. We're so delighted with what you've done that we're starting a college scholarship fund for you, with ten thousand dollars. We'll add to it over the next few years and it'll pay your tuition at a good college."

I gaped at them, unable to speak, and finally mumbled:

"I don't know what to say… Thanks."

"You deserve it," Cliff said, and Bill and Wally echoed him.

Part of me was all choked up and I was afraid I might cry.

"I gotta go. Thanks again."

I hopped on my bike and peddled furiously until I was out of sight. All I could think was how lucky I was.

Chapter 23

It took a while for me to settle down to a routine after the excitement of the tournament. I was a celebrity at school, due to the tv interviews and some of the guys resented the attention I was getting. The surfers were so protective of me that no one dared bother me. I was still coming to terms with the college scholarship fund. College was so far away it felt unreal, but the support of Cliff, Bill and Wally was very comforting. Wally had bragged about me to his customers and some of them were businessmen who wanted websites. I signed letters of agreement with two new clients, and was negotiating with three more. It was time to pick a business name for my design venture.

I was spending more and more time with Abby. She'd come to the shop with me after school, get her board and go to the beach. I had a few lessons every day and I'd give her a quick lesson between them. She started taking Ronnie's karate class, which now had more than 30 kids, who I reminded to pay him $10 a week. He found out from Davey that I was the one who started the kids paying and took me aside one day after class.

"I didn't know you got everyone to pay until Davey told me. That was real nice of you."

"Glad to do it. You deserve it. You're a great teacher."

"Thanks, Mike. Your lessons are free from now on."

"No way, Ronnie. You're a pro and should get paid. I can afford it and you're worth it."

"I'm getting the money because of you. How can I repay you?"

"You've looked out for me since I came to the beach. You don't owe me. You're a good friend."

"So are you. You really helped Davey. I appreciate that."

"He's my best friend. I was glad when he won his section… You can do something for me."

"Name it."

"Keep an eye on Davey. He's hanging with Zoey, Vicki and Carrie and I know they smoke pot all the time."

"I'll watch him. Thanks, Mike. If you need anything, just ask."

Abby started night surfing with me, Cliff and Davey and she fit right in, saying little, but loving every minute on the water. Afterwards I'd ride home with her to Jacar, then hurry home ot the boatyard, where I'd do my homework, work on my new client's websites, then fall into a deep sleep. I got up early, rode to the beach, ran two miles, then surfed until it was time to go to school. The best part of each day was riding the waves alone in the mornings, without anything on my mind but the joy and freedom of being on the water.

I should have known that everything was going too well. Davey came up to me in the lunchroom at school and looked worried.

"There's a rumor starting to go around school that you've been getting it on with Miss Fallon."

"What? Are you kidding?"

"No, Mike. I heard some girls talking about it in the hallway." He looked around to be sure no one was listening. "Are you getting any of that?"

"No, Davey. She's my teacher. That's all."

"Well they're saying she took surfing lessons from you and maybe other things."

"That's whack. There's nothing going on."

"Well I'll do what I can to cool it, but you know how word gets around."

I knew that. I also guessed who started the rumors; Zoey, Vicki and Carrie. They were becoming a real pain in the ass, but there was no sense talking to them. They'd just deny it and spread more rumors. I knew it was spreading like wildfire when Abby asked me if I had been involved with Miss Fallon. I assured her it was only a nasty rumor and she believed me. I hoped it would fade away, until I got a note to report to the assistant principal, Mrs. D'Angelo.

I looked at her office while she was on the phone. The walls were covered with some kind of colorful wool things on frames or something. I noticed her looking at me as she talked and I looked back. She wasn't very tall, judging by how low she was in her chair. She had stringy, grey hair, a flabby face with double chins, small sneaky brown eyes, a flat nose and almost no lips. Except for the fat, she would have made a great shrunken head in one of those National Geographic documentaries.

"I asked you here for a very delicate reason, Mr. Sanchez." She looked at me expectantly, but I just waited. "It has come to my attention that there is disturbing gossip going through the school about you and one of our teachers, Miss Fallon."

I played dumb. "What kind of gossip?"

"I don't know quite how to put this… That there is an inappropriate relationship between you and Miss Fallon."

I stayed dumb. "I don't understand."

"Students are saying you and she were seeing each other socially."

"What? That's crazy."

"Did you see her outside of school?"

"She took some surfing lessons this summer, but that's it."

"And did you do anything with her during the lessons?"

"No! They were on the beach, during the day, in full view of everyone, just like all my

lessons."

"And did you go anywhere alone with her?"

"Are you kidding?"

"No. This is a serious inquiry. If a teacher does anything inappropriate with a student there could be criminal charges."

"Nothing happened. I was never alone with her anywhere. She's my teacher and I like and respect her. She wouldn't be interested in a student, except as a teacher."

"How do you know that?"

I didn't, but what else could I say.

"Because she's a good person who encourages all her students."

"Well thank you for coming, Mr. Sanchez. Go to your next class now."

"Are you going to stop those rumors?"

"Why?"

"It'll hurt Miss Fallon if she finds out."

"Does that matter to you?"

"Sure. I don't want anything bad to happen to any teacher I like."

"We'll see about it."

Those nasty girls were doing a job on her, but there was nothing I could do. If anyone saw me talking to Miss Fallon alone, that would just confirm all the gossip. I couldn't tell for sure in class if she knew what was going on, but most of the students did. Some of them were always watching me, so I was very careful to seem my usual self, whatever that was. Things might have become stressful, except that my surfer friends were always supportive and Abby was fiercely loyal. She remarked:

"It's a sign of your good character. Most boys would brag about having a hot woman like that. You deny it."

"That's cause nothing happened and I don't need to brag about a lie."

"That's one of the many reasons I'm starting to like you a lot."

She was a really nice girl. It was weird. All my girls so far had been real nice. And they were rich. I had no idea how I'd act with a girl from the other side of the tracks, but I hoped it would be the same way.

Chapter 24

Business peaked at the shop a few weeks after the tournament, but had definitely increased due to the publicity and exposure. We were getting more and more sales through the website and Cliff raised my salary to $10 an hour. I told him I was making enough as I was, but he just laughed at me.

"You're one weird kid. I have to argue with you to give you more money."

I looked around to make sure no one could hear us.

"Would you rather give me an allowance, Dad?" which gave us a laugh. I added carefully: "There's a rumor all over the beach that you're my father."

"It doesn't look like I'm going to have any kids, so I could do worse."

"The rumor doesn't bother you?"

"Why should it? You didn't start it."

"Of course not."

"Then forget it."

"I think Zoey, Vicki and Carrie started it."

"I'm glad you didn't get involved with them."

"They started a worse rumor at school, that I'm having sex with Miss Fallon."

"That could be trouble. Teachers lose their jobs over things like that."

"What can I do?"

"Nothing. Just deny it to everyone who asks."

"That's what I've been doing."

"Good. Hopefully it'll die down as the school year goes on. Just make sure no one ever sees you alone with her."

"I'll try my best. How about I fix you up with her? She's hot and it'll stop the rumors."

"Lucy would skin me alive. No thanks."

"Just trying to be helpful."

"Try another way."

"Yes, Cliff," I replied innocently.

The rumors didn't die down at school and brought me a different kind of notoriety. I didn't like it. Lots of guys suddenly wanted to be my buddy and girls were coming on to me. I stayed cool and distant with all of them, except one kid. Milton was smart, small, shy and bullied. I saw some of the older kids pushing him around in the cafeteria and I invited him to sit with me and Abby at the surfer's table. Within a few days the bullies stopped bothering him and sought other helpless victims. I wish I could have defended all of them. Milton was so grateful he kept asking what he could do for me and I'm not sure if he understood, when I said:

"I did it for me as well as you."

I guess he thought I was a dumb jock, because he offered to tutor me and was shocked when I offered to tutor him in computer science. He was a very bright kid in a spindly body and I urged him to start physical exercise, running and karate. He almost fainted.

"I'd be too embarrassed to do that."

"I'd be embarrassed if I didn't try to improve myself," Abby told him.

One of the many reasons I was getting fond of her.

"Look, Milton," I said. "If you start work tomorrow, in six months you'll see definite changes. In a year you'll be a different person. How old are you?"

"Fifteen."

"Are you happy being a victim?"

"No."

"Then come to the beach around 5:00 p.m., run as far as you can, rest, then take Ronnie's karate class. It's $10 a week. Can you afford that?"

"Yes."

"Try it for a month. If you don't see any improvement, stop."

"I'll think about it," he replied.

"Don't think about it," Abby urged. "Do it."

"Okay. I'll try it."

"Good," she said gently. "Then you can continue to sit with us."

"You mean if I don't do it, you'll chase me away?"

"Why should we help you, if you won't help yourself?"

"I understand," and he scurried off to class.

"I'm glad you took him in," Abby remarked.

"I was bullied when I was a kid. I hate bullies."

"Why didn't you offer him surfing lessons?"

"First he's got to develop his body and build some self-confidence. If he's interested later, sure."

She suddenly stood up and kissed me hard, which set off a lot of cheering from the kids around us.

"What was that for?"

"For being a good person."

"I'm not, but I'm trying."

"You're dong pretty good with me so far."

"I'm glad. I'm really starting to like you."

Chapter 25

I took Abby to dinner Saturday night at Wally's restaurant. The manager, Frank, greeted me cheerfully and I introduced him to Abby. He showed us to a table, instructed the waiter to give the check to him and sent us a bottle of white wine. Before the waiter could open it, I told him to take it back, thank Frank for me and I ordered two cokes. A minute later Frank came to the table.

"Don't you like the wine? I'll get the list and you can pick anything you like."

I leaned forward and whispered:

"It's not a good idea to have two kids drinking wine in the restaurant."

He bopped the side of his head.

"You're so mature I forgot how young you are. Wally would kill me if I got you into trouble."

"Cliff would kill me if I got you into trouble."

He laughed. "Thanks, Mike."

Several adults had said hello to me when we went to the table. Now, as I looked around, others waved to me.

"You really are a celebrity," Abby remarked.

"No. Just a few people know me from the tv interview."

"Well a lot of people like you."

"A few."

Just then Wally came in with the chief of police and he introduced him, led him to a table, then talked to Frank. He came back to our table a minute later and thanked me for sending back the wine.

"The Chief is my pal and wouldn't have said anything, but if anyone complained, he'd at least have to take you out and send you home." He leaned over. "Now that the website is up, a lot of people want to order online. How do we do it?"

"I'll come by tomorrow and we'll look at a few apps and see what you like."

"Are you sure you don't want to work for me?"

"I'll be glad to help with projects, but my first commitments are to the shop and the marina."

"They're lucky to have you."

"Thanks, Wally."

"Enjoy your dinner."

"How come the manager told the waiter to give him the check?" Abby asked.

"I did a job for Wally and instead of cash, we agreed I could eat at the restaurant."

"Do you come here a lot?"

"Actually this is the first time. He'd be happy if I came every night, but that would be taking advantage."

We had a very nice dinner, steak for me, fish for Abby. As we biked home, I found myself thinking that we had been spending a lot of time together for the last few weeks. I liked her more and more, but despite her great body she felt more like a friend, then a girlfriend. We hadn't done anything sexual together and I didn't want to. I thought about it for a minute, then said:

"We haven't made out."

"Does that bother you?"

"No. I like being with you. Does it bother you?"

"No. Can I tell you something personal?"

"Sure."

"And you'll keep it a secret?"

"Sure."

"I'm not attracted to boys. You're the first one I liked, but not to make out with, as a friend. Does that bother you?"

"No. I like you as a friend. I could tell that sex wasn't happening for us."

"I'm sorry."

"No need. It's cool. I guess you prefer girls."

"I'm not sure. That's what I think about though. I just haven't tried it with anyone."

"Don't do it with Zoey, Vicki or Carrie, or they'll tell the whole school."

"How do I approach a girl?"

"I don't know. I can ask Cliff."

"Don't tell him it's me."

"No. I'll say it's a friend at school."

"And it really doesn't bother you? We're still friends?"

"Sure. You can kiss me once in a while at school, so everyone thinks you're straight."

"Oh. So now I'm an old lesbo?" and she smacked me playfully.

"Not old."

"You are bad."

Chapter 26

On Sunday I stopped by Wally's and set up an app for ordering and getting delivery online. He handed me a check for $500 and I told him it was too much. He laughed.

"I've made thousands of dollars in new business since you made the website and I'll make a lot more with ordering online. You earned the money. You never want to be greedy about money. It'll change you for the worse. But if you're entitled to it, take it. That's the ideal of doing business."

"I understand. Thanks, Wally."

"Just remember you're welcome here every day, if you like. You're good luck."

"I've been very lucky lately. I don't know how long it'll last."

"Enjoy it while you've got it. Try your best and maybe you'll make your own luck."

I waved goodbye and left, thinking how wrong my first impressions of him were. He was a generous, good-hearted guy who loved doing things for people. Now I had three friends who were doing things for me that were changing my life. I also had my surfer friends and Abby. That reminded me to ask Cliff how a girl… I wasn't sure how to say it… Tried to pick up another girl.

The rumors about me and Miss Fallon were still going around the school. I guess most of these kids led empty lives, or they would have lost interest already. I ignored the guys who asked me about it, though I came close to punching out one of the dumb football jocks, who told me he banged her and wanted to compare notes. Instead I laughed at him and walked away. That guy was barely down from the trees. Miss

Fallon would never have anything to do with someone like him. When a girl asked me about her, I insisted I had nothing to do with her.

In a quiet moment that afternoon, I asked Cliff how a girl could come on to another girl.

“Anybody I know?”

“No. A girl I know at school.”

“It’s Abby, isn’t it?”

“How did you know?”

“You wouldn’t ask for anyone else. Tell you the truth, I haven’t the faintest idea. If she was over 18, she could go to one of the lesbian bars. There are probably internet sites, but you never know who she’d meet.”

“Can you ask Lucy?”

“Sure. But she won’t know. If I think of anything I’ll let you know.”

“Thanks, Cliff.”

Without realizing it at first, something had changed between me and Abby. We were still close friends, but the urgency to be with her all the time had faded. I saw her every day at school, but she stopped coming to the shop every day. She still went to the beach after school and surfed, but only two or three times a week. She gradually stopped surfing with me and Cliff at night, and when she did I didn’t ride home with her. Not even Davey, my closest friend, noticed the difference. He was getting it on with Zoey, using my old spot on the beach at night.

“Hey, man. If you ever want your blanket for you and Abby, let me know. Zoey and I’ll find another place.”

“It’s cool, Davey. Enjoy it.”

"Thanks, Mike. We really don't have anywhere else to go. Ronnie won't let me bring her home and we can't go to her house."

"How's it going with you two?"

"Not cool. She gotta get high before having sex and she wants me to get high with her. She gets freaky when I won't. I tried to explain that I'm in training, but she doesn't buy that. Remember when you and I got high and Ronnie almost killed us… I don't think it'll last much longer… Maybe I'll try Vicki next."

I laughed. "You're a pig."

He looked at me indignantly.

"No, man. Pigs don't surf," which cracked us up.

Chapter 27

It was getting close to the Thanksgiving holidays and the rumor linking me and Miss Fallon had just about died out. Then a shock wave went through the school. There were claims that Miss Fallon had been seen kissing Abby in the computer lab. Abby had been sent home and suspended. Miss Fallon was put on leave pending a criminal investigation. I couldn't believe it at first and thought maybe Zoey and her friends were making trouble. Then the word was some of the computer students had come back to the lab to play a game and saw the pair. I don't know how it came to the attention of the school authorities, but I felt terrible for them. I celled Abby, but there was no answer. I decided to go see both of them after work. Part of me couldn't help thinking that if it was true, Miss Fallon was pretty stupid to do that in school.

Cliff was very sympathetic when I told him and gave me the afternoon off.

"We weren't helpful to Abby." he remarked.

"No. I feel terrible for them. I don't know what we could have done, but I wish it didn't happen."

I celled Abby as I rode to her house, but it went right into voicemail. I said I was coming to see her and disconnected. When I got there the house was dark. I rang the bell and no one answered. I waited a few minutes and rang again. When there was no response, I celled and left a message: 'I'm so sorry for what happened. If I can help in any way let me know. I'm still your friend'. Then I rode to Miss Fallon's house. I couldn't phone her, so I waited until someone came out and slipped in before the door closed. I went to her apartment, rang the bell, then knocked. She didn't respond. I didn't know if she was there, but I called through the door:

"It's Mike, Miss Fallon. Let me know if I can help," and I said my cellphone number.

It was frustrating not to be able to do anything for people I cared for, but I couldn't think of anything else. I rode back to the shop and Cliff could tell I didn't feel like talking. I canceled the two surfing lessons I had for today and changed them to tomorrow, but I put on a good face for the customers. I went to the beach after work and took Ronnie's karate class. He noticed how violently I was doing my forms, but didn't say anything. When it was over I grabbed my board and headed for the water. Milton called me and I stopped.

"I'm sorry about what happened to Abby, Mike."

"Thanks."

"Can I still sit with you at school?"

"Sure. As long as you keep working out."

"She was really nice…"

"She still is!" I snapped and rushed into the water.

I paddled furiously for a few minutes, then slowly relaxed. For some reason I didn't feel much like riding and just lay there on the board, adjusting if I drifted too far. Cliff came out a little later and didn't ride, just hung near me, not saying anything, but somehow his presence was very comforting. I felt a little better and when I sensed the next big wave, said:

"Alright, Dad. We hung out enough. How about a ride?" and I started paddling into position.

He joined me and a minute later we were high on the crest, a foot or so apart, and there was nothing else but the magic of flying on the water.

Chapter 28

As Christmas drew near, I still hadn't heard from Abby or Miss Fallon. They both knew they could reach me at the shop, so I assumed they didn't want any contact and I began to forget them. Our computer teacher substitute was an older man who didn't seem to know very much, so I continued to study on my own. Business at the shop was normal for this time of year, but mail order sales were going strong. I gave a lesson or two almost every day. My web design business was doing well. I got a new business client every few weeks, referred by satisfied clients. I also designed websites for some kids at school, charging anywhere from $100 to $250, depending on their ability to pay. I never let anyone know how quickly and easily I knocked them off. Between the shop, lessons and web designs I was earning almost $1,000 a week.

One afternoon, Cliff turned to me suddenly.

"Mike."

I jumped. "What?"

"You don't pay taxes."

"No."

"You're supposed to. I'm going to set up a meeting with you and my accountant."

"Do I have to?"

"Yes. I pay you by check. So do some of your web clients. The government knows. If you don't file, they could come after you and take your savings and your salary."

I didn't argue and met the accountant the next day. Ms. Lewison was real old, maybe 40 or 45, tall, thin, with grey hair, thick glasses, but a cheerful face. She had me list my income, collect receipts and my bank statements. Then told me she'd file for 2011 at tax time in April and not to worry about 2010. I wasn't happy when she told me my tax rate would be about 30%, unless I had deductions. I didn't know what deductions were and it turned out I didn't have any. She said she'd see what she could do and told me again not to worry.

Wally invited Cliff, Bill and me to Christmas Eve dinner at his restaurant, including wives and girlfriends. I met Bill's wife, Kathleen, for the first time and she was his direct opposite; short, petite, quiet and shy. She was real sweet and I liked her immediately. Wally had a special dinner for us, roast goose. It was delicious. After we ate we exchanged presents. I got gifts from everyone and I gave them gifts, but I gave Cliff an IPad, which he loved. Wally had instant IPad envy and asked where to get one. Christmas day I gave Ronnie and Davey presents. They were embarrassed that they didn't get anything for me. They felt better when I assured them they helped me all year round and I got some extra money last week.

School seemed strange after the holidays without Abby and Miss Fallon, but I got used to it after a while. A couple of girls made it obvious they were interested in me, but I didn't want to get involved with anyone right now. Davey, as he said, dropped Zoey, who came on to me, but I politely said: 'No, thanks'. Milton had been building his body and confidence for months gathering his nerve and asked Zoey for a date. He was almost struck dumb when she said yes, but managed to mumble: 'cool'.

Wally phoned Cliff in mid January to discuss a Spring surfing tournament. Cliff suggested we have it in mid-April, early enough so there was time between that and the end of summer tournament. I was brought into the first planning session and the goal was to do it bigger, with a lot more sponsorship and publicity. Cliff said there was enough lead time to arrange a sanctioned junior tournament, with points and ratings. Wally suddenly asked:

"Are you going to enter, Mike?"

"No."

"Why not? Cliff tells me you'd be the best surfer in the 16's and under."

"The same reason as last time. I don't want to compete against our customers."

"They wouldn't mind," Wally insisted. "They'd respect you for it."

"Tell you the truth. I'm just not very competitive that way. What I get from surfing is so special that it would change if I worried about winning or losing."

"Did you teach him that, Cliff?" Wally asked accusingly.

"I taught him to surf. He decided how he wanted to surf. I respect his choice."

Wally couldn't understand my lack of interest in competing and I didn't want to talk about it. As long as he still liked me, that was okay. We outlined what we had to do first, get sponsors, contact the media and spread the word. I reminded them that this time we should include the 18's and under, and bodyboards, since we said we'd do it.

Chapter 29

A girl in my computer class, one of the kids who supposedly saw Abby and Miss Fallon kissing, told me she had seen them standing close together, but she didn't actually see them kissing. She and the other kids finally admitted that to the principal. All charges against Miss Fallon were dropped, they arranged a compensatory payment for her trouble and she transferred with a clean record to another city. Abby's parents put her in a private school in San Francisco. It was a relief to know they were alright and hopefully getting on with their lives.

Cliff kept me busy, I think deliberately, to keep my mind off Abby and Miss Fallon. I was busy doing websites for the graduating seniors and preparing for the tournament. I made a website for the tournament with videos of Wally's restaurant, the marina and video clips from Cliff's surfing days. Wally insisted on paying me for the website and I got tired of saying no. Davey stopped seeing Vicki and took up with Carrie, and Milton was still dating Zoey. Davey confided in me that Zoey didn't do anything more then touching, so we joked together about what they did together. But Milton, by association, was now a fixture at the surfer's table. He finally decided to learn to surf and took lessons with me two or three times a week.

After the recent turmoil it was good to concentrate on my usual activities and everything seemed to be going well. But part of me never forgot that nothing lasts. More and more of the girls from school started hanging out at the beach with the surfers. Some of the jocks from the football and basketball teams started grumbling that the surfers were stealing their girls. A few of them came to the beach one afternoon while Ronnie's karate class was in progress. They watched for a few minutes, then melted away after comparing their mutual abilities. Fortunately, most of the jocks had their own girls and wouldn't get involved in any dispute resulting in a sports war that would cause problems for all of us.

A lot more girls wanted surfing lessons, due to the tv coverage of the tournament. It reached the point where I couldn't handle them all without giving up my time at the shop. I discussed it with Cliff and suggested we hire Ronnie as an instructor.

"That's a good idea," he said. "Let's pay him $15 per lesson and the other $15 goes to the shop."

I thought that was reasonable and I asked Ronnie if he would be interested. When he said 'yes', I brought him to the shop to talk to Cliff about how to treat customers, as well as general teaching practice. Cliff asked me to give Ronnie some demonstration teaching lessons and he was cool with me instructing him. He caught on quickly, as I knew he would and I told Cliff we could have confidence in him. He started the next day and I arranged for him to have at least 2 lessons a day, sometimes more, while I limited myself to 2.

It took me a while to realize that I was happy. When I finally did, a part of me denied it, a superstitious part that couldn't believe this was happening to me. But I had friends, I was making money, I had the pick of surfer girls and beach bunnies, and most important, a mentor, Cliff, who was the most important person in my life. He never told me what to do, but radiated honesty and fairness that made me admire him all the more. Without being aware of it, I had started walking and standing like him. I even got some of the same facial expressions and speaking mannerisms. I was talking to Milton after karate class, just before night surfing, and Davey, Zoey, Vickie and Carrie were hanging out with us. Cliff came up, tapped me on the shoulder and nodded to the water. Zoey said loudly:

"Look at them together. Don't they look alike? Cliff. Tell us. Is Mike your son?"

Cliff whispered: "Come closer." and when everyone leaned in, he murmured: "Don't ask. Don't tell," laughed, raced to the water and I followed.

We both laughed as we paddled out, but I had a sudden thought.

"Cliff. I know we think it's funny, but the rumor is at school, as well as the beach. Could it cause you problems?"

"What kind of problems?"

"I don't know. Reputation? Legal?"

"Has anyone we know treated you or me differently?"

"No."

"I can't think of any legal problems. Can you?"

"No. I just don't want to cause you any trouble."

"You've been a positive part of my life since the first day you walked into the shop."

"Thanks, Cliff. You're the best. I'll do anything for you."

"Right now, let's ride."

Chapter 30

A few days later I was at the beach giving an 8 year old girl a lesson. I happened to look around and Wally was standing there. I waved hello and said:

"Just a few more minutes. You're next," which made him laugh.

"Can you see me on a surfboard?"

"Sure. All it takes is practice."

I went over a few things with the girl, then turned to her mother.

"If you're both ready, Jan can go on the water tomorrow."

Mom was nervous and asked Jan:

"What do you think?"

"If Mike thinks I'm ready, I'm ready."

"Don't worry, Mrs. Tranchard. I'll be with her every moment."

"Well if you think it's alright…"

"I'll see you tomorrow. At 4:00 p.m."

I watched them walk away, little Jan reassuring Mom, and Wally said:

"You handled them pretty well."

"It's part of the job. Parents are always more nervous than their kids."

I started to tell him I could have him riding the water in 3 or 4 weeks, but he shook his head.

"Maybe another time. I stopped at the shop and asked Cliff if I could borrow you for a while. Get some clothes on and I'll take you to dinner."

"What's up?"

"I'll explain later. Do you like Mexican food?"

"Sure."

Wally ordered what seemed like half the menu and while I was gorging myself, he said:

"The Mayor resigned this afternoon because of health problems. They're holding an emergency election in two weeks to elect a new mayor. I want to be mayor."

He looked at me, waiting for my response, but I didn't know what to say. I knew nothing about politics and hadn't the faintest idea what a mayor did. I thought about what a good organizer he was and how well he dealt with people, and said carefully:

"You'll make a good mayor."

He laughed. "Thanks. I don't have a chance, but I'd like to try. I want your help and Cliff said it was alright."

"What could I do?"

"First make a website that'll make me look good. We'll get flyers, then you get all the kids at school to give them to their parents and ask them to vote for me. Ask all your surfer friends to give flyers to everyone on the beach. What do you think?"

"Sure. I can do that." My mind was racing. "We should have a rally on the beach on Saturday, with free hot dogs, burgers and soft drinks. If there's time, we should have signs made and put them up in store windows… If we can get a list, we can send emails to businesses and home owners. You should contact your friends on the newspaper, radio and tv. Get them to interview you. Buy ads…"

He was looking at me strangely.

“What’ll you come up with when you have time to think about it? Mike. You are my official campaign manager.”

“I don’t know if that’s a good idea. To people who don’t know me, I’m just a kid.”

“I’m confident you can handle it. Give it a try. If it doesn’t work out, no harm done. You’ve already come up with some great ideas.”

“Sure. I’ll start the website tonight and design a flyer. I’ll find out in the morning if there’s time to make signs.”

“Great. You’ll get $500 a week plus expenses.”

He waited for me to protest, but I just said ‘thanks’.

Later that night, after I started the website and flyer, I took a break and looked up elections, mayors, campaign managers, and how to run campaigns. I digested a lot of information quickly and a couple of facts. One. I was completely unqualified to run a campaign. Two. If you didn’t belong to a political party that would support you, there was no way to win a special election. I went back to work on the website, but resolved to have a serious talk with Wally tomorrow.

Chapter 31

I got up early as usual, ran, surfed, then went to school. I slipped out at lunchtime and went to Wally's restaurant. Frank teased me for playing hooky and I just shrugged and asked for Wally. He gestured back to the office and I went in.

"How's my campaign manager today?"

"We have to have a serious talk."

"Shoot."

"I did a lot of research about campaign managers and special elections last night. According to the data, special elections are always won by a Democrat or Republican, because only the major parties can organize fast enough to elect a candidate."

"Well I am a registered Republican. I'll talk to some of the boys and find out if they'll support me."

"I think you're supposed to do that before you become a candidate."

"We'll see how they respond. Besides, it doesn't really matter. This is a win-win situation. If I'm elected, I win. If I lose, I get great publicity for the restaurant, so I win."

"Alright. Your choice. But you need a campaign manager who knows the system, knows the players, knows how to arrange support, deal with the media, involve political and social organizations… The list goes on and on. I can't do any of that."

Wally looked at me and smiled warmly.

"Even if I knew how to find a campaign manager, by the time he came aboard the election will be over. We have to do the best we can. Are you in?"

"Sure. I'll post the website tonight. I'll get the flyer to the printer this afternoon and see if he can have signs in a few days. I need a good photo of you. Do we have a budget?"

"Yes."

"I'll get t-shirts made with your photo, 'Wally Custerback for Mayor', and hire some kids to wear them in the business district…"

"Great idea."

"Tonight I'll make up a list of all the political and social organizations, cultural clubs, any kind of organized groups I can find. We should make a phone script and hire someone to call all of them."

"What kind of script?"

"'I'm calling on behalf of Wally Custerback, who's running for Mayor in the special election'. I'll find something on the internet about why you're running and what you'll do for the city, and conclude with: 'He'd really appreciate your vote'."

"Mike."

"Yes?"

"Can you look up in the internet what a Mayor does?" Which gave us a laugh.

"Sure, Mr. Mayor," Which made us laugh even harder.

The next two weeks zipped by at a manic pace. I skipped school most afternoons to organize, meet people, take care of the tasks I assigned and deal with the constant demands to do more and more as election day neared. The local republicans already had a candidate and refused to support Wally. Despite their opposition, Wally got air time on radio and tv. I had some of my friends talk him up on Facebook, Twitter and chat rooms. People were definitely noticing him. The beach rally drew over a thousand people and the consumption of hot dogs, burgers and soda was prodigious. It was impossible to tell if any of the attendees were registered voters, but the odds were probable that some of them were. The exposure from tv coverage of the rally made the whole city aware of Wally's campaign.

There was a funny incident in the business district that gave Wally a big boost in attention. One of the surfers was walking around wearing a Wally for Mayor t-shirt. Someone complained about it, probably a rival supporter, and a police officer detained him. A local lawyer happened to be walking by and asked the officer why he stopped the boy. A discussion ensued and the officer threatened the man with arrest. A crowd gathered, the officer backed down, but people took camera videos and posted them. By nighttime, most locals saw the video and Wally got a lot of new supporters.

I was too nervous to go to school on election day, but Wally was completely relaxed. I made sure the surfers would keep walking around in their Wally t-shirts until the polls closed at 5:00 p.m. I made last minute phone calls to some group leaders I recently met, then I waited for the results. At 8:30 p.m. Wally got a call from the city clerk. The republican candidate got 36% of the vote. Wally got 34% . The other candidates were eliminated. Since 40% of the vote was required for election, there would be a run-off election in a week. It would be Wally versus the republican, a well known businessman with a long history in local politics.

Wally went wild with joy and babbled away about his forthcoming victory, then on to national politics and the inevitable march to the White House. I tried to calm, him without success, then left him to revel in his temporary triumph. We did what we could during the week, Wally almost jumping out of his skin with tension, while I was cool, certain of the results. When the day came, Wally couldn't sit still for a moment and almost chewed his fingers to the wrists by the time results came in. He got 48% of the vote. His opponent got 52%. Wally was crushed. I tried to console him, reminding him it was a foregone conclusion a party candidate would win, but he was miserable. He said a tense goodnight and went home. I biked back to the marina, exhausted, the last three weeks of frantic efforts catching up to me. I was too wiped to even get undressed and was sound asleep as I hit the bed.

Chapter 32

I was still tired when I returned to school, but the morning run and surfing raised hopes I would soon regain my normal energy. There was a message waiting for me in homeroom to report to Mrs. D'Angelo's office. After a lengthy wait on a hard bench filled with other offenders, I was finally admitted to her cutsey office. She seemed to take pleasure in talking down to me.

"We know you have become a tv celebrity, Mr. Sanchez, but that doesn't mean you can abandon school to go surfing…"

"That's not why I was absent."

"Do not interrupt me."

"Even if you have the wrong information?"

"What do you mean?"

"I wasn't surfing. I was working on Wally Custerback's special election campaign for Mayor."

"It's very commendable that you volunteered your services…"

"You don't understand. I was his campaign manager. He hired me to run his campaign."

"Do you expect me to believe that someone hired a boy your age to manage a political campaign?"

I took out my cellphone.

"Would you like to ask Mr. Custerback?"

She stared at me a long moment.

"You're telling the truth?"

"I wouldn't lie about something like that."

"Don't you think you should have requested permission to miss school?"

"It didn't occur to me. I had this great opportunity and I took it."

"Mr. Custerback lost the election."

"Yes, Ma'am. But only by a few points. He did incredibly well for a non-party candidate."

"I see. And do you think your efforts helped?"

"Sure. We just didn't win."

"You should go to a high school that still teaches civics. You'll certainly understand the subject. Thank you for coming, Mr. Sanchez."

"You're welcome."

I started to leave and she called me back.

"Mr. Sanchez."

"Yes, Ma'am."

"Try not to miss school."

"Yes, Ma'am."

Wally phoned me at the shop and asked me to stop by the restaurant that evening. Cliff, Davey and I did an early evening surf, then I biked to the restaurant. Wally was sitting at a table filled with men in suits, most of them talking faster than the speed limit on local streets. Wally saw me, waved, then yelled:

"Quiet, boys. This is my campaign manager, Mike Sanchez."

They gaped at my Wally Custerback for Mayor t shirt and cut-off jeans and the silence grew. I was used to this reaction and in a silly impulse said jauntily:

"Hi ya, boys," and wished I had a cigar in my mouth.

Wally burst out laughing and took me aside.

"These are important republicans. They were so impressed with my showing in the special election that they want me to run for congress. I want you to be my campaign manager."

"You've got to be kidding."

"I'm serious. You did an incredible job. It's because of you I'll be running for congress. You can work part-time until school lets out, then full-time in the summer. You'll get $500 a week part-time, $1,000 a week full-time. What do you say?"

"I don't know, Wally. You need a professional to win."

"You're my good luck charm, Mike. I'm putting $10,000 in your college fund to show my appreciation for getting me this chance. How does Congressman Custerback sound?"

"It sounds great. Let me think about it."

"Okay, Mike. But I want you on board."

"Thanks, Wally. You're a great guy."

The next afternoon I talked to Cliff about Wally's offer.

"You certainly did a lot for him and he's offering big money. What do you want to do?"

"I'd like to help him. And it's a challenge to find out what I can do. But not at the cost of giving up working for you."

"It won't change things for us."

"Sure it will. I wouldn't be surfing. I wouldn't be teaching and I wouldn't have time with you."

"Then you have to decide what you want."

"I just did. I'll do some volunteer work for Wally, but just a few hours a week."

I went to the restaurant that evening to tell Wally my decision, but he beat me to it.

"The party chairman insists that I use an experienced professional campaign manager. They're paying for everything, so what they say goes. We'll figure out a job and title for you once the new guy starts. Sorry, Mike."

"It's okay. This is the big time. You need a pro."

"Glad you understand. I'll call you."

Chapter 33

A week or so later I got a call from Wally telling me his campaign manager, Tony Belladonna, would stop by the shop the next day. Tony was short, fat, well dressed in an expensive light-weight suit, but he sweated a lot. He was loud, pushy and didn't really listen. He told me bluntly where I stood.

"Wally thinks you're a smart kid. He says you came up with all the ideas that almost got him elected mayor. But it's a different game now. Here's my card with my email. If you get any good ideas, send them along. I'll take a look at them. Take it easy, kid," and he waddled out.

We stared after him and Cliff shook his head, then said:

"You've got a lesson in five minutes."

I headed for the door, mimicking Tony's walk and said:

"Take it easy, kid." Which gave Cliff a laugh.

Wally was too busy running for congress to get involved in promoting the surfing tournament. He sent a check for $5,000 to Cliff, with a note asking him to coordinate publicity with his campaign manager, Tony. Cliff was not happy with the new arrangements, leaving everything to us.

"I really didn't want to be in charge of promoting the tournament," Cliff said.

"Nothing official went out," I reminded him. "We don't have to do it."

"If we cancel, Wally won't be happy with us."

I shrugged. "That's his problem. If you want to do it, I'll do most of the work. If you don't, that's fine with me."

“Do you want to do it?”

“No. I don’t need to be on tv again,” which gave us a laugh.

“Then I’ll return his check.”

I dropped the check off at the restaurant and as I was leaving, Tony walked in.

“How ya doing, kid?”

“Okay. I just returned Wally’s check to Frank. We won’t be holding the tournament.”

“How come? Wally was counting on it for publicity.”

A lot of comments raced through my mind, most of them sarcastic, but I just said:

“We can’t deal with it.”

“Too bad. Wally’s gonna be disappointed. Oh, well. That’s what happens when you rely on amateurs.”

I left before I said something really unpleasant.

I didn’t see Wally for a few days, then passed him on the boardwalk on my way to a lesson. He had a group who were handing out Wally for Congress flyers. He saw me and waved, but he didn’t say anything, so I waved back and kept going.

It was a relief not to be going 10-15 hours a day, learning how to do new things quickly, that had to be done. Yet part of me was pleased with how I had met challenges, and dealt well with many of them. I don’t know about being a politician, but with some study and practice I bet I could be a campaign manager.

Chapter 34

We got a lot of inquiries about the Spring surfing tournament, followed by disappointment when we announced that it was cancelled due to lack of sponsorship. We added that there might be a tournament at the end of the summer, figuring we might want to do it. One of the reporters from the tv station asked who the sponsors were that withdrew, but Cliff wisely responded that he didn't know, since he wasn't on the organizing committee. This distracted any anger possibilities away from us and people gradually stopped asking about it.

I actually spent more time on my schoolwork and the subjects I usually neglected. My grades improved, except in math, which didn't come naturally to me and required a lot more effort on my part. I decided not to worry about it now and work on it next year when I started high school. My teachers actually recognized my efforts and encouraged me to work harder. Even my Spanish teacher complimented me on my progress. I managed not to laugh in her face, because I spoke and understood Spanish. If she wanted us to read Don Quixote, and babble to us about Cervante's sublime language, that was her business. She didn't seem to know that the language in every Spanish speaking country was different. I bet she couldn't read the menu in a Mexican restaurant. But I didn't get angry. She wasn't mean. She just wanted us to learn refined Spanish.

My web design business was still keeping me busy and I got an email from a Lisa, who heard of me through a friend and wanted me to do her website. I emailed her what I needed and my rate and she requested a meeting to go into detail. I emailed that she should come to the surf shop and ask for me. She showed up the next day and I fell in lust. She had long black hair, a movie star's face, a model's body and just oozed sex. She went to Cliff and said:

"Hi, Mike. I'm Lisa."

Cliff pointed to me and said:

"He's Mike."

She turned to me and obviously didn't like what she saw. I was wearing a cut-off t-shirt and bathing suit, and had goggles on while sanding a board. I was sweaty, dusty and just a little ripe.

"Mike?" she asked tentatively.

I looked her up and down, which she didn't like, and answered:

"Yes."

"I'm Lisa… Are you really the web designer?"

Her attitude was beginning to annoy me, but I generously overlooked it, considering her body.

"Yes. Would you like to see my license?"

She didn't know how to respond to that, and said:

"Can we go outside and talk?"

"Sure. Do you want to wait while I wash up, or shall I come as I am?"

She wasn't amused and walked out the door. I looked at Cliff, who winked, and I followed her.

"This must be a mistake. One of my father's friends recommended you as a sophisticated designer. How old are you?"

Now I was really getting annoyed.

"You requested this meeting. Either we discuss what you want, or I have other things to do."

She wavered while I stared at her, but decided to stay. She explained that she wanted her website to list her academic and athletic accomplishments, so she could use it as part of her college admission package. That sounded simple enough, so I nodded and she told me she was applying to several California schools that had excellent Latin-American departments, her major, as well as the right athletic program. I switched to Spanish and asked whether she wanted stills or video. She was shocked.

"You speak Spanish?"

"Yes."

She told me, in hesitant high school Spanish, how important this was and how she needed to be sure I could do it properly. I was torn between growing dislike and growing desire and said:

"I tell you what. Let's have dinner together. I'll bring my laptop and show some examples of my work and you can outline what you want."

"Are you asking me for a date?" she said coldly.

I smiled sincerely. "I am arranging a meeting to exchange information. If you have an alternative place to meet, I'll be pleased to join you."

"What restaurant?" she asked suspiciously.

"Do you know Wally's?"

"Yes. My family eats there."

"Good. Tomorrow night? 7:30?" She nodded yes. "Just to show you it's business, if you don't hire me, dinner is on me. If you do, dinner is on you. Fair?"

"I'll see you there."

I watched her walk away. I had to find out what sports she did, because she had a great ass. This was a new experience for me. I didn't like her at all, but I wanted her body. I had to laugh at the thought that vampires must feel that way. She didn't know that I was a guest at Wally's, but she'd be impressed at how they treated me. She had to be at least 16, maybe 17. I'd have to figure out how to get around that. She didn't seem like the type to go out with a 14 year old boy.

Chapter 35

Lisa was waiting outside looking impatient when I got to Wally's, but I was 5 minutes early, so I ignored her surliness. We walked inside and Frank greeted me with a handshake.

"Hi Mike. How are you?"

"Good, Frank. What about you?"

"My wife says she's leaving me for a surfer."

"Anybody I know? I'll tell him to send her back."

"Tell him to keep her," which gave us a laugh. "Just you two?" I nodded. "Follow me."

He led us to a table, where the waiter, Paul, said:

"Hello, Mike. Miss."

"Hi, Paul."

"Something to drink?

"I'll just have water, but Lisa might want something." and I looked at her.

"I'll have a cocktail, if you will."

"I don't drink."

"Because of your age?"

"No. But have what you want."

"I'll stick to water."

Paul took our dinner order and the busboy brought rolls and water.

"Hola, senor Mike."

"Hola, Luis. Is Tito doing his homework?"

"Si."

Lisa was staring at me as if I had two heads.

"Everybody knows you."

"Yes."

"And the busboy called you 'senor Mike', even though he's older then you."

"I helped his brother."

"What did you do?"

"Nothing to discuss. Let me show you some website samples, then we'll talk about what you want."

I showed some of the business websites and Ronnie's site, which featured his teaching karate and surfing. She was favorably impressed and was about to tell me what she wanted, when Wally and a group of suits came in. Frank must have told him I was here, because he came straight to our table and called:

"Hey, Mike."

I stood up and he hugged me, then turned to his suits.

"This is the man who got me to the runoff for Mayor," He turned to me. "When I get to congress I'll owe it to you. There'll be a good staff job for you whenever you want."

"Thanks, Wally."

"How about designing a new website for my congressional campaign?"

"Sure. Let me know when you want to meet."

His campaign manager, Tony, was getting restless and muttered:

"Our guests are waiting."

"Gotta run, Mike. I'll call you tomorrow," and he rushed to his office, followed by the suits.

By this time Lisa was thoroughly dazzled and eagerly began telling me what she wanted. Academics were straight forward, then the surprise. She was a champion distance runner, who planned to train for the Olympics, 5,000 meters. I mentioned I ran and she condescendingly said:

"We'll have to run together some time."

"I run on the beach every morning at 7:00 a.m."

"How far do you run?"

"A mile or two, before I surf."

"I suppose you'll challenge me to surf, when I beat you."

"Why would I do that?"

"To prove you can beat me."

"I don't have to prove anything."

I was really starting to dislike her. We finished dinner, which I graciously said was on me, and we agreed on the cost. I charged her twice my usual rate, $500, which she agreed to and she said she'd stop by the shop with her material and a check. We said goodnight and I watched her get into a new BMW and drive off. I really wanted her body.

Chapter 36

I just started my run on the beach, along with Ronnie, Davey, Milton, Donna, the three witches, Zoey, Vickie and Carrie, and some of the beach bunnies, when Lisa joined us. She was wearing 500 dollar running shoes and a black spandex body suit that was spray painted on her taut body. We were a funny contrast. The guys were barefoot, in bathing suits, the girls were barefoot in bikinis. The girls stacked up pretty well to Lisa. The three witches dropped out at half a mile, bunnies at ¾ of a mile and Milton made a mile. Pretty good considering he couldn't do 100 yards six months ago. As Ronnie, Davey, Donna and I headed into the second mile, Lisa was a few feet ahead of us and kept looking back to see if we were trying to catch her.

We reached the two mile mark, turned and headed back to the starting point, where we kept our surfboards. Lisa didn't notice us turn and she kept going for a few moments, then realized she was alone. She rushed after us and when she caught up, panting, said:

"You didn't tell me you were turning back."

"You didn't ask me," I retorted.

The odds were probable that I wasn't going to get her body, so I wasn't going to be nice to her. She lagged further and further behind and was just about wiped when she reached us, as we were getting ready to surf.

"You ran more than 6,000 meters. You do that every day?"

"I miss a day once in a while," I replied pleasantly.

She looked at Ronnie, Davey and Donna, who were heading for the water.

"They're not even tired," she muttered, as she tried to control her breathing.

The competitive runner was so shocked that I softened for a minute.

"We've been running together for years. It takes time to build your endurance. Next time try it barefoot in a bikini…" She glared at me, suspecting I wanted to see her body, which I did. "When you feel yourself tiring, drop out…"

"I can run as long as you can," she growled.

I didn't bother responding.

"I'm going to hit the water now. It's the best feeling in the world after a run. You should try it."

"I suppose you want to give me lessons?" she said sarcastically.

I smiled. "I'm fully booked. I give newcomers to Ronnie," then I dashed to the water.

I finished Lisa's website a week later, then phoned her and asked her to stop by the shop. She loved it, particularly the last section, where I put in Olympic games running, and ended with a voice-over and the image of a gold medal: 'Lisa, like all Olympic hopefuls, thinks gold'. Her arctic exterior thawed like a glacier from climate change.

"It's wonderful. It's all I asked for and more. How did you come up with 'thinks gold?"

Duh. Her brain was definitely not as advanced as her body. Do hopefuls dream silver? Well, you can't have everything.

"I'm glad you like it."

"You're pretty cool about it."

"I always do my best for my clients."

She left happily, but even more confused about me.

Over the next few weeks, Lisa showed up on different days to run with us, almost as if she was checking that we really ran every day. She still ran in her running shoes and spandex and was tired at the finish, when the rest of us went into the water. I don't think we spoke other than to say 'Hi', and she didn't ask about surfing lessons. Yet she hung out sometimes with the beach bunnies while we surfed, and couldn't help noticing my popularity with the bunnies when I came out. I guess she was waiting for me to make a move on her, so she could blow me off. I mostly ignored her, which I knew irked her.

A few weeks before Easter break, Cliff said:

"Lucy and I have been talking about taking a vacation during Easter break. I was going to close the shop, but decided to ask if you wanted to run it while I'm gone."

I wouldn't have anything special to do, so that seemed like a good way to keep the business going.

"As long as I can phone you if there's an emergency."

"Sure. Just don't have an emergency."

I had keys, knew how everything worked, so it seemed simple enough.

"Where are you going?"

"San Francisco. Lucy wants to go the opera, concerts, plays, all the culture she can't get here."

"I'd like to learn that stuff someday."

"Next time we'll take you with us."

"Cool."

Chapter 37

Cliff left for San Francisco without any last minute admonitions, which indicated his confidence in me. The mornings were very quiet, so I worked on Wally's congressional website, which I started and stopped twice, because it was too historical. I finally found the right approach, which was 'What your congressman does for you'. I looked up the duties of a congressman on the internet, and did a voice over using images in the public domain. I finished with a winning looking photo of Wally, and the voice over: 'Congressman Custerback works for you. You hired him to always do his best for you'.

I phoned Wally and told him I'd bring it to the restaurant after I closed the shop, but he was so urgent to see it that he said he'd come to the shop with Tony, and a few aides. Lisa came in just before he got here and was upset after I didn't make a fuss over her. Wally stormed in, yelling: "Lemmee see it. Lemmee see it," and almost knocked her down.

I set up my laptop on a counter and showed the website. The group waited for Wally's response before commenting. Tony looked ready to dismiss it.

"Mike. You're a genius. This is terrific."

The aides said nice things, then Tony asked:

"How did you come up with that 'works for you' angle?"

For once he wasn't confrontational, so I answered:

"I looked at congressional campaigns in Southern California. They all seemed to have one or two big issues they focused on. When I looked up this congressional district on the internet, I found there was a large poverty population and a few thousand Hispanic voters… These guys traditionally vote democratic…"

"How do you know that?" Tony demanded.

"I looked up voting patterns on the internet. Business people and the wealthy vote republican, so this seemed like a good way to get the popular vote."

"It's a brilliant idea, kid," Tony acknowledged, totally won over. "Can you make a short video like that?"

I had no idea how to do it, but there was always the internet.

"Sure. I can make different kinds. 10 seconds, 30 seconds, a minute, 2 minutes, 5 minutes, so they can be used in different ways."

"You were right about him, Wally," Tony said admiringly. "How soon can you do them?"

"Figure out how you're going to use them and decide which one's you want first. I'll do a production schedule and a budget."

"Come to dinner tomorrow night and we'll talk about it," Wally said. "Bring your girlfriend."

Before she could protest this indignity, he headed for the door, then paused.

"When will the website be ready?"

"As soon as you approve it."

"It's approved."

"I'll post it tonight."

He waved and was gone, followed by his team. Meanwhile, Lisa was fuming.

"Did you tell him I was your girlfriend?"

"No."

"Then why did he call me that?" She demanded.

Even the thought of her body couldn't curb my annoyance.

"Well he saw you having dinner with me. Now he saw you hanging around like a groupie."

Her face blanched, then turned red with anger.

"That's not why I was here."

"Why are you here?"

She didn't know what to answer, then stammered:

"I… I… Wanted to thank you for doing such a good job on my website."

I smiled cheeringly and said warmly:

"You're welcome, Lisa."

She was completely confused by my friendly response.

"You can be very nice, when you want to be."

"Can you?" But before she could reply, I asked: "Would you like to join us for dinner tomorrow night?"

"You're impossible," she growled and stormed out.

Chapter 38

I studied video production that night. It took a while to sort through big studio productions, but I found desktop, or in my case, laptop production. It was incredibly simple if you had digital material and knew how to edit special effects, text and music. I quickly did a ten second rough cut with the text, and a music intro, then I did a voice over, 'Wally Custerback for Congress', then I did a slow zoom in on a photo of Wally, and voiced over. 'I want to work for you', then text 'elect Wally Custerback to Congress', text and more.

I briefly considered doing a 30 second rough cut, then decided no. I looked up budgets for video production, but couldn't find helpful info. I arbitrarily chose $1,000 for 10 seconds, $3,000 for 30 seconds, $5,000 for 1 minute, $10,000 for 2 minutes, $25,000 for 5 minutes. I drew up a letter of agreement, with a proviso that the quotes were rough estimates, to be renegotiated if necessary.

In the morning I brought my laptop to the shop before I ran. I wasn't surprised that Lisa didn't show up for the run, and I idly wondered if I'd see her again. During the morning, at odd moments, I added some bars of music from the song 'Sweet Georgia Brown', to the rough cut. Ronnie and Davey came in about 11:00 a.m. and made themselves useful. I had mentioned that I'd be running the shop alone, and they showed up without being asked. I had Ronnie give my lessons in the afternoon. After he left, Davey asked:

"When are you going to let me give lessons?"

I laughed. "When you stop being so horny that you come on to the little kids mommies."

He actually blushed, then said in a hurt voice:

"You don't trust me."

"I'll trust you with my life, but not Cliff's business."

He understood the difference and grinned.

"I can't help it if I think about sex all the time."

"The three witches seem willing."

He almost fell over laughing.

"Is that what you call them?... Holy shit. You're right. They're like those great looking witch girls in one of those movies."

"Don't tell Milton. He's still into Zoey."

"Just between you and me, Mike."

I went to Wally's restaurant after I closed the shop. Frank sent me to the office where Wally was talking to Tony and his aides.

"Glad you can make it, Mike," Wally said. "I'll be through here in a few minutes and we can talk during dinner."

"Sure. But I'd like to show you a rough cut of a 10 second spot."

Tony almost dropped his jaw.

"You made something already?"

"Just a sample."

"Let's see it," Wally urged.

I powered up the laptop, then played the spot.

"Again," Wally urged.

I ran it and Tony urged:

"Again."

There was a long silence, then Tony murmured:

"I don't know how he did it so quick, Wally, but we gotta have him do these ads."

"Agreed," Wally said. "We'll talk while we eat."

He led us to his table and Frank rushed up to me and pointed to the bar.

"Someone's waiting for you."

I looked and saw a gorgeous dark-haired woman, in a short black cocktail dress that revealed flawless skin and incredible legs. I couldn't take my eyes off her and it took me a moment to notice that all the male eyes in the room, and most of the female, were fixed on her. It was Lisa. She knew the effect she had and smiled coolly.

"Did you forget I was invited?"

"I forgot a lot of things when I saw you."

This was the first time I reacted to her in a way she expected and she sat there calmly as I looked her up and down. The dress, set off by a pearl necklace that must have cost a lot of oysters their lives, was cut low and displayed firm, shapely breasts that would distract any man who liked beautiful women. I smiled, thinking about the response she'd get when I brought her to Wally's table.

"What are you smiling at?"

"How nice it would be to have you with me if I wanted something from someone who disliked me."

"What a nice thing to say."

"Will you join us for dinner?"

I held out my hand and she took it as she got up from the bar stool. The eyeballs clicking sounded like the ball on a roulette wheel at a casino. Wally, Tony and the aides leaped to their feet and jostled each other to hold a chair for her, and look down her dress. Wally prevailed.

“Gentlemen.” I said. “This is my friend, Lisa. Lisa this is Wally, Tony and… I’m sorry I don’t know your names,” I said to the two aides.

“I’m Eric.”

“I’m Carl.”

Wally signaled Frank, who kept looking at Lisa.

“We’ll start with a nice champagne.”

“Yes, Wally.”

“Then bring shrimp cocktails, lobster and steak. How do you like your steak, Lisa?”

“Rare.”

He ogled her. “You are rare indeed.”

“Why thank you, congressman.”

“Not yet. Wally.”

“I have a feeling if you rely on Mike, it’ll be congressman.”

I couldn’t help thinking what a partner this brunette bombshell could be.

The Lisa effect was incredibly successful. Wally agreed to everything I suggested, signed the letter of agreement without reading it and wrote a check for $9,000 for three spots, 10, 30, 60 seconds. The food was really good. So was the champagne. Everyone else was so intent on gaping at Lisa that they ate mechanically and probably didn’t taste anything. Wally kept the champagne flowing, no doubt hoping that Lisa would get high and reward him with her body. But I knew she valued herself more than that. She passed on dessert, stood, and everyone leaped to their feet.

"Mike and I have to be going now. Thank you for a very nice dinner, Wally. And very nice company."

I followed her out and actually felt glances of envy that I was leaving with this beautiful woman.

"Where did you learn male hypnosis?"

She laughed and replied coyly:

"Whatever do you mean?"

"You know what I mean. You dazzled those guys. I'd like to give you a fee for your efforts tonight. How about $500?"

"Are you kidding?"

"Not at all. You helped me make the softest sale of all time. Would you consider going into business with me?"

"Is this some kind of line?"

"No. With a little training and practice you could sell electric blankets in the Sahara."

"You are serious."

"Yes. Would you like to go somewhere and discuss it?"

"Like where?" she asked suspiciously.

"A cocktail lounge. A hotel. Your choice."

"You live with your parents, right? What about your room?"

"I don't live with my parents."

"Where do you live, o man of mystery?"

"It's a secret. If you go into business with me and I learn to trust you, I'll show you."

"Now I'm really curious. I bet I can get you to tell."

Before I could reply, she grabbed my shoulders, pulled me against her and kissed me. I felt myself sinking into her and wanted the kiss to go on and on. She slowly moved away.

"Wow," she said. "I thought I was going to thaw you. You're some kisser."

"Thank you. Glad to please."

"I'm going home before I do something dumb."

"Will you think about my offer?"

"You really want me to?"

"Yes. Come to the shop tomorrow and we'll talk.'"

I watched that sleekly constructed, aerodynamic body go to her car and drive away. Perhaps the fantasy for possession wasn't as far-fetched as I thought it was.

Chapter 39

I wasn't surprised when Lisa showed up for the morning run. She stretched and loosened up with us, then took off her spandex and running shoes. She was wearing a modest black bikini that made her look sexier than the thongs the bunnies wore. She ran with us, not competitively, enjoying the run, not trying to impress or compare. That was a nice change. When we got back to our surf boards and prepared to go in the water, she got dressed and said 'she'd see me later'. The waves were running big and I got three great rides before I had to go open the shop.

It was a quiet morning with very few customers, so I worked on Wally's ads. I outlined the final version of the 10 second spot, and sketched out a rough cut of the 30 second spot. I calculated I could finish them both tonight. Unless there were complications, I could finish the 60 second spot over the weekend. Assuming Wally approved them, and I'd try to bring Lisa along for insurance, I'd make $9,000 in one week. Not bad for what was 6-8 hours of work. If I could figure out a way to do that 30 or 40 weeks a year, I could keep my potential partner in the manner she was accustomed to.

Lisa came in just before I closed the shop, wearing jeans and a t-shirt that she made look stylish and sexy.

"I'm taking you to dinner and we can talk about your offer."

"Sure. Do you want to wait here while I do my karate, then surf, or should I meet you there?"

"How long will you be?"

"I usually stay out for an hour. If you decide to wait, I'll be 30 minutes."

"Alright. I'll go to the beach with you and talk to the bunnies. I'm sure they can tell me all about you."

"Just don't talk about business. The three witches will babble about it to everyone."

She laughed. "Agreed. Only personal stuff."

The waves were running beautifully and I had to force myself to go in. I waved goodbye to Ronnie and Davey and paddled in. I went to the shower, rinsed off, dried, then put on shorts and a t-shirt. I could feel Lisa watching me, but I didn't react. I turned, smiled at her, then waved for her to join me. I didn't want to talk to the witches now. She led me to her car, we got in, and she drove off waiting for me to ask where we were going. I didn't. I just looked out the window, willing to go anywhere with her.

"The three witches told me you're quite a lover boy."

"Don't say that!" I snapped. "It makes the girls I've been with sound cheap."

She was startled at my defense of previous girls.

"But you do have a reputation."

"I would like to think it's for being smart and a good friend."

"Zoey, Vickie and Carrie hinted you slept with all three of them."

I laughed. "They're not my type."

She was startled. "They're beautiful, sexy, rich…"

"I like nice, smart girls."

"I didn't know you took karate. Do you like to fight?"

"No. I hate violence. But it's been around me all my life. The more capable I become, the easier it is to avoid it."

"Zoey told me you never compete with anybody."

"That's right."

"How come?"

"It took me a while to prove my abilities to myself. I always try my best, so I don't have to compete with anyone."

"You're a strange one."

I grinned fiendishly. "You have no idea."

Chapter 40

We drove for about 45 minutes and Lisa was definitely irked that I didn't ask where we were going. She pulled into the driveway of a fancy French restaurant and a valet took the car. The maitre d' looked dubiously at me and said:

"We require gentlemen to wear a tie."

I gave him $20 and said:

"Bring me a tie, please."

Lisa gaped at me, but he didn't bat an eye. He went to his reservation desk, took out a flowering monstrosity, and handed it to me. As I slipped it on, he said:

"Follow me, Monsieur. Madame."

He led us to a table, held the chair for Lisa, bowed and sailed off. The waiter asked:

"Something to drink?"

"A glass of a nice red for the lady. Water for me."

"Sparkling or still?"

I had no idea what he meant, but replied:

"Sparkling. Like the lady."

He handed us menus and they were in French.

"I don't read French. What do you recommend?"

We ordered and he went for the drinks. Lisa was staring at me like I was a peculiar creature who suddenly became personal.

"I've never seen anyone so poised. You paid for a tie as if you've done it before. You. weren't the least bit self-conscious about saying you don't read French. How old are you?"

"14."

"When's your birthday/"

"July."

"Why don't you say you're 15?"

"I'm not 15 yet."

"I don't understand. How can you be so self-confident?"

"Did you bring me here to try to embarrass me, or test me?"

She blinked. "I'm sorry. I'm just trying to figure out who you are."

"Let me know when you do... Did you think about my offer?"

"You want me to charm your clients?"

"I want you to learn the basics of the video production business, help find clients and help sell them. I'll pay you 25% of the fees.

"That could be a lot of money. My family is rich, but it would be nice to earn my own money. What about you and me personally?"

"That's up to you. You're smart, beautiful, and good with people, despite your insecurity..."

"Is that so, Dr. Freud?"

"And I find you very desirable."

"I feel a little awkward about our age difference."

"I know. That's why I said it was your choice."

"You're not even going to try to persuade me?"

"I want your brains and your body. If I can only get one I'll take your brains."

"That's either the best compliment I ever got, or an insult. In any event, I'm going to an Olympic training camp as soon as school is over. I won't be back until September. When school starts again I'll be 17 years old."

"Then why don't we try to be friends for now. If you're interested in working together when you come back we'll talk about it then."

We made light conversation during the rest of dinner and I ignored the frequent stares we attracted. When the waiter brought me the check I gestured to Lisa, who paid with a credit card. She had a lot of them and I made a note to get a few more. She was quiet on the drive south and when we got to Chula Vista, asked:

"Shall I drop you at the shop?"

On an impulse I asked:

"Can you keep a secret?"

"Yes."

"No matter what?"

"Yes."

"Even if you decide you hate me?"

"Yes. What's the big mystery?"

"I'll show you where I live, but you've got to swear never to tell anyone."

"Alright. I swear. Do you live in a homeless shelter?"

"Do you know where the Imperial Beach Marina is?"

"Yes."

"Drive there."

"You live near there?"

"I live there. On a boat."

"You live on a boat?"

"That's what I said."

She started asking all kinds of questions, but I said:

"I'll answer them when we get there."

The drive only took a few minutes. I showed her where to park in the parking lot. Old Tom, the night watchman, woke up and came to the office door.

"Is that you, Mike/"

"Yes, Tom. With a friend."

He cackled: "I wish I had a friend like that," and went inside.

I led Lisa to the boat and she stared.

"It's a big sailboat," she said in amazement.

"Actually it's a ketch."

She stared at me like I was speaking Icelandic.

"And you live alone in it?"

"On her, not in."

"I don't think I can deal with this tonight," and she pecked me on the cheek and fled.

I shrugged, tried to forget my fantasy of shipboard sex and went to work on the video ads.

Chapter 41

Lisa ran with us in the morning the rest of the week, but didn't speak to us and left when we got back to our surfboards. I didn't see her during the weekend and finished the 60 second spot for Wally on Saturday night. I met him at the restaurant on Sunday after I closed the shop. He was noticeably disappointed that Lisa wasn't with me. He cheered up considerably when I showed him and Tony the three finished spots. They loved the 10 second and 30 second spots, but went wild for the 60 second version.

It opened with 'Happy days are here again' music and Wally standing in front of the Capitol building. The voiceover said: 'You hired Wally Custerback to work for you'… Various exterior, then interior shots. 'This is where he does his job to make sure you get what you voted for'. Then shots of Wally on the beach with a group of people who were glad to see him. 'He's there for you. Write or make an appointment to let him know what you need'. The last visual was a close up of sincere looking Wally. 'He'll do his best for you'. Fade to 'Happy days, music'.

Tony gazed at me admiringly and muttered:

"Mike. You're a genius. I've worked on big campaigns where the ad agency didn't do as well in three months. These spots are terrific."

Wally echoed him and I replied modestly:

"Glad you like them."

"We love them," Wally enthused. "How do you come up with that stuff?"

"Creative secret, Wally."

He laughed. “Tony. We’ve got to find other ways to use Mike’s talent.”

“Sure, Wally. For now we’ll start with the 60 second spot for two weeks, then the 30 second spot for 1 week, and the 10 second spot for 1 week. We’ll poll the response, then decide whether to go for the 2 minute spot. Is that any problem for you, Mike?”

“No. But if you want the 2 minute spot, I’ll need some material and at least 2 or 3 weeks to put it together, and I may have to revise the budget, depending on the material.”

“No problem,” Wally assured me.

I took out a disc and handed it to Tony.

“Here are the 3 spots. Tell me your email and I’ll send you the online copies.”

Wally invited me to eat with them and I accepted. I mostly nodded politely while I ate, then said a quick goodnight.

Sunday was really busy at the shop. By the time I closed I just wanted to get out on the water. It was a bright, moonlit night, with good waves, but I didn’t feel like riding. I just lay there, paddling occasionally to stay outside the breakers. My thoughts drifted to everything that had been happening lately. Somehow I kept coming back to Lisa. I had to tell myself that nothing would come of it, even though I hoped it would.

I stopped at the shop Monday morning, just to be sure Cliff was back and opening on schedule. He was just unlocking the door when I got there and we hugged. I said we’d talk later and rushed to school. It felt like a long time since I’d been there, not just the Easter break. I had a positive attitude and resolved to work hard for the rest of the term. At lunchtime, the three witches wanted to know what was happening with me and Lisa. Zoey said:

"We have a bet. I bet you won't get in her pants because she's too old for you. Vickie thinks you will."

I smiled pleasantly, then turned to Milton.

"Will you tell your harem to stop talking about Lisa, or they'll have to sit at another table."

Milton didn't know if I was kidding or not, but he said firmly:

"Don't bother, Mike, girls," and they actually listened to him.

Nice going, Milton. I looked at him more closely and saw that running, karate, and surfing was changing him. He was tan, his body was filling out with new muscle, and he looked confident. No one treated him like a nervous nerd anymore and he fit in at the surfer's table. I knew that he was smart, but I realized I didn't know anything else about him and made a note to find out more. Ever since he learned I was more computer savvy then he was, he had attached himself to me. The physical stuff followed and he would probably do anything I asked. I'd have to find out what he could do. He might be useful in my business ventures.

When we surfed that evening I asked Cliff about his trip. He laughed.

"It was a cultural whirlwind. We went to the symphony twice, saw a terrible show at the theater that Lucy loved, went to the Museum of Modern Art, the DeYoung Museum, The Palace of the Legion of Honor…"

"What's that?"

"A funky arts museum. … The Asian Art Museum and lots of art galleries. The worst event was a poetry reading at a coffee shop. These weirdoes were yelling, screaming and hopping about like ants on a hot stove. I didn't like the opera, but the ballet wasn't bad. Those dancers are real athletes. Lucy wanted to see the Gay Men's Chorus, but I declined. We ate at a lot of fancy restaurants and I did my cultural duty for the next five years."

"Talk about weird. You were on vacation with a beautiful woman and you're still complaining?"

He grinned sheepishly. "I didn't while I was there and some of that stuff wasn't bad."

"I wonder if I'm morally obligated to tell Lucy what you said?"

"Surfers have been known to drown out here," which cracked us up.

I was very busy for the next month doing much more school work than usual. My web design business kept growing through word of mouth referrals by satisfied customers. Then a high-end car dealer, recommended by Wally, hired me to make a 1 minute video ad. I immediately had business cards printed for my company, Sleek Productions, video and web design. It turned out to be a simple, profitable job. They had stock footage of the cars and showroom, so I just wrote a short script and shot a 10 second sequence with the manager sitting in a Jaguar convertible, saying: 'We'll put you in the seat of a luxury car.' It only took 4-5 hours and I charged him $5,000. I kept reading more and more about digital video production and my bank account kept growing.

Although I kept waiting for things to go wrong, nothing bad happened. Despite growing in confidence and ability daily, part of me always expected disaster. Maybe that goaded me to try harder. My ongoing frustration was Lisa. She ran with us three or four mornings a week, but wouldn't talk to me. I knew there was no point in trying to approach her, so I just smiled pleasantly if she happened to look at me. Either I would wear her down and she would come to me, or she was gone.

Chapter 42

I guess it was the attitude change, but I really enjoyed my classes, even math. I couldn't help thinking about it as I biked to the shop. Then I fantasized that next year, at this time, I'd be riding a motorcycle. Cliff and I hugged as if we hadn't seen each other for months, even though he had only been gone for two weeks. He complimented me on how well everything was maintained and the volume of sales. Ronnie was standing nearby, looking self-conscious, and Cliff said:

"Ronnie asked for a job during the day when you're not here. What do you think?"

"Sure. Ronnie did a great job while you were gone. It'll be great to have him here."

He turned to Ronnie.

"You heard what the boss said. You're hired."

"Thanks, Cliff. Thanks, Mike. You can rely on me."

"We know that," Cliff said warmly.

The three witches teased me about Lisa, and I couldn't get angry at them because they were right. Their bodies kept flashing neon signs advertising their availability, but I wasn't interested. I had casual sex a few times with some of the older beach bunnies, some of them Lisa's age, but it was never serious. Neither they nor I wanted a relationship. I was finally forced to admit to myself that I really wanted Lisa. It wasn't as far-fetched as yearning for a movie star, but it came close. I did know I intrigued her. Maybe more. But she had lots of reasons for not getting involved with me and I couldn't argue with her, because they were valid. I consoled myself that it was a test of wills. Either she'd give in, despite all reasons to the contrary, or she'd forget me. I decided to give it a little time before making myself forget her.

Chapter 43

My middle school career finally ended and I graduated with a 3.8 grade average, up from 3.1 the year before. I showed it to Cliff and he was as proud as a parent. He told Ronnie to watch the store and took me to a men's clothing shop and bought a blue, pin-stripe suit, shirts, ties and shoes for me as a graduation present.

"Your son will look great in this, sir," the clerk said.

"Thank you," then he told me: "You might need this for some of your business meetings."

"Thanks, Dad," which made us both grin.

We went back to the shop, closed it, then went to the beach and took Ronnies karate class. I was surprised that Cliff was at least advanced brown belt level, maybe even black belt, because he never joined the class before. Then we surfed. It was a beautiful, calm spring night and the waves were gentle, so we mostly paddled in place and talked. At one point, Ronnie moved next to me and said:

"Thanks, Mike."

"For what?"

"Looking out for Davey."

"No need to thank. He's my best friend and he looks out for me."

"You helped me keep him away from drugs. I owe you big time for that, as well as for the money from karate and now the job. I don't forget. Anything I can do, just let me know."

"Thanks, Ronnie. You're a good friend."

Davey had edged closer and was trying to hear what we were saying, so I whispered to Ronnie just loudly enough for Davey to hear:

"I don't know if those pills are strong enough to keep him from getting a hard on…"

"Hey. What are you guys talking about?"

"The horniest kid in Chula Vista," Ronnie said.

"It's not my fault I like girls," he protested.

"It's how many we're worried about," I replied. "If you start getting them pregnant, Ronnie'll have a whole tribe to support."

We joked for the rest of the time on the water. Later, Cliff and Lucy took me to dinner and plied me with champagne. By the time they dropped me at the boatyard, I was about ready to surf without a board. The sky was brilliant clear, with thousands of stars flickering their light from thousands of years ago, just reaching my gaze now. I put a cushion on the foredeck and lay there, all kinds of thoughts racing through my head with slightly drunk clarity. I heard footsteps nearby and it wasn't Old Tom. I knew his walk. Then I heard someone coming up the ladder. I grabbed a 2" x 4" board and slowly moved towards the gangway. A big shadow loomed and I drew my arm back and was just about to smash the intruder, when I recognized her.

"Lisa!"

I startled her, she slipped and started to fall backwards. I grabbed her and pulled her to me. She fell on top of me and we tumbled to the deck. Her hot body was pressed against me, I got an erection that she noticed, and I said urbanely:

"Welcome aboard."

She tried to move off me, but I held her tightly and murmured:

"You have to ask the Captain for permission to disembark."

She adjusted on me so my erection wasn't pushing in her stomach, and said:

"You almost scared me to death."

"Next time knock, or announce yourself. I wouldn't go to your house and just barge in… But now that you're here, let me give you the hospitality of the boat."

"I'd like to see it."

"Not it, Her. And you'll see her later," and I kissed her.

She was very tense, so I kissed her again more gently and stroked her hair and shoulders. Her mouth softened and I ran my hands down her body. She moaned with pleasure, but tried to move away. I held her with one arm and slid off her t shirt, then mine. Her body was burning hot and I slipped her bra off and she moved closer. I reached down, unbuttoned her jeans, opened the zipper and slipped them down, then her panties. I caressed her back and buttocks, then her thighs and gently turned her over. I stared at her delicious body and she closed her eyes.

"I've never done anything like this," she whispered.

I didn't answer, kissed her more passionately, ran my hands on her breasts which were firm, and sleek, with small but erect nipples. When I caressed them, she moaned and clung to me. I moved down and kissed them gently and she gasped. Then I licked them and I felt her body pulse against me. I sucked one nipple and squeezed the other and she moaned louder. I moved my hand down her belly, over her soft pelt, then on her taut clitoris and she came with a rush.

She started mumbling something that I ignored and I moved my head between her legs and started licking her. Her moans grew louder and when I slid my tongue inside her she came in my mouth. I put my cock in her wet opening and she stiffened, but I just lay still until she relaxed. Then I moved slowly, in and out, each time deeper, until I felt something pop and I slid deeper inside. She came with a flow of hot juice and I immediately pulled out before I came in her. She lay there panting like an animal. I took her hand, put it on my cock and said:

"Squeeze it and rub it until I come."

I guided her hand up and down, then let her do it until I spouted like a porpoise.

"I never touched a penis before." I didn't respond. "In fact, I've never been naked with a boy. I don't think I've ever had an orgasm."

"I promised you the hospitality of the boat."

"Why did you stop before shooting that stuff?"

I suppressed a smile at her ignorance.

"I wasn't wearing a condom. If I came in you and you got pregnant, you'd look pretty funny running the 5k with a big belly."

I ran my hand on her belly and she stirred. I leaned close and kissed her and she kissed me back. I started to caress her, but she said:

"I've got to go. I didn't mean for this to happen."

"No need to apologize," I teased.

She was flustered, stood, turned her back and got dressed.

"Did anyone ever tell you that you have an intelligent looking ass?"

"Don't talk that way!"

She rushed to the gangway and started down the ladder. I followed and said:

"Aren't you going to kiss me goodbye?"

She paused, scrambled back up, grabbed my head and kissed me hard.

"I'm leaving for summer camp in the morning."

I sighed dramatically. “Shipboard romance never lasts.”

“You’ve made my life very difficult. And you have a weird sense of humor.”

“Thank you.”

Chapter 44

In the morning I realized that Lisa might have a great body, but she wasn't a very good lover. Maybe it was because of inexperience, but I couldn't find out until school started again. Meanwhile I was feeling almost as horny as Davey. I found myself eying the three witches' bodies, which were hot, and, as usual, had 'to let' signs on them. But I decided it would be more trouble then it was worth. There was always casual sex with the older beach bunnies, but I guess I wanted more, a regular girlfriend. That could be a problem. I wouldn't hit on the customers, I didn't smoke, drink or use drugs at the surfer parties, where most of the girls preferred to get high. I'd have to see who I could pick up at the beach.

Cliff and Lucy took me to dinner for my 15th birthday and it was an incredibly warm family experience for me, one that had been growing more intense lately. The next morning, Cliff gave me my birthday present, a beautiful hybrid surfboard that he custom designed for me. It looked killer with its red and black jagged lines. Cliff insisted I take it for a quick ride. I was really pumped and I didn't have to be told twice. I ran to the beach and got a perfect barrel that I rode all the way in. I went back to the shop and thanked Cliff.

"This is the best board ever, made by a true artist."

Ronnie and Davey admired it and we praised Cliff, getting more and more extravagant. When I said:

"You are the Rembrandt of surfboard artists," he said:

"Enough! We've got work to do," but he couldn't help smiling when I mouthed Rembrandt at him during the day.

So far, it had been a very nice summer. I had grown another inch, and at 5'11", 180 pounds, I was trim and fit. It took me a while to realize that I hadn't been feeling the doom and gloom lately that was always part of my life. I had no dreams for the future, just some vague plans for studying computer science and video production in college, I barely believed in my present good luck day by day, without having positive expectations. So it was a refreshing change not to feel apprehensive each morning when I woke up.

Wally phoned Cliff and asked if we would organize the end of summer surfing tournament. Cliff said he'd get back to him and discussed it with me. I told him if we kept it as simple as last year, an amateur event, we could easily manage the second annual Imperial Beach surfing tournament. We agreed that it would be for 16 year olds and under, and no body boards.

Cliff grinned. "There are going to be some angry youngsters."

I laughed. "We'll blame the anonymous sponsors."

I called Wally and told him we'd do it, then added that I'd like to make a video for his restaurant, Wave Length and the Imperial Beach Marina.

"What about a plug for my congressional campaign?"

I thought quickly.

"This isn't a political event. I'll shoot a short segment with you in front of the restaurant, saying what a wonderful community experience this is. You'll be the honorary chairman of the tournament and get great publicity as a man of the people."

"That sounds great, Mike. Do it. Stop by the restaurant tonight and I'll give you a check."

Then he told me how well the ads were doing, especially the 30 second version and he'd need a new one in September. I asked about the one minute ad and he said it didn't poll well, so they didn't use it.

Cliff was a little edgy about organizing the tournament, so I reminded him that we did everything already last year. All we had to do this time was change the date on the t-shirts and posters. He felt much better when I said:

"All you have to do is oversee the events and look official. We'll let Wally hand out the prizes."

"You convinced me."

Chapter 45

The tournament turned out to be bigger than last year, with a lot more entrants, as well as sulking over 16's and body boarders. But it went well. We actually had more sponsors and better prizes, courtesy of the sponsors. Wally got tremendous exposure, Davey won the 16 and under group, Milton came in third in the novice group, and I was on tv several times. The same blonde plastic reporter as last year asked me again why I didn't compete. When I gave the same answer, 'I didn't want to compete with my customers', she had tried to be clever. 'Wouldn't they respect you more if you showed your skill?' Did she take a year to think of that? 'All the people I surf with are different. My best friend, Davey, who won the 16 and under group, is a great competitor. He respects why I surf and I respect why he surfs. On the other hand, I do have to compete for clients in my website design and video production business.' She actually asked about my business and I got two minutes of television air time describing what I did, including plugging the videos I made for the sponsors.

Everybody was happy with the tournament. Well almost everybody. Some of the body boarders mumbled threats, so I referred them to Ronnie, and they quickly dispersed. Once again, Wally, Big Bill and Cliff put money in my college tuition fund. This time Wally put in $10,000, Big Bill $3,000, and Cliff $2,000. The fund was up to $35,000. A few more years like this and I could go to Harvard.

School started and high school wasn't much different than middle school, just bigger, with more kids. The surfers had two tables and they welcomed me and Davey cheerfully. Fortunately, none of the older guys held me responsible for excluding 17 and 18 year olds in the tournament. Ronnie spread the word that it was the anonymous sponsors who did it. Everyone believed him, because the surfers knew and respected him. Milton joined us cautiously and was pleasantly surprised when he was accepted as a matter of course.

There were a lot more good looking girls in high school and some of them were friendly, so prospects for a girlfriend were improving. The three witches approached me, offering anyone of them, or two, or all, but I politely declined. I was too familiar with their petty ways, jealousies and possessiveness. They didn't seem upset at my rejection of their shapely bodies, and consoled themselves with the 16 and 17 year old surfers.

My classes were okay, only advanced math and computer science were a challenge, but that was fun. The big change was in my language requirement. I took Chinese instead of Spanish. There were less than 15 kids in the class and one very cute Chinese girl, so it could be interesting.

I didn't see Lisa the first day and I didn't look for her. The only problem I had was when some of the football jocks asked me to try out for the team. I told them politely that I worked seven days a week and didn't have time. Some of them resented my lack of school, team or football spirit. One of the larger hulks even started muttering threats. I just smiled and said softly: 'Thanks for asking, guys', and they drifted away.

Lisa came to the shop a few days later and asked to talk to me. She hadn't been running with us, so I didn't know what to expect. She was very skittish, so I suggested we take a walk and she said:

"I think about you a lot. I can't forget that night on your boat. I went out with several older guys this summer, but I didn't feel anything when I did things with them. I can't go anywhere with you officially. You're too young. It would be embarrassing. But if you like, I'll come to your boat at night and you can do things to me."

I didn't know whether to laugh at her, or hit her, so I decided to be cool.

"That doesn't work for me. But you're welcome to run with us. Ronnie'll give you surfing lessons, if you like."

"I don't want to surf."

"Suit yourself."

"You don't want me?"

"Not that way."

"Do you know how many men want me?"

"I don't blame them."

"But you don't?"

"You're two years older than me. I understand if you can't deal with that. But I'm not going to be your secret sex toy… If you want to work with me we can talk about that. Did you think about my offer?"

"I can't. Too many people would think I was your girlfriend."

"Good luck at the Olympics, Lisa," and I walked away.

I didn't look back and headed for the shop. I started to laugh when I thought I could have asked her how much she'd pay me for sex services. I was still smiling when I got back to the shop, but Cliff sensed I was upset.

"It didn't work out?"

"No."

"Too bad."

"Maybe not."

"So you're not getting it on with her?" Davey asked.

Ronnie smacked him on the head, and said:

"Don't be a jerk."

"That's alright," I said to Ronnie. "We know what a pig he is. You're welcome to try," I told him. "I'll even give you a reference, if she asks. You can also use the three witches as references," which gave us all a laugh.

Chapter 46

For the first time in my life I was actually enjoying school. Between my television appearances for the surfing tournaments and word of mouth about my web designs, I was very well known. Lots of kids wanted to be friends. I told them all I didn't have time to hang out, but invited them to surf with us, or take Ronnie's karate class. I met a lot of girls, some of them hot, but I took my time getting to know them, figuring once I got involved, the whole school would know about us. I only saw Lisa at a distance. If she noticed me, she pretended not to. It didn't matter anymore.

Things were going well at the shop. Business had been picking up steadily since the tournament and Ronnie was really good with the customers. We were so busy that we let Davey start giving surfing lessons, but only to boys who came with their fathers. He sulked about this at first, but when I announced loudly to Cliff and Ronnie:

"This way we won't have to cut off his thing for messing with the mothers," he cheered up immediately.

Cliff ran with us three or four mornings a week, then surfed with us before we went to school. He also kept coming to Ronnie's karate class, which he seemed to enjoy. This was good for me, since I loved being with him. Considering he had been a world champion surfer, he was incredibly modest about his accomplishments. He wasn't really a businessman, but he had common sense and treated everyone fairly and respectfully. He had a serene attitude and dealt with everything calmly. Like true surfers, he never fought the waves, just went with the flow. I learned a lot from him and tried each day to live up to the examples he set.

The one unexpected benefit from a big high school population was that everyone seemed to need a website. I got so busy, so quickly, I couldn't make them all. The kids kept offering money, so how could I refuse? I asked Milton if he wanted to join my company as an associate... I was proud at using that term... and he leaped at the chance. I offered him 25% of the fee for every site he worked on, which he accepted gratefully. I found out while discussing the commitment that he came from a poor family and he could really use the money. Well at least he had a family.

I gave Milton two training sessions in my style and technique of web design, as well as showing him how to use the online content that was free. I had business cards with his name printed and gave him his first assignment. He did a fairly good job on a rough cut in about 4 hours, took my revisions with a good attitude and finished a final version in another two hours. It was a $250 deal, so he got $62.50, which thrilled him. When I told him he could do 3 or 4 a week, he pledged eternal loyalty.

Wally called and asked me for a new 30 second ad right away. I hired Davey and Milton as production assistants for a video shoot in the business district. I did street interviews, asking well-dressed men and women what they thought of Wally. Out of 20 interviews, we got three useful, positive responses. I edited them into 8 second segments and ended the ad with a shot of Wally at the surfing tournament, being applauded by a large crowd. I recorded a voice over, 'Wally Custerback has always served his community. Send him to congress, where he'll work for you.' Wally loved it and cheerfully paid the $4,000 I billed him. I paid Davey and Milton $150 each, which they thought was great for three hours work.

Unlike his disappointing close loss in his mayoral campaign, Wally was elected to Congress in a landslide. Tony invited me to the victory party and urged me to bring Lisa. I said I hadn't seen her lately, but gave him her email address so he could send an invitation. The party at his restaurant was a raucous affair, with lots of people trying to get close to Wally. A brass band blaring fight songs and marches added to the commotion. Cliff had been invited, but declined to go. I brought Ronnie, Davey and Milton, figuring they had helped Wally in various ways, and would get a free meal.

Wally was surrounded by prosperous looking men and women who were eager to worship the man of the hour. Wally spotted me and yelled:

"Mike. Mike. Come here."

His new suitors reluctantly parted to let me through and he hugged me enthusiastically, then announced loudly:

"This young man was the second most important worker on my campaign, after Tony. I promised you a job. Tony is my chief of staff now. Talk to him about what you want. Just name it and it's yours."

"Thanks, Wally," I yelled to be heard. "Congratulations. Good luck in Washington."

Others were demanding his attention and he patted me on the back fondly and turned away. Tony said:

"You have my number. Call me."

"Thanks, Tony."

I had no intention of working for Wally, but I could tell him another time. I stayed long enough for Ronnie, Davey and Milton to stuff themselves, then we left.

Chapter 47

As it got closer to Thanksgiving, Cliff invited me, Ronnie and Davey for holiday dinner at his house. This was thoughtful, since Ronnie and Davey's family were back East somewhere. The brothers lived in a surfer's house that lots of our crowd crashed at. I asked if I could bring Milton, who was increasingly involved with us, and he said 'yes', but stipulated:

"Only if he doesn't bring the three witches."

I reassured him that they had moved on to older boys, which Milton was still brooding about.

Lucy was a great hostess, making everyone feel at home. I had been to their house many times, but it was the first for the other guys. I adored Lucy, who was beautiful, kind, smart, whose only flaw was that she didn't surf. I suppressed a smile when Ronnie smacked Davey on the side of the head for ogling her body when Lucy went to the kitchen. I smacked him also and he apologized to Cliff and promised to behave. Everyone cracked up when I said:

"The only place I'm taking you from now on is the zoo."

Ronnie and Davey ate and ate and swore it was the best meal they ever had. Milton was too shy to gorge the way they did, but he raved about the meal. When we finished, we managed to get to our feet and say goodnight. Davey was very respectful, so I wouldn't have to pound him for being a low dog. Milton thanked Lucy properly and I thanked her and kissed her on the cheek. Just as we got to the door, Lucy said:

"Oh, Mike. Is Davey the boy who tries to hit on the mothers at the beach?"

He turned beet red and fled into the night and we followed, laughing at his embarrassment.

The morning after Christmas vacation started, the disaster I always feared struck without warning. I was just leaving the marina to go to the beach, when Big Bill stepped out of his office and beckoned to me. He looked unusually somber and I instantly sensed something was wrong.

"I need to talk to you, Mike."

I hadn't seen Bill often lately, we were on two different schedules. But he knew I was always helping out at the yard and thought well of me.

"Sure. What's up, Bill?"

"I have some bad news. After years of dispute over the estate, the heirs finally reached an agreement that includes selling the ketch."

My heart sank as I realized I would be losing my home, my secure nest that kept the world out. It was the only place that had ever been mine, since growing up in the trailer was a nightmare. I said the first thing that came into my head.

"Can I buy it?"

Bill was incredibly gentle and didn't laugh.

"It's an Irwin 41 center cockpit ketch. The book value is about $65,000."

"I can put $10,000 down and pay it off monthly."

He shook his head sadly. "They won't go for that. Their lawyer instructed me to make a cash sale. I told him you were living aboard to maintain it. He was grateful for that and said he'd give you a $500 fee when it sold. He didn't have to do that."

"Maybe I can get a loan from the bank and buy it."

He put his arm around me comfortingly.

"The only way to get a loan would be if you had collateral."

"My web design business is making about $1,500 a month. I could pay back a loan in five years. Maybe sooner, if my video production business makes money."

"They don't work that way. You have to have something of value that they could sell if you couldn't repay the loan. I'm sorry. It'll be at least four or five months at the earliest before the boat might sell, probably much longer. The economy is still depressed and the ketch is too big for a small boater, and too small for a yachter. It could take years."

Part of me was getting used to the shock. Another part was in denial.

"When do I have to be out?"

He shrugged. "It could sit there for years. But to be safe, in three months or so, start thinking about where you'll go if it's sold… I asked the owners of some of the big boats in the yard if you could live aboard, in exchange for maintenance, but they said 'no'. I really like having you here for security, and you've been a big help in the yard. I just don't have another boat."

I managed to thank him and rode to the beach. I didn't feel like running and just sat there. Cliff noticed how distressed I was, joined me and asked what happened. He was very concerned when I told him, and said we'd have to figure out what to do. I was miserable, but felt a little better knowing that he cared.

Chapter 48

Despite all the good things happening to me and around me, I didn't enjoy Christmas. I was too disturbed about losing my boat. It was funny in a way that I had come to think of it as mine. I guess I figured I'd live there for years, at least until I went to college. Maybe it was a strange place for a young guy to live, but it was perfect for me. I had everything I needed and my prospects for getting on in the world were great. I kept kicking myself for developing a false sense of security and harshly reminded myself of my mantra, 'nothing lasts'. I tried to put a good face on when I was running and doing karate, but my unhappiness stood out like a lighthouse when I was on the water. Just before we went in one evening, Cliff paddled to me and said:

"Do you want to talk?"

I didn't know whether to curse, cry, or find the boat heirs and kill them, but I didn't feel like talking.

"I know it feels awful now, but you've dealt with much bigger problems in your life and come out stronger, just as you will from this."

I just lay on my board, listless, feeling sorry for myself, almost hoping a giant wave would wash me out to sea and end my suffering. Cliff ignored my apathy and said firmly:

"You have so many opportunities ahead of you that where you live isn't important. You earn enough money to get a room, a small apartment, or you can even live with me."

It took a minute for what he was saying to register, then it began to sink in.

"You mean you would let me live with you?"

"If that's what you wanted."

"I don't know what to say."

"Then don't say anything."

"I wouldn't let you do it because you're feeling sorry for me."

"I don't feel sorry for you, Mike. I admire how you built a life for yourself, instead of giving up…" He looked around and saw that Ronnie, Davey, Donna and Milton had gone in. "My father died when I was one year old. My mother started using drugs and died of an overdose when I was four. I was put in a foster home until I was seven, when my aunt found out where I was. She brought me to live with her in Chula Vista, in what's my house now. She left it to me when she died. I learned to surf and that changed my life. I became a star, made enough money to open the shop, then learned that I didn't want fame, or a lot of money. I just wanted a quiet life and to surf for myself, not in competition, not for others… Maybe I should want to do something more important in the world, but I'm no genius and can't change anything…"

"You're the smartest man I know."

"I'm not smart, Mike, I just have some common sense and I try to be fair. It took a long time to get over those years in foster care. I still dream about them. That's one of the reasons for overcoming your childhood."

"I didn't. I'm still full of anger and hate."

"But you don't show it and you don't take it out on others. That's what's important. Now think about this. Bill told me…"

"You talked to Bill?"

"...Yes. May I finish?" I nodded. "Bill says the boat market is so weak that the ketch could sit for years. And if it sells you'll have plenty of time to find another place. Or like I said before, you could live with me."

"You'd really want me to live with you?"

"Everybody already thinks you're my son. Why not?"

A wave of love rushed through me and it was the deepest feeling I ever had.

"Thanks, Cliff. I'd be proud to live with you."

"Just never bring the three witches home," which ended the solemn moment in a laugh.

Chapter 49

I tried very hard to put a good face on every day, but I felt hollow inside. I was going to lose my boat. I felt like screaming to the world it was unjust, but I already knew the world didn't care. The only thing that kept me from going crazy was Cliff's offer to let me live with him. But part of me couldn't help wondering if he was doing it out of pity. I spent a lot of time thinking about my Christmas list, which helped me maintain self-control. I actually spent hours thinking about the right gift for the right person. There was Cliff, Lucy, Ronnie, Davey and Milton. I debated whether Big Bill should get a gift.

Deciding about Big Bill took a lot of time going back and forth. I sort of worked for him. Well I did. But we had no personal arrangement. He was my landlord. But again there was no formal arrangement. He didn't lose anything by my living on the boat. In fact he gained, for I maintained it. Yet I didn't pay rent. I helped keep the premises secure, since Old Tom wasn't very efficient. I did boat repairs, well simple ones, and did a lot of maintenance, especially in the summer. I got my first laugh in a while when I realized how silly I was being, and decided not to get him a present.

By the time school started again I was back to my old self outwardly, but inside I was waiting for what would happen next. Only Cliff knew that I was still troubled, but he didn't pry, ask questions, or offer advice, which I loved him for. He knew I had to work it out on my own, but I could tell he was worried. A few nights later I was on the boat, lying on the deck looking at the stars. I was having a fantasy about talking to a really smart girl, while eating a pizza and drinking wine.

I heard footsteps and it wasn't Old Tom. It was Lisa. She knocked on the hull and called:

"Mike. Can I come up?"

"What do you want?"

"I want to talk to you."

"Talk."

"I can't do it from down here."

"Sure you can. There's no one else around."

"I feel foolish..." When I didn't answer, she said: "I want to be with you."

"Why?"

"Don't make me say it."

"Say what?"

"You know."

"No, I don't."

She blurted: "I want you to do things to me."

"Three hundred dollars."

"What?"

"You heard me."

"You want me to pay you?"

"Sure. Whores get paid."

"You're not a whore."

"Then stop treating me like one. If you want to be with me, it has to be at school, the beach, wherever we go."

"I can't do that."

"Then pay or go."

She didn't answer me, but I heard her rush off in the dark and she might have been crying. I shook my head in wonder. She was beautiful, smart, rich, had a family that loved her and was going to be a world class athlete. She was so screwed up she was snuffling around the boatyard looking for sex, with a half-breed Mexican-American kid two years younger than she. I guess I wasn't as bad off as I thought I was.

Chapter 50

One nice thing happened to help me fight the fear of losing my boat. On January 10th, I was exactly 15 ½ years old, so I went to the Department of Motor Vehicles and applied for a motorcycle learner's permit. I probably should have started the paperwork and qualifications earlier, because it was a lot more complicated than I expected. I had to make an appointment for a test at the Department of Motor Vehicles, but first fill out a form DL44 and get my mother to sign it. I had to pass all kinds of tests at the appointment, vision, traffic laws and signs, motorcycle laws… I kicked myself for not getting the information earlier… And I had to present proof of completing a motorcycle safety course, given by the California Highway Patrol.

My computer teacher, Mr. Corliss, was one of the Driver's Ed. teachers, so I asked him to enroll me immediately, which he did. I got the DL44 from the DMV, then I went to see my mother. I hadn't seen her in at least three years, so I wasn't sure until I got there that she'd be living in the same place. The trailer was even filthier and more run down then I remembered. So was Maria. She was fat, dirty, bedraggled and stank of beer. Her eyes had the vacant look of heavy drug use. I wasn't surprised that she didn't recognize me, because I had changed considerably. Her current boyfriend, a short, skinny guy with the shakes, thought I was a gringo bill collector and tried to get rid or me.

"I'm Maria's son," I said in Spanish. "Mike Sanchez."

She stared at me, then gushed, "My son,", her mouth missing half her teeth. She hugged me and it took all my self-control not to shove her away. I couldn't remember her ever hugging me before.

"What do you want?" Boyfriend demanded.

I didn't look at him.

"I need my birth certificate and I need you to sign something."

"That's when you think of your mother, when you want something," boyfriend sneered.

I was tempted for a moment to pick him up and toss him out the door, but that would freak out Maria, so I said pleasantly to her:

"I brought you some Christmas money."

"Give it to me," boyfriend demanded.

"It's for my mother."

He stared at me and saw how much bigger and stronger I was then he. I guess he didn't have a pistol, because instead of threatening, he muttered:

"Give him what he wants."

Maria went to her chipped black cardboard dresser and took out an old blue candy box, stuffed with letters, ribbons, movie stubs and plastic stirrers. She rummaged through it, took out my birth certificate and handed it to me. I looked at it curiously. There was no father's name. I put it in my pocket, took out the DL44, gave her a pen and showed her where to sign. When she signed it, I put it in my pocket, gave her $25 and headed for the door.

Boyfriend snatched the money from her.

"Is that all there is?"

"Next time," I said, and I left, hoping there wouldn't be a next time.

I phoned the California Highway Patrol to register for the motorcycle training course and they told me there was a six month waiting list. I couldn't wait six months to get a permit. I phoned Tony in Washington and asked as a favor if he'd call them, which he cheerfully agreed to do. He did it right away, because I got a call a few minutes later from

Lieutenant Rawlings of the Highway Patrol, informing me there was an immediate opening for the course. I thanked him, got the information, hung up and called Tony.

"It's good to have powerful friends."

He laughed. "Anytime, Mike. We owe you big."

"Thanks, Tony, How're you doing/"

"Busy planning the Wally for Senator campaign."

"Let me know if I can help."

"Sure thing. We'll be in town soon. I'll call you and we can talk about that job."

"Thanks again, Tony."

Chapter 51

The motorcycle safety course was 15 hours, 6 ½ classroom, 8 ½ on a motorcycle. With Cliffs approval, I took some time off at the shop. I took the course in a week, two days in class, three on a bike, and passed with flying colors. I got an appointment at the Department of Motor Vehicles for the following week to take my learners permit test, but I needed a bike. I had to laugh at my carelessness. I had been dreaming about a bike for more than a year, but I neglected to figure out how to get one.

I talked to Ronnie, who told me he had an ex-surfer friend who didn't use his bike anymore. We went to his house and Ronnie introduced us. Gus was an old guy, at least 40, and drinking too much beer according to his pot belly. But he was friendly and showed us the bike, a Kawasaki sport bike. It was grey and black, sleek, powerful looking and was calling my name.

"It's an older bike," Gus said. "A 1995 model, but it's cherry. She just needs a clean up, a tuning and some parts changed, because she's just been sitting here for years."

Ronnie had told me that he'd do the bargaining, so I just stood there and pretended I knew what Gus was talking about.

"How much do you want for it?" Ronnie asked.

Gus thought for a moment, then replied:

"$3,000."

Ronnie shook his head no.

"Alright. $2,500 and I'll do the work to get it ready. You pay for the parts."

Ronnie looked at me and I said:

"It's a deal."

I would have paid $3,500. I don't know why, but from the moment I saw it, I knew it was for me. Gus went over the entire bike carefully and made a list of what needed replacing, or repair, including new tires. We agreed on $500 to cover everything, and Gus said he'd take me to the test. I thanked him and said I'd take him to dinner at Wally's after the test, which he thanked me for profusely. My appointment was for the following Monday and he promised to have the bike ready by then. I gave him a check for $3,000, and he told me I'd have to get insurance to get a license plate, because his last plate was from 2008. I didn't know anything about insurance so I asked Cliff, who referred me to his agent, a nice lady who settled everything quickly. I took the insurance form, Gus's old registration and the bill of sale to the DMV, paid my fee and got my new plate. It felt weird to have a license plate for a motorcycle I owned, but didn't have and couldn't drive..

That evening after we surfed, I took Ronnie to dinner at Wally's and thanked him for his help in getting the bike.

"You know I owe you for all you've done for me and Davey. Anything I can do for you, just ask."

"Thanks, Ronnie. You're a pal… I was thinking. You're a great teacher. Did you ever think about teaching at a dojo? You'd probably make good money."

"I don't think I'd enjoy working indoors. I love being on the beach and until I decide what to do next, I'll stay there. But thanks for thinking of it."

"I just want you and Davey to be okay."

"We're managing. I'm happy Davey can compete on the surfing tour when he's 17, and start making money… How do you think he'll do?"

"He's good. I know that. But I don't know how good. Why don't you ask Cliff to assess him. He knows surfers."

"I will."

"Do it alone, in case he has some comments that you wouldn't want Davey to hear."

"Good idea. Thanks, Mike. See you later."

"Thanks again for your help with the bike."

"It's cool."

Chapter 52

Part of me didn't like to face it, but my inner confidence was shaken with the uncertainty I was feeling on losing the boat. I tried my best to put on a good face and be positive, but it was difficult. It was a big help that I was getting my learner's permit. Gus took me to the DMV on my new bike that I'd be able to drive, if I passed the tests. I gave them the form DL44, passed a written test, gave them my thumbprint, passed the traffic laws and signs test, passed the motorcycle laws test, presented proof of completing the motorcycle safety course, presented my birth certificate and my social security number. I paid the $33 fee and, voila, secured my learner's permit. Then I took Gus to dinner at Wally's, which he really enjoyed.

Of course Gus had to drive us to his house, since I couldn't carry passengers with a learner's permit. I thanked him for all his help and started to go. He asked me to wait a moment, went inside, and came out with two helmets with faceplates, saddlebags, heavy gloves, and boots.

"You may as well take these. I have no use for them anymore."

"That's real generous, Gus. Let me pay you for them."

"No. Enjoy your bike. Take it easy."

"Thanks, Gus."

I rode off carefully. Part of me wanted to zoom, but I restrained myself, thinking what it would be like if I got arrested the first day for speeding. It felt great. I rode around for a while, getting used to the bike at several different speeds. By the time I got to the shop I was feeling comfortable on the bike. I decided to get a leather jacket, brown, not black, so I wouldn't look like a gang member. Cliff, Ronnie and Davey admired the bike and Davey wanted a ride. He moped when I explained I wasn't allowed to take passengers, but perked up when I promised him the first ride when I got my license.

The bike was a real pleasure, my only frustration was that I wasn't allowed to drive at night. I rode it whenever I could and it definitely helped me feel better as other things started going wrong. My web design business slowed down and I was only getting one or two orders a week, some weeks none. I gave Milton his share of each project, but his income dropped drastically along with mine. He began acting strangely and I couldn't help wondering if he thought I was holding out on him. But I had bigger worries. My video production business went absolutely nowhere. I hadn't heard from Wally. When I called his office the secretary said he was unavailable and took a message. He didn't call back. I tried Tony's number and got the same kind of response, with no return call. I guess Washington transmitted a disease: forgetting your friends.

I tried to forget my growing anger at Wally. It was just one more thing going wrong. But I still ran every morning and surfed at least once a day, generally twice. When I was on the water other problems faded away, at least for a while. Cliff was really good to me during this time of growing troubles. He never pried, but was always ready to listen and made sure I knew that. I never complained. I learned a long time ago it didn't do any good and only made me feel worse. But he knew I was struggling and always let me know that he was here for me. He's the best.

I had opportunities to pick up girls on the beach who were hot, but I had lost interest in any kind of relationship. I had casual sex with some of the older beach bunnies and that satisfied me for the time being. Then a funny, pathetic thing happened one night. Lisa came to the boat, knocked on the hull and when I answered, said:

"It's Lisa, Mike. I brought money. $300."

I felt terrible that this beautiful, smart, proud girl was so desperate that she had to come to me like this. I went down and talked to her.

"I don't want your money, Lisa, That was a bad joke. I can't give you what you want and you can't give me what I want. Maybe when you graduate from high school things'll be different."

She just stood there staring at me and tears flowed from her eyes. I couldn't believe how breathtakingly beautiful she was. It was tempting to take that gorgeous body on the boat, but I had my pride, sometimes the only thing that kept me going. I watched without saying anything as she got into her car and drove away. I found myself thinking that I could have done things to her and made her a sex slave. But the idea was repulsive and I pushed it away. I was lucky that I wasn't low enough to exploit her.

Chapter 53

My status at school had been pretty high. Now that I had a bike, it was even higher. Since it was obvious that I wasn't a gang member, I became more appealing to girls my age, or even a little older. Of course I couldn't take passengers, but I discouraged attention from any girl who seemed more interested in being with a glamorous surfer, then wanting to know me as a person. Maybe it was false pride that made me suspicious of new acquaintances, but in a way that was almost all I had.

As well as the coming loss of my home, which I only forgot for short intervals, mostly while surfing, I was worried about my loss of income. For a while I had taken the web design business for granted, as a steady source of income. Then the gold rush in high school brought in a lot of money quickly. Between that and the expectation of a growing video production business, I never worried about where my money would come from. It seemed to come on its own. I wracked my brain thinking of ways to promote my business. I put an ad for web design in the school newspaper that cost $25 for four weeks. it was cheap enough. I only got one response, and he only wanted to pay $50, so I gave the job to Milton.

Video business was even more unproductive. Without Wally's referrals, I didn't have any contacts. I thought about making a video ad for my production services, which would be easy and fun. Then I got the advertising rates at the local tv station. That ended that idea. I looked up ad rates at various sites on the internet and some of them were very reasonable. The only problem was that they may have been for a yak herder's site somewhere in outer Mongolia, who would pay in curdled milk. I would obviously have to give serious thought as to how to revitalize my income.

My salary at the shop was now my only reliable income source. It was sufficient to pay for my expenses and still allow me to save a little each week. But my casual attitude towards making easy money was rapidly changing. Business was slower at the shop, except for mail order. Ronnie had become very competent at filling orders, otherwise Cliff might have laid him off. Surfing lessons were fewer until early spring. Except for three of my regulars, I gave new lessons to Ronnie, who I knew needed the money. After discussing it with Cliff, I let Davey give lessons to girls with their mothers, with the stipulation that we would castrate him if he came on to the mothers.

I spent a lot of time thinking about my current situation and finally concluded that despite how I felt it wasn't the end of the world. I was doing well in school, my relationship with Cliff was solid and I earned enough money to pay rent when I lost the boat. An incident at the shop put things in perspective for me. A shabby looking guy bought a waxing rag for $2 and gave me a ten dollar bill. When I handed him the change, he said:

"I gave you a twenty."

"I'm sorry, sir. I thought you gave me a ten."

"It was a twenty. Check your till."

I was 99.9 percent sure he gave me a ten. But I got the feeling he ran this scam regularly and would argue about it. There were customers in the shop, so to avoid a scene I gave him $10.

"Here's your change, sir."

He looked surprised that I gave in so easily, snatched the bill and scurried out. Cliff walked over. "Everything alright?"

"Yeah. That guy beat me out of ten bucks. I'll put ten in the register."

"Are you sure he scammed you?"

"99.9."

"But not a hundred?"

"No."

"Then you handled it the right way. You bought $10 worth of good will for us, cause we always look bad if we're seen arguing with a customer over change. If he comes in again, you put his bill on the counter while you make change. That way he can't dispute it."

"Good idea. Thanks, Cliff."

Somehow, this silly episode and Cliff's support, made me feel a lot better about things.

Chapter 54

It was always nice when something unexpected happened that turned out well for someone. We had just come in from surfing and were standing on the beach talking. I noticed a skinny, young kid, about 10 years old, using a Styrofoam board in the shallow water that he probably got at the local supermarket. I had a momentary flashback to my first efforts to surf and got a warm feeling watching him. He had no idea what he was doing, but he kept trying. I understood that. Two older boys, 12 or 13, started teasing him, but he ignored them and kept trying to stand on the board. I didn't like them laughing at him, but it didn't seem serious until he fell off his board and the wave carried it onto the beach. One of his tormentors grabbed it, yelled: 'It's a piece of shit', and broke it. The brave kid ran to him and started punching him. The two boys were about to beat him up, so I ran over and grabbed both of them.

"What do you think you're doing?" I demanded.

"The kid was bothering us," one of them whined.

"I saw what happened. You bullies broke his board. Do you have money to pay for it?"

They shook their heads no and were getting nervous.

"Get off the beach. If I see you bullying anyone again, I'll spank you in full public view and ban you permanently from the beach. Now get out of here."

They ran off and the kid looked at me worshipfully.

"Thanks, Mike."

I looked at him but didn't recognize him.

"Do I know you?"

"No. But I know you. I'm Frank's son."

"Who's Frank?"

"The manager at Wally's restaurant."

"Oh. Frank. Sure. He's a good guy. What's your name?"

"Tommy."

"Tell you what, Tommy. Come to the shop and I'll give you a loaner board."

"Gee. Thanks."

I called Davey. "Tommy. This is Davey. He'll give you a couple of lessons, then you can decide if you want to be a surfer."

"I'm going to be a surfer," and he started to run off.

"Tommy," I called.

He stopped. "Yes?"

"Get those pieces of your board and dump them in the trash."

"Yes, Mike."

He grabbed them and ran off, a gawky, lesser shorebird, full of energy. It felt good doing something for the kid. Of course it didn't make up for any of the bad things I did, but it was a nice change to do something for someone else.

A few days later, Frank stopped by the shop.

"Hi. Mike. I haven't seen you at the restaurant lately."

I didn't want to tell him that I wouldn't be a freeloader if I wasn't doing anything for Wally.

"I've been pretty busy."

"I want to thank you for what you did for my son."

"He told you?"

"Only after I asked him why he was sleeping with that surfboard." I had to laugh at that and he laughed with me.

"That was real nice, what you did for him, Mike. He likes Davey, but he wants you to teach him. He wants a lesson every day. I'll pay for them."

"I tell you what. I can't give him one every day, but I'll give him one or two a week. The rest of the time he's with Davey. Alright?"

"Sure. I won't forget what you did for him. Remember. You're welcome at the restaurant every day of the year."

"Thanks, Frank. I'll see you there."

Chapter 55

I found myself getting interested in a girl in my computer science class, named Elena. She was tall, slim, dark haired, pale-skinned, with enormous dark brown eyes, and a shapely body. She was very shy, so I made sure not to stare at her. One day, Mr. Corliss paired us for a coding exercise, and it gave me an opportunity to talk to her. When the bell rang, I said:

"Can I meet you after school?"

"You want to take me somewhere on that big bike?"

"I'm not allowed to take passengers. How about I walk you home?"

"I don't think so. Some of the local boys wouldn't like it."

"Is one of them your boyfriend?"

"No."

"Then let me worry about it."

I waited for her after school, then walked her to where she lived in West Chula Vista. It was a long walk. Halfway there she told me she usually took the bus, but this gave us time to get acquainted. I found out she was on the soccer team at school and played for an amateur league on weekends. She wanted to be a professional soccer player and a computer programmer. Nice combo. Just before we got to her block, she said:

"We should say goodbye here."

"I'll walk you to your house."

She recognized my determination and shrugged. We turned the corner and three young, tough looking kids were hanging out.

"Hey, Elena," one of them yelled. "Who's the gringo?"

"A friend from school."

They walked to us and the same boy said, glaring at me:

"We don't like gringos here."

I smiled pleasantly and said in Spanish:

"Sorry, friends. I didn't know I strayed into Mexico. I thought I was in the U.S.A."

They gaped at me in surprise and the first kid said:

"You speak Spanish."

"Yes."

"Hey. I know you," another boy said. "You're that surfer dude. You're famous."

"My name is Mike Sanchez. If it's alright with you I'd like to visit my friend."

"You're Spanish," the first kid announced.

"Yes."

"It's cool, man. You're welcome here."

"Thanks, man."

They ambled off and Elena said:

"You handled them well."

"Thank you." Then I said without thinking: "I'd like to handle you well."

She stared at me and I wondered if I had been too rash.

"You are fresh. It's a good thing I know you're intelligent. Now it's time to meet my mother. If she decides you're human I won't have to sneak around to speak to you."

"I'm very good with mothers. Almost as good as I am with daughters."

"You are very fresh. But you haven't met my mother."

Mamacita turned out to be an older, slightly shorter version of Elena, who could have passed for her older sister. She seemed to be bright, educated and poised. She liked me immediately, which surprised Elena.

"I've seen you on television at the surfer's tournament. It was good to hear a young man who wasn't driven to compete. What else do you do?"

"I work at the Wave Length Surf shop. I have a web design business and a small video production company."

"Impressive. What do you study?"

"Computer science, math, Chinese, karate and I'm beginning to get interested in politics."

"You want to be a politician?"

"No. But I recently worked on political campaigns for a friend of mine and I want to learn how the system works."

"A friend at school."

"No. Wally Custerback."

"Our Congressman?"

"Yes."

"You worked for him?"

"I ran his mayoral campaign and assisted with his congressional campaign."

"I see. You're not the usual teen age boy."

"I hope you won't hold that against me."

She laughed. “You may visit my daughter. But if you get her pregnant, you’ll feel the

wrath of my Aztec ancestors.”

“Mama!” Elena protested.

“Do I embarrass you, Mike?”

“No, Ma’am. I like your style.”

“I like yours. But don’t tell my husband what I said. He’s old fashioned and prefers a machete.”

“I like Italian food too.”

She burst out laughing. “I’ll see you again.”

Elena walked me to the door. “You are an evil magician. She never liked anyone I

brought home before.”

I whispered:

“I told you so,” and left before she could reply.

Chapter 56

I quickly discovered that Elena was another difficult person to get close to. She refused to sit at the surfer's table in the cafeteria. She did invite me to sit with her and her friends, a gaggle of young hispanic girls who babbled non-stop about their favorite rapper, the best shade of lipstick and where their boyfriends would take them as soon as they got some money. She took it gracefully when I declined to join them. She wouldn't let me put my arm around her when we walked in the hall and avoided me after school, leaving with a protective cordon of her friends. On top of those obstacles to get closer to her body her father wouldn't let her go out at night, except if he or her mother was with her.

I wasn't sure if it was worth it to pursue her. The only free time I had was at night. She'd probably be in bed by the time I finished karate and surfing, which I wouldn't give up for anyone. Things between us sort of took care of themselves. She was friendly in school, the only place we met, and I didn't pressure her in any way to do anything with me. I did invite her to stop by the surf shop on the weekend and I'd give her a surfing lesson, but she countered with an offer to give me soccer lessons, if I came to her weekend practice. So it was an impasse. She was a nice person so I didn't have any negative thoughts about her. I was just beginning to wonder why nothing seemed to work out with the girls I liked. Maybe the trouble was they were all too nice. Could it be time for a low-life slut? Even that was complicated. I couldn't hang out with someone like that at the beach or school, it would affect business. Late night visits for cheap sex? Unappealing. The obliging older beach bunnies were fine for that. Oh, well. Maybe next year.

Meanwhile, I had more important problems. How to revitalize my web design business, then how to get video production customers. I designed a flyer, had it printed, then handed it out to all the stores I knew near the beach and asked them to post it. I posted it on bulletin boards at school, at the public library, anywhere I could think of. I didn't expect a stampede, but hoped it might help a little. I ate at Wally's two or three times a week to save money. On one visit I asked Frank if I could l leave my business cards at the counter.

"How's business?" he asked.

"Slow. Wally was going to introduce me to some people for video projects, but I guess he's too busy right now."

"He's completely involved in planning a run for the Senate." He looked around and made sure no one was listening. "Wally made me a partner in the restaurant and put his share in a trust, so he wouldn't have any conflicts of interest. I know most of the people he knows. I'll ask around and see if I can connect you with anyone."

"Thanks, Frank. I appreciate that."

"In fact, come to dinner Friday, Saturday and Sunday nights regularly and I'll introduce you to whoever's a potential customer."

"That's great. Thanks."

"I always liked you, Mike. You were always respectful and didn't let Wally's attention turn your head, and I would have been glad to help you. But you made a real friend for what you did for my son. I'll do what I can for you."

"I was glad to help, Frank, He's a brave, determined kid. He didn't back down when those bullies were going to beat him up. I admire that."

"He looks up to you. He thinks you're special."

"I'll try not to disappoint him."

I rode back to the boat yard, feeling good about Frank's support. I guess I could suffer through the great food at Wally's on the weekends.

I checked my bike to make sure the tarp was snug. I had gotten into the habit of wiping it down at night and in the morning, to keep the dampness from causing erosion or rust. At Cliff's suggestion, I waxed the surfaces for a protective coat. It also made the bike look great.

Chapter 57

Cliff, Ronnie, Davey, Donna and I were surfing one evening just as it was getting dark. The waves were swell and we were getting good rides. I just paddled out when I heard Cliff shout, 'outside'. I saw a large wave coming in and turned to catch it. I heard Cliff shout again, then something hit me with a tremendous crash and I went underwater.

I opened my eyes slowly. Everything was so bright that it hurt. I blinked a few times, then saw I was in a white room. For a crazy moment I wondered if I was dead. Then I saw Cliff sitting by the side of the bed. I said 'Hi', but nothing came out. I reached for water, but my left arm wouldn't move. It was in a cast. Cliff noticed the movement.

"Thirsty?"

I nodded and it hurt. I croaked something and Cliff put a straw in my mouth. A minute latter the most delicious drink ever started clearing my throat. I guessed I was in the hospital.

"What happened?"

"What do you remember?"

For a moment I couldn't remember anything and I got scared, then images of surfing came back.

"We were surfing. You yelled 'Outside', then something else and I guess somebody hit me."

"A jet-ski boat hit you last night."

"It's today?"

"It's tonight. Late. You've been unconscious for more than 24 hours. I was really getting worried. You were hit in the head and your arm's injured. Can you sit up?"

"Give me a minute to be sure my head's on tight."

Cliff slowly cranked the bed up and stopped when I held up my right hand. I was in a hospital gown and the sheet seemed too heavy to lift.

"Do I have any other damage?"

"Some cuts and bruises. You got off lucky."

"I don't feel lucky."

"If he had hit you head on, he would have killed you."

A flash of memory returned.

"When you yelled I turned my head."

"That's what saved you."

Just then the doctor came in, a bored, tired looking Indian or Pakistani. I couldn't tell which.

"So, young Mister. You have rejoined the living."

He shined a light in my eyes, took my blood pressure and pulse, felt my head with clumsy fingers that hurt, asked if I was dizzy or nauseous, then said:

"You will stay tonight, so we are sure you do not have concussion. You have a slight fracture of the humerus, which could heal in a week to ten days. If your head is clear and you can walk without dizzy, then you'll go home tomorrow.

I wasn't happy about his hurting me, but muttered:

"Thanks, doctor."

After he left, Cliff said:

"Ronnie, Davey and Donna stayed all last night. I sent Ronnie to open the shop, and Davy and Donna went to school. They came back today and were here until two hours ago."

“Thank them for me.”

“Sure.”

I must have fallen asleep. When I woke up the room was dark, my head felt at least as good as the average water balloon and Cliff was sleeping in the chair next to the bed.

I reached over and patted him gently.

“Cliff… Cliff… Wake up.”

He slowly stirred, yawned, then looked at me.

“You’re feeling better?”

“Yes. Go home. I’ll be alright.”

“You sure?”

“Yes.”

“Okay. I’ll see you in the morning.” He squeezed my good arm fondly and left.

Chapter 58

I must have fallen asleep instantly. What felt like minutes later I woke up with a big, heavyset woman shaking my arm.

"What? What is it?"

"Juice."

"What time is it?"

"5:00 a.m."

"And you woke me for juice? Why didn't you just leave it on the night stand?"

"Hospital regs. You gotta wake up and drink it."

"Are you kidding?"

She folded her arms across her formidable chest and glared at me.

"Are you going to give me trouble?"

I wasn't sure if I could have taken her with two good arms and a clear head, so I drank the juice. It tasted more like sugar water then anything from fruit.

"Now what?"

"You can sleep until breakfast at 7:00 a.m."

I wanted to say a lot of nasty things, but her bulky arms persuaded me to shut up. She galumped out and I lay there trying to figure out why some idiot wanted patients awakened at 5:00 a.m. to drink juice, and then go back to sleep. It didn't feel strange when an orderly woke me for breakfast at 7:00 a.m. I was usually up and out for my run by them. But breakfast was inedible, funny brown looking eggs that tasted even funnier, strips of fat they called bacon, two pieces of cardboard they called toast. The orderly wasn't happy when I said I wasn't hungry and he made a note on my chart. A demerit for not eating? I sat up, went to the bathroom, a little awkward with one arm, but my head was clear.

Cliff came in an hour later and I asked him to find the doctor and get me out of here.

"Are you sure you're alright?"

"I'll get worse if I stay here."

Cliff went to find the doctor and returned in ten minutes.

"He'll be here after rounds."

"They have boxing here?" I joked.

He wasn't sure if I was kidding and replied:

"That's when the doctors visit all the patients."

"Including me?"

"I guess so."

"Good. Then we'll get out of here."

"They helped you and would have saved your life, if it was serious," he said gently.

I started to argue, then realized he was right and nodded agreement. We talked for a while and discussed whether or not to do the surfing tournament without Wally. I said we could do it with Frank's support. Just then, the doctor came in. I couldn't tell if it was the same bored, tired looking Indian or Pakistani. He checked me carefully, then said if I was up to it I could leave.

"Thanks, doc. Where are my clothes?"

Cliff helped me put on my t-shirt and pants, pushed the wheelchair they made me ride, paid the bill, $475, which I vowed to repay, and took me to his house.

"You're staying here until your arm's well enough to go back to the boat. Are you hungry?"

"No. I'd like to sleep for a while."

He led me to a small room in front that faced the beach. I lay down and began to fade out.

"Thanks, Cliff."

"Get some rest."

"Cliff."

"Yeah?"

"Don't wake me for juice."

Chapter 59

It was dark when I woke up. I went to the kitchen, where Cliff was eating.

"Lucy went to San Francisco to give a lecture, but she made a big pot of pasta. Are you hungry?"

"Starving."

He filled a plate and said:

"Dig in."

I devoured the pasta, salad, Italian bread and several more helpings of pasta. Then I sat back.

"I'm full."

"How about some ice cream?"

"Sure."

"Davey and Donna will come by tomorrow after school. Ronnie said he was going to find the jet-ski boater and either get the money for the hospital bill, or beat the guy senseless."

"If he does, he'll save me the trouble. I'd like to run in the morning."

"Are you up to it?"

"If not. I'll stop. I won't be able to surf or do karate until my arm heals. At least I can run."

"You have to stop if you feel the least bit dizzy."

"Sure. I'd like to take off one more day of school, then go back. This way I won't miss too much and I can ride my bicycle."

I went to the beach in the morning for the run and everybody greeted me tumultuously. Davey told me how he raced ashore to call an ambulance, while Cliff and Ronnie brought me in. Ronnie pledged to get the jet-ski boater and Donna said she brought in my board and it was at the shop. Cliff and Ronnie looked me over carefully before they allowed me to run. I started tiring at a mile or so, stopped and slowly headed back. When the other runners came back I ran with them and when we reached our beach area I wasn't feeling too bad. Cliff sent Ronnie to open the shop, Davey and Donna to school and took me to breakfast at the Beach Café. I gobbled pancakes, scrambled eggs, sausages and lots of rye toast and jam.

"I guess you won't starve to death until lunch," Cliff teased. "There's turkey and cheese in the fridge. Make a sandwich or two. I'll see you after I close the shop."

"I'll meet you there for the evening run. I'll rest until then."

"Can you make it home alright?"

"Sure."

"Then I'm going to the shop. I'll see you later."

"Thanks, Cliff."

"De nada, buddy."

It was a strange feeling not having anything to do but eat and sleep. I almost felt guilty for not being at the shop, or working on a web design project. I found myself thinking about school. I had a small bandage on my head, one eye was black and half-closed and I had a cast on my arm. It would look like I was in a fight. Maybe I'd get a patch for my eye and tell the kids who asked that I was attacked by a Great White. All the surfers knew what happened by now. They would think that was very funny.

Instead I slept until one p.m., ate two big sandwiches slept until five p.m., showered, careful not to wet my head or cast, then went to the shop just at closing time. Everyone fussed over me, then I ran the full 2 miles out and back, and waited for Cliff to surf. Then I took him to dinner at Wally's, where Frank treated us like VIPs. He had heard what happened to me and offered to find the jet-ski boater, but I told him someone was doing that already.

"Okay. But if you don't have any luck, I have some friends who could find him and request damages."

"Thanks, Frank. I'll let you know. We were talking about the surfing tournament this year. Do you want Wally's to be a sponsor?"

"Of course. It's great publicity. What do I have to do?"

"We'll let you know the details in plenty of time. It's mostly the money donation."

"No problem. Let me know when. Do you want to meet some people?"

"We should wait until my eye heals, so I don't look like I've been fighting."

"As soon as you're ready."

"Thanks, Frank."

Chapter 60

It wasn't too difficult riding to school with my arm in a cast. I wasn't even tempted to take the motorcycle. I got a lot of strange looks, but the only person who asked me what happened was Mr. Corliss, my computer science teacher. When he heard a jet-ski boat hit me while I was surfing, he ranted unexpectedly, shocking the class.

"They should be restricted to certain areas and required to not make a wake there and back. They are a menace to boaters and I would prefer to see them banned altogether, though that won't happen."

"They have some use for lifesaving," I reminded him.

"I'm talking about the mindless yahoos who don't care who they disturb."

"Are you a boater, Mr. Corlis?" I asked.

"Yes. I have a 32' sailboat."

"I'd like to talk boats with you sometime."

He looked at me for a moment, then said:

"Okay. Now lets get on with the class."

At lunchtime, the surfers were glad to see me and the three witches were very protective, insisting on getting my lunch and bringing it to me. They would have fed me if I let them. They had gone through some changes lately, dropping out of the surfer party scene and taking surfing more seriously. This was the first time they weren't suggestive or manipulative with me and I looked at them closely. They even looked a little different, more clean-cut, less predatory. I felt like I was being tended to by a caring flock of Ibis, or some other beautiful shorebirds. It was hard to resist peeking at their shapely bodies, but I knew if they caught me looking they might come on to me and they were looking good enough to be tempting. I'd rather wait a while and see if they really changed, before encouraging them.

The only unpleasant incident was when I passed Lisa in the hall as I was leaving and she said:

"What were you fighting about?"

I didn't bother answering someone who obviously thought the worst of me. I rode to the shop with Davy and several other surfers who went straight to the beach. I did a little work, checked out my board that Davy had cleaned and waxed and felt good doing something useful. I ran with the group and the three witches asked Ronnie if they could run with us and he said 'yes'. They managed more than a mile and joined us on the way back. I sat on the beach and watched as they surfed with Ronnie, Davy and Donna. Cliff surfed by himself and I waited for him when the others left. He put my bike in the back of his pickup truck and drove home. We had another big pasta meal, chilled awhile, then went to bed. Just before I fell asleep I remembered that Milton had said hello, but didn't ask about the business. I told myself I'd talk to him tomorrow, then fell into a deep sleep.

Even with the cast on my arm I began to feel better, but Cliff insisted I not ride the motorcycle until it was removed. One good thing happened. Ronnie found the jet-ski boater who hit me and gave him choices; the sheriff, a beating, or pay for the hospital. The choice was payment and he gave Ronnie a check, made out to Cliff, for $500. We spent the extra $25 on a pizza party at the shop that included Ronnie, Davey, Donna and the three witches.

I went to the hospital ten days later. After waiting for two hours, the same Indian or Pakistani doctor, or his clone, removed the cast, pronounced the arm healed, but cautioned me to use it carefully for another week or so.

I put in a full afternoon at the shop, took Ronnie's karate class, using my arm very cautiously, then surfed with Cliff. This had been the longest period I hadn't surfed since I first started years ago. It felt like coming home. I didn't do much, a couple of easy rides and I paddled only with my right arm. Cliff didn't talk, aware that I was immersed in the rapture of the water, but he stayed close, in case I had a problem. I gave myself up to the sensation of being where I belonged and cherished every moment.

When I came out, Ronnie, Davey, Donna and the three witches were waiting for me. Davey took my board and said:

"Holy shit. You're glowing like someone stuck a light bulb up your ass."

"Crudely put, my eloquent friend, but true. It was incredible to be out there again. I don't know if could live without surfing."

Everybody nodded and Ronnie said:

"Amen, bro."

The three witches grabbed towels and dried me. On an impulse, I announced:

"As some of you may remember, I nicknamed these three beauties 'the three witches'. I now officially change that to 'the three graces'. Please correct anyone in future who uses that former name."

Zoey, Vickie and Carrie hugged me, kissed me, petted me and kept fussing over me. I wondered if I made a mistake, then admitted their attentions were delicious. We said goodnight and I told Cliff I was going to sleep on the boat tonight.

"Are you sure you can manage the ladder?"

"Yeah. I feel fine."

"I got used to having you at the house. You're welcome anytime. And if the boat is sold you're living with me."

"Thanks, Cliff. You're the best."

Chapter 61

I got back into my regular routine during the next few weeks. As we got closer to summer, business at the shop increased. There were also more surfing lessons, so I was able to share with Ronnie and Davey. There were some requests for websites, but nothing like the flood when I entered high school. Frank had been introducing me to well-to-do people at the restaurant and mentioning that I was the video producer who Wally used. Some preliminary talks for projects started, but no one seemed very urgent to get to the point of signing a contract.

School ended and I got A's in all my subjects, with particular praise from Mr. Corliss. It was a relief to know I probably wouldn't see Lisa again. There hadn't been much web design work, so I didn't spend much time with Milton. Even though he ran with us, took karate and surfed, he seemed aloof. I assumed it was because of the lack of business, but a part of me didn't care. I had mentored him. If he wasn't grateful that was his problem.

I turned 16 in July and got my motorcycle license, at least an interim license until I got my photo license in the mail. Now I could take passengers, ride at night and on the highways. As promised, the first passenger was Davey and he told me he and Ronnie were saving to buy their own bike. The three graces were next on the bike and Zoey's hot body pressed against me felt entirely different from Davey's.

We started planning the 3rd annual Imperial Beach surfing tournament and it was even easier then last year. Frank helped recruit new sponsors, who paid me $5,000 to make a video, and I hired Ronnie and Davey to assist me. We updated the posters, t-shirts, and I got paid for updating or making new websites. We followed the same format as last year, 16s and under, no bodyboards and Ronnie discouraged all complainers. The plastic blonde tv reporter showed up at the shop. She heard about my work on Wally's campaign and wanted to do an in-depth interview with me.

"I heard you were instrumental in getting Wally elected."

"I did what I could," I replied modestly.

"You produced his video ads and did other things."

"Right."

"Those ads were pretty sophisticated. When did you learn that?"

"I've been studying video production for several years. I started with a few small projects and went on from there."

"Where's your studio?"

"I have space in the surf shop."

"I understand you're very active in the local beach life."

"What's your name?"

"Merry."

"Short for Merriweather?"

"How did you know?"

"You look like an explorer type."

"Are you coming on to me?"

"Just appreciating you. Why don't you spend some time with me on the beach. We run in the mornings, then surf. I give surfing lessons in the afternoons. When the shop closes at 6 p.m. we do karate, then surf." I looked her up and down. "You look pretty fit. Bring your camera crew and work out with us, take a surfing lesson and you'll see all the outdoor stuff. If you join me for dinner at Wally's, we can talk about other things."

"You're pretty self-assured for a young guy. I'll think about it."

"I hope you won't hold it against me that I'm not insecure."

She waved and walked off. Her face may have seemed a plastic mask, but her body sure wasn't made of plastic.

Chapter 62

Merry and her video crew showed up a few mornings later at the beach. She did an interview with me, then ran with us, wearing a simple warm-up suit. She dropped out at ½ mile, but her crew continued shooting. She rejoined us on the way back and her crew ran along with us, sprinting ahead at the finish to show her arriving with the other runners. She had a few words with everyone on camera, another interview with me, then Merry and her merry men, I couldn't resist it, left for another assignment. She said they'd be back tomorrow afternoon to shoot surfing lessons and karate. I guess her body was becoming more appealing, because she looked less plastic each time I saw her.

It's not that I didn't like school, but summer was the best time for me, when I could spend all day at the shop, or the beach. The only school obligation I had was from Ms. Yee, my Chinese teacher, who made me promise to study during the summer and work with a language learning tape. I made it part of my regular routine, two or three nights a week.

That evening, on prime time news, Merry's first segment on me aired. She made me look passionate about what I did, intense in how I did it and committed to encouraging others to improve themselves. Everything was so positive about me that I willingly overlooked the clever editing that made it look like she ran all the way with us. All the comments from my friends that she included were either praising me, or thanking me for helping them. I came out looking like a saint or something.

Merry and her crew showed up late the next afternoon, when I was giving a lesson to Tommy, Frank's son. We were working on balance at the edge of the water and she had the crew start shooting and recording what I was saying. I sent him into the water for a quick ride before karate, and Merry got me talking about how it felt to surf. When Tommy came out, she interviewed him. Of course he told her how I saved him from bullies. Merry felt very self-conscious trying karate, but I put her with Tommy and a few of the newbies and led them carefully through the beginner's forms. Her crew focused mainly on her, me and the newbies, with additional footage of the big group with Ronnie.

She had her crew shoot us as we got ready to surf, then as we headed out, and when we started riding in. When Cliff arrived, she talked to him for a few minutes, but he was more interested in surfing than the interview. I came in from a ride as the crew was packing up and I reminded Merry of my offer of dinner at Wally's.

"You were serious?"

"Sure."

"Wally's expensive. Can you afford it?"

"Yes."

"Where do you get your money?"

"I'll tell you over dinner."

"You are persistent… All right. Strictly professional though. I'll interview you."

"Sure. Do you want me to pick you up?"

"You have a car?"

"Motorcycle."

"I'll meet you there. 8:30?"

"It's a date."

"It's not a date. It's business."

"See you later."

Chapter 63

I really didn't understand why I was making a play for Merry. The age disparity was even greater than with Lisa. Merry had to be at least 25. She may not have been as old as Cliff, but she was no kid. She wasn't a celebrity, just a little weather girl on the local station. Granted she had a great body, but there was something cold and ruthless about her. Could that be it? She wasn't a nice girl and I needed a change from all the nice girls I had been involved with?

Merry drove up to the entrance just as I arrived and I parked the bike myself, not trusting the valet, who parked her two year old Beemer. She waited at the door and we went in together. Frank greeted me warmly.

"Hi, Mike. Glad to see you," then he recognized Merry. "Ms. Dennison. Glad you could come. Niece piece that included my son."

"Who's your son?" she asked.

"Tommy. The boy Mike was giving a lesson."

"He's a nice kid."

"Thanks. Come this way."

He seated us at a good table, which Merry was quick to appraise. Paul greeted me:

"Hi, Mike. Good to see you. Good evening, Miss. What can I get you to drink?"

"Bring the lady a martini, please."

He nodded and walked away.

“You didn’t order,” she remarked. “And how did you know I drank martinis?”

I was about to answer, when Luis brought water and hot rolls.

“Hola, Senor Mike.” and we spoke Spanish. “How are you?”

“Good, Luis. When is Tito coming to the beach?”

“I’ll remind him.”

“You should come in the mornings.”

“You know I work late and I’m too tired.”

“You’re always welcome.”

“Thanks, Senor Mike.”

Paul brought Merry’s martini and sparkling water for me.

“He’s older than you. Why does he call you senor Mike?”

“I helped his younger brother and he’s grateful.”

She drank her martini quickly and I asked:

“Another?”

“Trying to get me drunk?”

“No, Merry. I don’t like drunks.”

“You’ll be able to drink when you’re old enough.”

“They’ll serve me anything I want. I just don’t drink.”

“Too pure?” She taunted.

Paul, who was waiting to take our order, gave her a disapproving look.

“I’ll have the broiled lobster and asparagus,” she said.

I ordered a steak and salad and we chatted, me relaxed, Merry tense and trying to probe me. She had another martini, then 2 glasses of wine with the lobster and was feeling the liquor. She babbled about how hard it was to advance at the station without sucking off the producers.

"Maybe you don't suck well enough," I quipped.

I didn't know if she wanted sympathy or admiration, but that shocked her. We finished and I left $30 for Paul and Luis, said goodnight to Frank and led her outside.

"You didn't pay," she said.

"They'll put it on my tab. You've had a little too much to drink and shouldn't drive."

"Is this where you offer to drive me home?"

"No. This where I call a cab for you. You can pick up your car in the morning."

"Don't you want to take me on your motorcycle and feel me pressed against you?"

"Another time."

Just then a cab dropped off some passengers and I bundled her into the back.

"Tell the driver your address."

She mumbled something I didn't hear, I closed the door and the cab drove off. I knew I could have slept with her, and she probably wasn't as drunk as she seemed, but she just wasn't appealing. I rode back to the boatyard, said goodnight to old Tom, studied Chinese for an hour, then went to bed. I didn't stir until 6:30 a.m., when I got up to start a new day.

Chapter 64

Merry and her crew showed up in the afternoon for her surfing lesson. She didn't look worse for wear after drinking last night, but she definitely looked plastic again. Her crew set up and I was about to give her the introductory talk, when she took off her warm up suit. She was wearing a very small blue string top and an even smaller thong. I immediately told the cameraman: "Cut", and took her aside.

"What do you think you're doing wearing a few strings like that?"

"I'm showing that my body is as good or better than the girls on the beach."

I couldn't believe how dumb she was.

"Unless you want to spend the rest of your career sucking off producers, put your warm up suit back on. We'll do a land lesson today. If you want a water lesson, wear a very modest one piece bathing suit and make sure your camera guy erases any footage he may have shot once you peeled."

"I just want to fit in," she said weakly.

"Well if you want to show off your body, I have a friend who makes porno flicks, or you can do private showings for me some night."

She glared angrily at me, but put on her warm up suit, spoke to the cameraman, then turned to me.

"I'm ready for my lesson."

I went through the usual description of the pleasures and risks of surfing, had her do a few warm up exercises, then had her practice balancing on the board, followed by standing from the paddling position. She did alright, all things considered and after 20 minutes, I said:

"That covers the basics. If you want to try the water, come back tomorrow afternoon, at 3:00 p.m."

She nodded, told her cameraman to shoot the crowd that had gathered, then they packed up and left. I couldn't figure out why I stopped them from shooting her in her string and thong. Maybe because she was doing a big story about me that would help my business. Whatever the reason, I knew I was right to do it, but I had to admit I wouldn't mind getting my hands on that body.

Merry and her crew showed up early the next afternoon to set up for her lesson. They shot the end of my lesson with Tommy, who was doing well. He had eagerly said 'yes', when I suggested he enter the 12 and under novice group at the surfing tournament. This year we had made t-shirts well in advance and I had given them to the running group and karate class to wear regularly. I gave Tommy the smallest size and it swam on him, but he was proud to wear it. Of course we sold the t-shirts at the shop, Wally's, the Marina, and several other places.

Merry told me she was ready and I quickly went through paddling, standing and riding. I cautioned her that she'd probably fall and might not even get a ride, but she was undeterred. I gave her a big 'ready', for the camera, she nodded yes and I said:

"Grab your board."

She took off her warm up suit and displayed her shapely body in the skimpy blue top and thong she wore yesterday. She may not have been as firm as the three graces, but she had a fine looking ass. I didn't comment on her sparse attire, and just said:

"Let's go."

We waded out, then paddled and I showed her how to cut through the waves, which weren't very big, or go under them. We got out far enough so I could show her how to pick a wave, paddle into position, then get up on the board. She had absolutely no feel for the water, or the waves, so I told her when to turn and paddle. She tried and fell several times and was getting frustrated. I told her softly:

“This isn’t easy, or everyone would be doing it. Stay relaxed and don’t think about it. I’ll tell you when to go at the next half decent wave. You just go.”

We waited for a few minutes and a medium size wave started rolling in, and I said: “Go”.

“It’s too big,” she protested.

“Go. Go.”

I watched her turn and paddle and kept pace with her, not too close, just enough to help her, if necessary. I didn’t say that when I surfed I wouldn’t have bothered with a wave like this. She managed to get into position, I yelled: “Get up”, and she stood, managed to keep her balance, headed for shore, threw her arms up triumphantly and her top flew off. It took a moment for her to realize her breasts were bare, then she jumped off the board, totally embarrassed. I moved close and said:

“Hold onto the board with one arm and paddle to shore with the other. Stop where you can stand and I’ll get your warm-up jacket.”

“Thanks, Mike. I feel so stupid.”

“Well you looked pretty good for a moment.”

Her camera crew got a great shot of her riding high, almost naked. People on the beach had been standing with their camera phones, recording every moment, and waved goodbye to Merry and her crew when they packed up and left. By the time they got to the station someone had posted on YouTube and it had gone viral. Her producers loved the shot and aired it with breasts blurred as part of the beach segment. The show got the highest rating ever for the station. In the morning Merry was a celebrity.

Chapter 65

One response to Merry's ride on tv was we got a flood of new students eager to learn how to surf. Most of them were young girls and boys, between 5 and 10 years old. There were some older guys in their 20s, who thought this was a great way to meet girls. I talked to two of them, just to get an idea what was going on in their not overly bright heads. They figured if they hung out on the beach in a wet suit, with a board, they'd be chick magnets. I let Ronnie teach them, so if there was a problem he could quickly settle it.

I set up a schedule with Ronnie and Davey, so one of us would always be in the shop with Cliff. We had so many young kids that I hired Donna to teach some of them. From her first minute with them she did so well that I kicked myself for not hiring her sooner. I appointed Tommy our official assistant. With Cliff's approval, we paid him a stipend of $5 a day, as well as giving him free lessons. When he didn't have any particular tasks, he followed me around like a puppy. He was underfoot so often that I had him assist Donna with the kiddies. In just a few short months he had put on weight and muscle and loved every moment he was with us. A good kid.

Merry and her crew returned a week later to do another interview with me and they immediately drew a crowd. She greeted me with a kiss that amused everyone but the three graces, who had taken an intense dislike to her. She confided that she got a weekend anchor slot and a big raise, which she owed to me. Then she invited me to dinner, and I accepted.

When her crew was ready, she began the interview, which was different than the earlier ones.

"We've shown our viewers the happy beach life of surfing. But there's another side of the story, a darker side, with drugs, wild parties, forced sex. What can you tell us about that?"

I couldn’t believe she was doing this and it really pissed me off, but I replied pleasantly:

“I know all the regular surfers and I’ve been to their parties. I never heard of anyone pushing drugs, or forcing a girl to have sex, or fighting. Surfing is an individual activity and the people who surf aren’t angry. They find peace and beauty on the water. Surfing movies always show some crooks, drug dealers or violent animals. Maybe it’s like that somewhere else, but not at Imperial Beach.”

“So you’re saying there are no drugs at those parties?”

“Some people may enjoy getting high, but it’s not like those high school parties, where the kids get sick, crazy or violent.”

“Do you use drugs?”

“No. And I don’t drink, Neither do the friends I surf with. We get our high being on the water.”

“You just heard from Mike Sanchez, who reminded us not to believe everything we see in the movies. Thank you, Mike.”

“You’re welcome, Merry.”

She told her crew to shoot the kiddie’s lessons and she’d put voiceover in later. We chatted for a few minutes and she suggested:

“How about dinner at a Chinese restaurant tonight?”

“Fine.”

She gave me the name and address and told me to meet her at 8:00 p.m.

Chapter 66

Word about my interview spread like wildfire along the beach. Surfers kept coming up to me and thanking me for defending them publicly. 'Grizzly', a huge, hairy guy, even older than Cliff, naturally gave me a bear hug that could have crushed my ribs if I didn't get my arm in the way.

"Well said, Mike. You know some of us get a bad rap."

I had to laugh. He was married to a tiny woman, tough as tungsten, who ruled their lives, which satisfied both of them. Despite his ferocious appearance, 'Grizzly' was a gentle soul, who'd go out of his way to avoid violence. I couldn't resist teasing him.

"I promised the reporter I'd reveal all your evil ways on camera."

He shook his head sadly. "I told Cliff he should have drowned you when you first showed up."

"I'll remember that and tell her how you kidnap girls off the beach and make them use drugs."

We grinned at each other and he gave me another squeeze.

"Take it easy, Mike."

Merry was waiting at the door when I got to the restaurant, looking sexy in a short skirt and tight top. I greeted the manager in Chinese and we chatted for a minute, Merry looking on in amazement. I didn't tell her that I looked up some Chinese social and food phrases on my IPad.

"I didn't know you spoke Chinese."

"I'm just learning."

"What else do you know?"

"If we become better acquainted I'll tell you."

"Maybe someday. I'm leaving for San Diego after dinner. I got a morning anchor slot at a major station, starting tomorrow. They want to meet with me tonight."

"Congratulations."

"Thanks. I owe it to you. Look me up if you're ever in San Diego and need a favor."

We finished dinner, she paid the check, kissed me on the cheek and was gone. I wouldn't miss her, but I had a momentary pang of regret that I didn't get my hands on her body. Her last surfing segment had aired earlier that evening. By morning, anyone who didn't thank me on the beach, stopped by the shop. Cliff and I had to laugh at how many of the guys were drug users, but we both knew they didn't deal, or push anyone to use. The truth was in all the years I was surfing at Imperial Beach, I never saw any of them get violent. I did have to admit that some of the parties got wild, but never ugly.

That evening, after surfing, the three graces were waiting for me. Vicki said:

"Zoey never really had sex with anyone. She touched guys and let them touch her, but that was it. We want you to have sex with Zoey, because we know you'll be gentle with her."

Six months ago I would have laughed in her face. Three months ago I would have said 'no thanks'. But they had changed.

"When?"

"Tonight?" Vicki asked.

I didn't say a word, took Zoey's hand, led her to my motorcycle, gave her a helmet and got on. She got on behind me, held me tightly and we drove off. We stopped for a traffic light a few blocks away and she whispered:

"I'm so excited I'm wet down there. Do you really want to do this?"

I took her hand and put it on my cock, which was stiff. She felt the heat through my jeans, and squeezed hard. I almost came in my pants. When the light changed, I put her arm around me again. I drove to the marina, led her to the boat and when she started to ask about it I told her we'd talk later. I guided her ahead, then helped her below without putting on a light, pulled her to me and kissed her. Her mouth was sweet and eager. I ran my hands down her body and she moaned. I lit a candle, put on some soft music, then took off her clothes, first caressing her breasts, then stroking her clit until she came in a rush. I got undressed, put on a condom, led her to the bed, got on top and slid gently inside her. She was wet and hot and I slowly moved in and out, going deeper each time, She suddenly cried out, then opened like a flower. She moved with me and we came together. We lay there quietly for a few minutes, then got dressed. I told her about living on the boat and made her promise not to tell anyone, even the other two graces. I drove her home, she kissed me and I drove off. We hadn't said a word since we left the boat.

Chapter 67

The three graces were at the beach for the morning run and Zooey was glowing. They greeted me with approving pats and hugs, while I took off my t shirt and shorts and stretched. They ran almost a mile and a half and were proud of themselves. So was I. I complimented them when we got back to our surf boards.

I heard Tommy ask Davey:

“Why are they fussing over him?”

“They’re his harem.”

“What’s a harem?”

Davey looked around helplessly, unsure how to answer the curious kid. Donna smacked him on the head, then turned to Tommy:

“Davey was joking. They like him.”

“Do you like him?”

“Sure. He’s a great guy.”

“Are you a harem?”

“No. He’s my good buddy. Davey just made up that word.”

Ronnie led everyone into the water, ending that conversation. Just before I left for the shop, Zoey took me aside.

“Thank you for last night, Mike. You were wonderful.”

“You were pretty good yourself. Thank you.”

She actually blushed and raced to join the other graces.

Last minute preparations for the surfing tournament kept me busy, but everything moved along quickly and efficiently. We had done it twice before, so it wasn't a surprise, but it was reassuring that there were no problems once it started. Except the crowds. Whether the growing awareness of the tournament, or Merry's series with her final triumphant ride, the beach was packed with spectators. The Chief of Police, a short, stout, red-faced man, stopped by the shop to complain about the crowds. I played innocent and dumb and told him Congressman Custerback's office was coordinating the event and he should talk to them. I must have been convincing, because he told me he knew who I was and to keep up the good work. Cliff gave me that funny look, raising his eyebrows, at my performance.

The first week went off without a hitch, with no protests, no complaints, no injuries and a happy crowd. On the final's day, the crowd was enormous and Merry came from San Diego with a crew to broadcast live. In a very short time she had slicked up her image and looked slightly less plastic. Naturally she interviewed me and wanted dirt or scandal. I blandly told her about the competition and praised the sponsors. Just then Wally and entourage arrived. I signaled him to join us, introduced him to Merry, then found a reason to leave them.

As expected, Davy won the boy's 16 and under, and Donna won the girl's 16 and under. Tommy placed 2nd in his novice class and it was hard to tell who was more thrilled, he or his Dad. Wally awarded the trophies, broadcast on tv regionally, and everyone went home happy. Well maybe not the clean-up crew. The beach was a mess. I guess it was too much trouble for people to put bottles and other garbage in the many trash cans placed all over the beach and boardwalk.

The next morning, when Cliff mentioned that in a few months we should decide whether or not to sponsor the tournament next year, I knew he didn't like the fuss and effort. I had to admit that it wasn't the fun it used to be. So whatever he preferred was fine with me. I just wanted to enjoy the few weeks before school started. Then I got an unexpected visitor. A man from a major surfing magazine came to the shop and offered me a job traveling to surfing tournaments for three months, narrating events on camera and interviewing surfers. It was tempting and the money was very good. I'd certainly make connections that would be useful. But there was my way of life here and school, so I told him I'd think about it and get back to him. Cliff hadn't said anything, so when the man left, I asked:

"What do you think?"

"You were smart not to answer right away. Take your time to consider it. It's a big commitment."

I had a fantasy picture of Tahiti, Australia, Brazil, then reality set in. I had school and I knew Cliff would never let me be a drop-out. So farewell adventures, glamorous places, foreign beauties… I turned to Cliff.

"Well at least I have you."

"Don't you have a lesson now?"

As I walked out the door, he threw a sponge ball that hit me in the head, and grinned cheerfully.

Chapter 68

Another exciting result of the tournament was that Davey got an offer to join the junior section of the World Surfer's Tour. Obviously, if he did well, he'd move up to the men's tour, where fame and fortune might wait. He had a long talk with Ronnie and convinced him that school wasn't important and that he really wanted to do it. Ronnie asked me to ask Cliff to assess Davey's chances. Cliff described the intensity of the competition, evaluated Davey's prospects, pointing out areas he could work on, then assured him he had the potential, and concluded:

"If you do it, make some friends who aren't competition off the waves. That'll make everything easier."

After surfing that evening, Davey took me aside, made sure no one was nearby, then said:

"I really want to do this, but it's scary."

"Of course it's scary. You're going into a whole new world. But if you think about it, you did that when you went into high school. You've got nerve, you're smart, tough, a great guy and a hell of a surfer. I know you well enough to tell you you'll do fine."

"I wish you were going with me."

"That wouldn't help your surfing and that's all that counts on the tour."

"What if I don't make it?"

"Then you come back after seeing the world, having met beautiful girls, made money and decide if you want to try again. Don't be a dope. You've got everything to gain and nothing to lose."

He hugged me. "Thanks, Mike. You've always been there for me."

"As you have for me. That's what best friends are for."

"I'll send you pictures of my girls," and he walked off jauntily.

Two days later Davy was off on his great adventure, first stop, Hawaii. Ronnie thanked me for encouraging him to go, and I told him that after Cliff, he and Davy were my closest friends. With Cliff's approval, I hired Donna to work at the shop, so we'd alternate lessons when school started. Milton heard about Davey's departure and my hiring Donna, and he resented it. He came to the shop and confronted me.

"Why didn't you hire me to work at the shop?"

"You're a bright guy, Milton, but you're not easy going with people. That's important in a retail business."

"I get along well with people," he protested, raising his voice.

"Come on outside, so we don't disturb anyone in the shop," I urged.

"Why? Are you going to threaten me?"

"Of course not. I wouldn't do that. You're still my associate for web design."

I eased him outside and he mumbled:

"If you don't want me here, I don't want to work with you," and he rushed off.

"Talk to me in a day or two when you cool down," I called after him.

I turned around and the three graces were standing there and had heard every word.

"He's a real jerk," Vicki said, "after what you did for him." Zoey sort of stood shyly behind Carrie, her pattern since our night together.

“He’s sore because he wants to belong,” I explained, “and he thinks working here will do that.”

“The only reason we accepted him was because of you,” Carrie said.

“He was lucky that three beautiful girls accepted him,” I replied.

“So what’s with you and that tv reporter?” Vickie demanded.

“Nothing. She’s in San Diego.”

“Showing off that flabby body like that,” Zoey muttered.

“It wasn’t that flabby,” I protested.

“You need to take a close look at us,” Vicki teased.

“I do all the time. You’re the hottest girls I know.” And I had to admit to myself that I was thinking about them a lot lately. “I’ll see you beauties later,” and headed into the shop.

“Bye, Mike,” they crooned, and I couldn’t help looking after those sleek, taut bodies as they walked away.

Chapter 69

The day school started, for the first time I could remember I was looking forward to class, particularly Ms. Yi in Chinese and of course Mr. Corliss in Computer Science. The Chinese class was even smaller than last term, only six of us and the cute Chinese girl was gone. So Ms. Yi decided to concentrate on conversation for the semester, and if the school didn't drop the course, reading and writing next term. I thought it was a great idea. I'd rather talk to people then write to them.

The surfers still had two tables in the lunchroom. The seniors from last year were gone, but new freshmen were here to fill the ranks. Between the surf shop, the tournament and all my tv exposure, I was well known throughout the school. A few of the surfers always seemed to be near me wherever I went and the three graces hung out with me outside of class. I couldn't figure out why the guys were always around, until Jimmy Longboard, a big rangy senior, told me Ronnie had asked some of the guys to look out for me, now that Davey was gone.

"I can take care of myself," I said.

"I know, man. But you're our spokesperson and we don't want anyone messing with you. Besides, Ronnie asked us. We cool?"

"Sure, Jimmy. Thanks."

Not that they made up for Davey, but it was a good feeling that my buddies were at my back. I briefly wondered if Ronnie prompted the three graces to hang out with me, then dismissed it, knowing how strong-willed they were.

It was really good to see Mr. Corliss again in Computer Science. I'd have him again in computer lab, normally only open to seniors, but he arranged it for me.

"Now that you're a famous surfer," he teased, "did you forget your code projects?"

I showed him what I had been working on during the summer and he was surprised at my progress.

"Stay after computer lab for a few minutes. I want to talk to you about something."

"Sure, Mr. C."

Class was interesting and Mr. Corliss made sure to challenge us, which was one of the reasons I always enjoyed his class. Milton ignored me, elaborately looking away when I happened to look at him. He was no longer welcome at the surfer's table, so he was throwing away all the good things he had started building. Someone in the class told me he was trying to get web design jobs on his own, especially from the new freshmen. Fine by me. I had learned the hard way that the web gold rush only lasted a short time, so I needed another money maker.

I assumed Mr. Corliss wanted to talk to me about another project, but he surprised me.

"Mike. I have an M.S. from San Diego University and I'm working on my PhD there. I spoke to a few of my professors about you and they'd like to meet you. If they like what they see and you keep up your grades next year, they'll offer you a four year scholarship. All expenses paid. Tuition, books, fees, dorm, cafeteria. A full ride…" I didn't know what to say, so I just stood there… "Well? Say something."

"It sounds great. Is it a good school?"

"A very good school. It's a private Roman Catholic University near the beach. They have a fine curriculum and graduates with a B.S. get a well rounded education in math and business. You'll love it."

"When do I meet them?"

"I'll arrange it in a month or so, if you want it."

"I want it. Thanks, Mr. C. I don't know if I could afford to go to college otherwise."

"I'm glad to help. You've got a lot of potential… By the way. One of my professors is a surfer and he's seen you on television. He thinks you're very mature for your age."

"Thanks, again, Mr. C. I really appreciate this."

Chapter 70

Milton got about half of the freshman who wanted web design, but I didn't begrudge them. I knew he needed the money and I didn't pay attention to his activities. For some reason, the three graces had decided he betrayed me. I only found out accidently that they told some of the freshmen not to work with him. I took them aside and asked them not to do anything against him.

"He's got enough problems. Leave him be."

"But he's bad mouthing you to the freshmen," Vicki protested.

"That's their problem if they believe him."

"Don't you care what he says?" Carrie asked.

"No. My friends know who I am. If those kids don't know better, I don't need them. Now do me a favor. Forget about him."

"You're so good," Zoey crooned. "We've been talking about making you our boyfriend."

I had to laugh. "You've got to be kidding. I could never deal with the three of you. One of you would be more than I could handle."

"You think we're that special," Vicki preened.

"Absolutely. If I was an arab sheik, I'd give all my camels to get you in my harem."

This cracked them up and what could have become awkward, ended in laughter.

Over the next few weeks I established my regular school schedule: run and surf in the early morning, school, the shop and lessons after school, karate, and the highlight of my day, surfing with Cliff. It was a very satisfying routine that always felt different day to day, so it was impossible to get bored. Cliff got sick with some kind of virus in early October and he was going to close the shop for a few days. I persuaded him that Ronnie could man it until I got there and he agreed, as long as Ronnie could call my cell phone if he had an emergency. Ronnie ran the shop well from Wednesday to Friday, and I was there all day Saturday and Sunday, having Donna give my lessons which she did well.

Cliff came back on Monday, pleasantly surprised to find the place neater then he left it, and Ronnie had made a lot of sales. Cliff gave him a bonus and raised my salary again, which I didn't object to. Then he told us we were getting health insurance, paid for by the shop, which was cheap since we were young and healthy. His accountant, Ms. Lewison, worked out a formula and the shop got a tax deduction, so Cliff, Ronnie and I got coverage and it didn't cost much.

In late October, Mr. Corliss arranged a Friday meeting for me at San Diego University, with an invitation to spend the night at his professor's house. I drove up the coast on Route 5, enjoying the scenery, especially the beautiful beaches. I realized halfway there that this was the longest trip I'd ever taken and resolved to have travel in my future. I met Professor Orsini at the Computer Science Department office and liked him immediately. He was tall, slim, dark-haired, with a friendly face and the deep tan of the dedicated surfer. He was much older than Cliff, maybe 40 or 45.

Professor Orsini introduced me to the department members in the office, then gave me the grand tour. I saw the classrooms, the labs, the dorms, the bookstore, and we had lunch in the cafeteria, which had much better food than my high school cafeteria. Everywhere there were serious, but happy looking students, working, studying or playing ball on the campus. I even enjoyed the old looking buildings that Professor Orsini told me were designed in the 16th century Spanish Renaissance architectural style.

The last stop of the tour was back at the department office where two other professors questioned me about my computer work. I told them about my web design and video production business, then went through the languages I studied, the ones in progress, and the ones planned ahead. We talked about coding and they told me they were impressed with my progress and I was an excellent scholarship candidate.

On the way to Professor Orsini's house, naturally on the beach just north of the city, he asked me what I thought of the school.

I couldn't suppress the enthusiasm in my voice.

"I love it. It's a great place. I'd love to go here."

"Well you made a good impression on the department chairman and vice chairman, and you won me over."

"Thanks, Professor Orsini."

"Call me Charlie."

Chapter 71

The Orsinis lived in what Charley called a charming old Victorian style house in Ocean Beach. I got a good look at the community as I followed Charlie to his house on my motorcycle. It looked as nice as Imperial Beach. When I pulled up on my bike, his wife and two children were waiting for us. They looked a bit startled to see the leather jacketed, space helmeted biker, but when I got off the bike and took my helmet off they saw I wasn't a wild beast. Mrs. Orsini introduced herself and the kids.

"Hi. I'm Sandy. This is Nicky and Holly."

"Hi. I'm Mike. Nice to meet you ."

Nicky was about 12 years old and he looked at me intently.

"I know who you are," he declared. "You're that celebrity surfer who's on tv all the time."

Holly, who was about 10, asked:

"Are you famous?"

"No. I just help run a surfing tournament and the tv station keeps interviewing me."

"Did Dad bring you here to get us to surf?" Nicky asked suspiciously.

"Of course not. He's interviewing me for a scholarship at the university, so if we get to know each other say good things about me."

"We'll see," Holly said teasingly.

"Can I ask you a question, Nicky?"

"Yeah."

"Why don't you surf?"

"I don't know… I just don't want to bother."

"Did you ever try it?"

"Not really. Dad keeps pushing me…"

"What about you, Holly?"

"I feel the same way Nicky does."

"Well I hope it won't bother you if I surf while I'm here."

"It's okay," Nicky said.

"I do other workouts every day. I run in the morning, surf, then go to school. I work at the surf shop from 3-6 pm, then I do karate and surf. Do you guys run?"

"Not really," Nicky said.

"You should consider it. It's a great exercise. I run with a group of guys and girls and everyone does different distances."

"Could we try running with you in the morning?" Holly asked shyly.

"Sure. You'll have to be up early though. I run at 7:00 a.m. Would you like a karate lesson after dinner?"

"That'd be cool," Nicky said.

"Me too," Holly added.

Charlie grilled hamburgers, hot dogs, corn on the cob and potatoes on the deck and we ate watching the ocean. The Orsinis made me feel right at home and I liked all of them. Charlie noticed me watching the water and said:

"I bet you'd like to hit the water."

"I have to digest, or I'll sink like a stone. And I'm going to give Nicky and Holly a karate lesson, if it's alright with you."

"Why, sure. Did you ask them?"

"They asked me."

"Oh. Should I join you?"

"No, Dad," Nicky was quick to say. "You can surf with him later."

The kids really took to karate and they listened intently that it was a tool to build self-confidence, not a way to learn to hurt people.

"So what if someone starts a fight with you?" Nicky demanded.

"First I try to talk my way out of it, then I run away."

"What if they hit you?" Holly asked.

"I'll defend myself. I study karate so I won't have to fight. I don't like to hurt people."

"You're pretty good though, right?" Nicky asked.

"My teacher thinks I'm at black belt level. We train at the beach, not in a dojo, so we don't test."

"You do all the physical stuff, yet Dad says you're an advanced Computer Science student," Nicky remarked.

"I do a lot of things. I have a web design business, a video production company," I grinned at them. "Brains are more important than brawn."

The kids really enjoyed the lesson and I suggested if they wanted to continue they should check out the local dojos, or find a club. I got my board and was about to hit the water, when on impulse, I asked them:

"Would you like a surfing lesson?" They looked at me warily and I added:

"I'm a better surfing teacher than a karate teacher. Try it. If you don't like it, don't do it. You're both athletic and in good condition. You might like it."

They agreed to try and I skipped my usual introduction of the pleasures of surfing and went right to the basics.

"Surfing is all about getting up and staying up."

I started them lying down on the sand and paddling, then standing up. Once they got the hang of it, I let them take turns practicing standing on my board. They both had the knack, so after a few more minutes, I said:

"That's enough for the first time. If you want to continue, we'll do it in the morning."

"Will you be disappointed if we don't do it?" Holly asked.

"No. It's up to you. Did you enjoy what we did today?"

They nodded 'yes' enthusiastically.

"Then I think you'll enjoy tomorrow, but it's your choice."

I surfed for a while with Charlie, who was pretty good for an old guy. We were waiting for a good wave and I had to laugh when he said:

"You don't do many tricks for a young guy."

"I just want to enjoy the waves on a new beach. I'm not too big on tricks. I just like to get great rides."

"I saw you giving the kids a surfing lesson. Thanks. I've been trying to get them to surf for years. What's your secret?"

"Wait and see if they go in the water in the morning… I've been teaching for three years and I like working with smart kids."

We surfed til it got dark, then went in, showered and dressed. Nicky and Holly got me into a video game where we were an explorer team, dropped on an alien planet and we had to face beasts and climate threats. They were really nice at coaching me through ambushes. They went to bed at 10 p.m., exhausted by the exercise. Sandy, a nurse, left for her

11:00 p.n. shift at the hospital and Charlie and I talked for a while, he telling me about life at San Diego U., and me telling him about my activities. He led me to a guest room at 11:45 and said goodnight. I went right to sleep, completely relaxed after a real good day.

Chapter 72

Nicky and Holly were waiting for me when I went out on the beach to stretch before my run. They were wearing warm-ups and running shoes and when I peeled to my bathing suit, Nicky said:

"We didn't know what to wear."

"You should wear whatever you're comfortable in. I prefer to run in a bathing suit and barefoot." They stripped down and I told them: "Always stretch before you run to make sure your body is loose. Keep in mind this is exercise, not a competition. It should be satisfying and fun. Don't over do it. I've been running for years, so I go a long way. Go as far as you can without stressing yourself. Even if it's only ten feet," which made them laugh. "Ready?"

Then nodded 'yes', so I led them off, setting a careful pace and monitoring them closely so I could stop them if they overdid it. They did fine for ¼ of a mile, then started to tire, so I stopped.

"That's enough for your first day out. Walk back slowly. You did great. I was about your age, Nicky, when I started running. I didn't go as far. I'll see you in a bit and you can decide if you want another surfing lesson."

I ran about a mile out, then ran back, to be sure the kids didn't wander off while I was gone. They were waiting for me with surf boards, so I went right to standing and balancing with them. They both did well and fifteen minutes later, I said:

"Now comes the big decision. Do you want to try the water?" They both nodded eagerly, so I said: "Alright. Nicky first, then Holly, then both of you together."

I led Nicky into the water, reminding him this wasn't a test or a competition and he seemed to get the idea. He fell the first few times, but instead of getting angry or quitting, he became more determined. And a few tries later he caught his first ride. He babbled about how he felt as we went in to get Holly.

"Can I go again?" Nicky asked.

"Wait until Holly gets her first ride, then we'll surf together."

Holly dashed in, scrambled onto her board like a monkey, paddled out, caught a nice wave, was up in a flash and rode it all the way in. Charlie and Sandy were watching from the porch, but wisely stayed there, leaving the kids to me. We surfed for the next hour, and I made adjustments to their stance which they quickly adopted. When I finally said: "That's it for day one," they wanted to keep going, but I insisted we stop. I sat them down on the beach and they didn't notice Charlie and Sandy come up behind them.

"You guys did great for the first day. I hope you enjoyed it as much as I did."

"But you were just teaching us," Nicky objected.

"I love teaching and I was surfing with you."

"Why did you stop us?" Holly asked.

"It's never good to overdo it. The ocean will be there a long time. If you decide to keep surfing, you'll learn to stop when you've had enough."

"Aren't you going to tell us to surf." Nicky asked.

"No. That's up to you."

"They why give us lessons?" Holly asked.

"So you have a choice. I'm not here to push surfing. You're healthy, capable and you have talent. I just wanted to give you a chance to make up your minds after trying it."

“Would you dislike us if we don’t surf?” Nicky said.

“Of course not. I like you because you’re smart, strong-willed and willing to try new things.”

Holly jumped up and hugged me.

“Thanks, Mike. You’re cool,” she murmured.

Then Nicky hugged me. “Holly’s right. You are cool…Can you stay the rest of the day and do karate and surf again?”

“I really should be getting back. I have a job…”

“Grab him, kids,” Charlie ordered. “Make him stay.”

They grabbed me and chanted: “Stay. Stay. We won’t let you go.”

“Let me get my cellphone and call my boss and see if he needs me.”

“Here. Use mine.” Sandy offered.

“What’s your boss’s name?” Holly asked.

“Cliff.”

“Is he nice?” Nicky asked.

“He’s a great guy. My best friend. He taught me to surf… Hi, Cliff. How’s it going?” Quiet? Are Ronnie and Donna there? Good. Listen. Have Donna take my lessons this afternoon. I’ve been mugged by a couple of young hooligan surfers and they won’t let me go. Okay. Don’t forget to make out a check for the health insurance. I don’t think I’ll get back in time to surf tonight. I’ll see you tomorrow.”

“You told your boss what to do,” Nicky remarked.

“Well I manage the shop.”

“And you surf with your boss,” Holly added.

“Every night, after we close the shop. He’s a great surfer and I learn from him every time we’re out.

“What’s his name?” Charlie asked casually.

“Cliff Landers.”

“Are you kidding? He was a world champion. I always wondered what happened to him. He just disappeared one day.”

“He lost interest in competing,” I explained. “He’s so good he could compete again, but he just wants to enjoy the water.”

“Well how about some lunch,” Sandy urged, “and maybe you’ll stay another night with us.”

Before I could reply, Nicky and Holly grabbed my arms and yelled: “Stay. Stay.”

Holly said: “I’m not letting you go.”

I shrugged. “I guess I’m your prisoner.”

Chapter 73

It was a really nice day with the Orsini family. We hung out on the beach all day. Sandy brought out sandwiches and soda for lunch. Later I did karate with the kids, which attracted a crowd that they coolly ignored. Then we surfed. The kids had a blast and made Charlie promise to surf with them whenever he could. The Orsinis took me to dinner at a Mexican restaurant and were dazzled when I spoke Spanish to the manager and waiter.

"What other languages do you speak?" Holly asked.

"Well I'm studying Chinese, but I can't speak it yet."

By this time Charlie was almost as wild about me as the kids were.

Sandy didn't have to work that night, so after the kids went to bed, we sat up pretty late talking. They were bowled over when I told them about my video production company and my work helping Wally get elected.

I was up and on the beach at 7:00 a.m. and the kids joined me as I was stretching. Charlie and Sandy asked if they could join us.

"It's up to Nicky and Holly."

They both welcomed their parents and we set off at a careful pace. Charlie tactfully stopped when the kids did, but Sandy ran on for another ½ mile and I went another ½ mile. On the way back two girls were jogging and one of them called out as I passed them:

"Hey. You're that famous surfer guy."

I waved and they ran with me. When we got to the Orsinis, they were still trying to make conversation and one of them said:

"How about a lesson?"

"I'm surfing with my friends now."

"Here's my phone number," the aggressive one said. "Give me a call."

I followed the Orsinis into the water, and Nicky asked:

"Do girls do that a lot?"

"Wait'll you're an experienced surfer," I teased.

We had a great time. When we left the beach I showered and dressed, then said goodbye. They tried to persuade me to stay for karate, surfing and dinner, but I told them I had to leave. They all hugged me goodbye and Charlie walked me to my bike.

"I've been trying to get my kids to surf for years and you did it in a few minutes. You made a friend for life," and he hugged me again. "Just keep up your grades and you're in at San Diego U."

"Thanks, Charlie. I don't want you to do it because I got the kids to surf."

"It'll be on your scholarly merit. Does that reassure you?"

"Sure."

"You'll have to come visit us again."

"Sure. That'll be fun."

On the way back to Imperial Beach I felt real good knowing I took a big step in insuring my future. After I cleaned the bike, I did some much needed house-keeping on the boat, then grabbed my board and headed for the beach. I got there in time for Ronnie's karate class, then Cliff, Ronnie, Donna and I surfed. It was a little strange at first without Davey, we had been surfing as a group for years, but we gradually just gave ourselves up to the water and had a blast. Cliff took us for pizza and told me to tell them about my visit to San Diego. I described the University and the Orsinis and they congratulated me on making a good impression. When we said goodnight I realized that these were my closest friends in the world and on an impulse I hugged them one at a time.

Chapter 74

I got a sudden rush of website orders from freshmen who I hadn't thought were interested. It turned out that the three graces spoke to a lot of them and advised them not to work with Milton. He confronted them and told them to 'mind their own business', and Vicki replied: "then don't bad-mouth Mike". He started to get angry, but some of the surfers intervened and he slunk off. When I heard about the incident I tried to talk to Milton, but he blew me off.

"You turned everyone against me," he accused.

"That's not true. You got upset when the web business slowed and it grew from that. Just apologize to the three graces and we'll se if we can rebuild our friendship."

"Not a chance," and he stormed off.

His choice. It wasn't hurting me.

Except for the complete lack of video projects, everything else in my life was going smoothly. In school, Mr. Corliss was thrilled at the feedback he got from Charlie about my visit to San Diego U. He assigned special projects to me suggested by Charlie that would impress the Computer Science department. Ms. Yi was happy with my progress in Chinese and I kept high grades in my other classes. I finished the last of the websites in early November and invited the three graces to dinner, as a thank you for their help. I gave them a choice and they picked Wally's. I hadn't been in for a few weeks and Frank was delighted to see me. I introduced the graces and he welcomed them warmly. He led us to a table and when we were seated, said:

"I want to talk to you before you leave."

"Sure.

Luis brought hot bread and water and I asked after his brother, Tito, who I hadn't seen at the beach or school. He told me in Spanish that Tito dropped out to work for a while, but promised to go back to school.

"If I can help in any way, let me know."

"Gracias, senor Mike."

Paul came to take our orders and after I introduced him, I asked him to bring the graces a glass of nice burgundy. The graces were wearing black cocktail dresses, pearls and other expensive jewelry. They didn't look like high school girls and every male eye in the room, and some female, kept wandering to them. They sat with their glasses, looking so sophisticated it was easy to forget that they weren't even 17 years old.

"They treat you like royalty, Mike," Vicki remarked. "How come?"

"I did a lot of work for Wally and got to know everyone here. Besides, it doesn't hurt that I brought three beautiful girls."

It was a very pleasant dinner and the graces really enjoyed themselves. When they finished I signed the check, but left a big cash tip for Paul and Luis. I told the graces I was staying to talk to Frank and walked them to their car. They took turns kissing me goodnight, each one more sensual. Zoey was the hottest and she whispered:

"I haven't forgotten that night."

I watched them drive off, wondering how I was going to resist those beauties. Frank took me into the office and said:

"I've been talking to a friend of mine about you, Carl Weatherstone, who owns a chain of upscale furniture stores. He wants to do tv ads, but the agencies wanted too much money. If you get me your reel, I'll give it to him and if he likes it, I'll set up a meeting."

"That'll be great. Thanks, Frank."

"I feel terrible that I haven't been able to do anything for you."

"Maybe this'll work out."

Later that night I looked up what a reel was on the internet and found out it was a sample of your work. The next night I put together cuts of Wally's ads, the surfing tournament, the car dealer, the marina and the surf shop. I brought it to Frank after school and left, telling myself: 'Don't count on it. Don't count on it'.

Chapter 75

I hadn't heard from Frank about the reel by the end of the week. I kept repeating my latest mantra, 'Don't count on it. Don't count on it', yet one part of me was hoping. I went to Wally's for dinner Saturday night and Frank told me he hadn't heard anything yet.

"If I don't hear from him by Wednesday, I'll give him a call. He's tight with money, so it's better if he comes to you. He may come to dinner tomorrow night and if he does I'll question him. I'll let you know what happens."

"Thanks, Frank."

"After what you've done for Tommy, if he doesn't come through, I'll have you make a video for Wally's."

"I appreciate that, Frank. But it would be a waste of money without airing it on tv and that would be expensive. Everybody knows Wally's and the website works fine for you."

"You're a good guy, Mike. Most people would jump at the chance to make money."

"My friends are more important to me then a few bucks."

I managed to shut Weatherstone's out of my mind and was busy with school, work and my other activities. Frank phoned me Wednesday night with news.

"I spoke to Carl a little while ago. He loves your reel and wants to meet you. I can set it up for tomorrow evening at his store. Is 7:30 good for you?"

"Sure."

"If there's a problem, I'll let you know. Otherwise it's confirmed."

After work the next day, I only caught two rides with Cliff, in order to get to the meeting on time. Carl was gruff and loud, obviously to intimidate people because he was rich. I was calm and polite and let him run on for a while about how important he was. He finally looked at me strangely and said:

"You don't talk much."

"Only when I have something to say."

He stared stonily, then grinned.

"Alright. What can you do for me?"

"That depends on what you want. It's obvious your stores are upscale, so one approach is the appeal to the well-to-do, perhaps using the art gallery technique of snobbish exclusivity, without being crude."

"That's exactly how I feel about my stores. I appeal to the wealthy. How do we do it?"

"Are you prepared to spend money on tv advertising? Because there's no sense in making videos, unless you air them."

"I have three stores from here to Los Angeles. I'm planning to open two more, with one in San Francisco. I'll buy the air time."

"Are you thinking about one ad, or a campaign?"

"A campaign. Definitely. I'm going into a new market and it'll take time to reach people."

"I'm glad you understand your situation. That'll make my job easier. If this is agreeable, I suggest I make three rough cuts as samples of different ads. If you like them, we'll use them as a basis for finished ads. They'll cost $1,000 each and we'll sign a letter of agreement. If we continue, we'll discuss cost and draw up a contract."

"The agency wanted $25,000 for a 30 second rough cut."

"I'm a small production company, not an agency."

"Agreed. I'll write a check."

"I brought a camera. Can I shoot some furniture ?"

He looked at my small camera dubiously.

"That doesn't look very big."

"It's high-tech digital. The same quality you see on tv."

"Oh."

I shot several couches, a dining room set, and a few room set-ups. Then we wrote out a letter of intent, signed it and he gave me a check. I got his cell phone number, told him I'd have the three rough cuts in a week or so, then I'd phone to set up a meeting to show them. Just as I was leaving I got an idea for a rough cut.

"Can I bring a model in for a quick shoot some evening this week?"

"Certainly. Do you need us to set up anything?"

"No. It's just for a rough-cut."

I quickly wrote out a script, a girl getting ready to go to college, saying: 'Daddy bought me a new Mercedes as a going away to college present. Now I need a couch. I'll spend more time on it and have it longer than my car, so its got to be good.'

I laughed to myself on the ride to the marina, thinking of Vicki as the pampered daughter. Then I thought of another 30 second cut of the three graces furnishing their dorm rooms. One more good idea and this would be a snap.

Chapter 76

Vicki was thrilled to star in a commercial. To make sure there were no jealousies, I scripted the other 30 second spot to include all the graces. I pointed out that they might not want to be in the actual tv version, because of parental concern, unwanted attention, even stalking. I guess I said the wrong thing because that excited them to be involved even more. We went to Weatherstone's the next night and Vicki nailed her part on the first shoot. I shot a medium close up of her sitting on a luxurious couch, then slowly zoomed in and ended on a close up shot of her looking smug. The room shoot with the three graces took a little longer, but they did well together and I was satisfied with the result. I paid Vicki $200 for her individual shoot, and the three of them $100 each for the room shoot. They were delighted with acting and getting paid for it.

I drew a blank for the third rough cut and was about to do a another version with the three graces, when I remembered the art gallery reference and got an idea. I wrote, then recorded a script: 'We're not an art gallery. We don't have champagne openings. But if you want furnishings to go with your Picasso, Weatherstone's is the right place'. I laid the audio over a slow montage of elegant furniture and added some soft background music.

I phoned Carl at lunchtime and arranged to see him that evening. Once again I cut my surfing short with Cliff to get to my appointment. Carl flipped when he saw the rough cuts. At first he tried to be cool, but finally raved about how much he liked them. We signed a contract for three 30 second spots, based on the three rough cuts, for $5,000 each, for a total of $15,000, to be ready in three weeks. Carl assured me that if the ads played well, we'd do some more.

Just before we surfed in the morning, I took the three graces aside and told them I would be making three tv commercials and I would like to use them as actresses, if they signed a video release and got a parent to countersign. The next morning they each handed me a release, countersigned by their Daddys. I told them Vicki would get $500, and Zoey and Carrie $250. In the event we had to do more shooting, they'd be paid more. They were like little kids and kept asking what channel it would be on. I told them it would be a while and I'd let them know as soon as I had an air date.

I did a lot of extra schoolwork to get ahead of the curricula, so I wouldn't fall behind when I started working on the final cuts of the ads. The next few evenings I surfed a little later then usual with Cliff.

"You don't have to make up for a few early nights," he remarked.

"Surfing with you is the single best thing in my life. I love every minute of it and don't like to miss time with you."

"Don't we spend enough time together at the shop?"

"You're so easy-going that you don't always notice how fast the day goes. You've helped me become more easy-going, which changed my life."

"I'm real proud of how you've been growing up."

"Thanks, Cliff."

I delivered the three finished ads to Carl a few days before Thanksgiving. I also emailed them to him and he loved them. He wrote a check for $15,000, which I cheerfully accepted. Then he thanked me and told me he'd let me know when they aired, and keep me up to date on the results. I didn't tell him how many times I redid the voice over for the art gallery spot, until I got a slightly superior tone. It was an easy job for a nice chunk of money. I took the graces to a celebratory dinner at Wally's, gave them three checks, for which I received a lingering kiss from each of them, definitely arousing my libido. But once again I managed to resist temptation.

"Just think," Vicki declared, "if we become big stars, we'll owe it all to you."

Carrie, usually the quietest of them, suddenly said:

"Why don't you do a tv show about us?"

We stared at her in surprise and the words spilled out of her.

"We were three spoiled girls, who just shopped and hung around. Then we changed. We run, do karate, surf and now we're actresses."

"Carrie. Sometimes you're brilliant," Zoey gushed.

"What do you think, Mike?" Vicki demanded.

I didn't know what to say, so I stalled.

"You're beautiful, smart, athletic and you did well on camera, but we'd need some kind of story to make it interesting."

"We know you can write one," Zoey enthused.

"I don't know if I can, but I'll think about it."

"We have confidence in you," Carrie crooned.

Well I'd have to figure out how to get out of this one. But part of me couldn't help preening my feathers at being praised by three hotties. I saw them to their car, then went back to talk to Frank. I told him about the successful deal with Carl and he was happy for me.

"I'd like to give you a fee for arranging it."

"Are you kidding me? I should be paying you for what you're doing for Tommy."

"I'm glad to do it, Frank. He's a great kid."

"Well he's been neglecting his schoolwork lately."

"I'll tell him unless he gets top grades, I'll suspend him from the shop and karate."

"Don't tell him I told you about it."

"Don't worry. I'll question him about other things too."

"Thanks, Mike. I owe you big time. I have a few more video prospects. I'll keep you informed."

As I rode back to the marina, I couldn't help thinking how lucky I was to have so many good friends. For a moment I flashed back to childhood in the trailer, then gave thanks I escaped that prison world.

Chapter 77

Cliff and Lucy invited Ronnie and me for Thanksgiving dinner and it was a warm and pleasant evening, but seemed a little strange without Davey, who was riding the waves somewhere in the Philippines. He sent a letter to Ronnie that he read to us at the table, which gave us a laugh. It included a section for me, with instructions that Ronnie shouldn't read it. At Ronnies urging I read it aloud, including the part about the beach bunnies and groupies he was having sex with. He ended it with: 'you're better than most of the group here. You could do well on the tour, if you wanted to.' Lucy asked:

"Why don't you compete? Isn't it unusual for a young man your age not to? Is it Cliff's influence?"

"I had to fight my way out of poverty and squalor. I compete with myself to get better and better. I don't want to compete with others. Cliff's influence is great. He always encourages me to believe in myself. He and Ronnie are my role models."

"Me?" Ronnie exclaimed in surprise.

"Yeah. You're only a few years older then me, and you don't drink or use drugs, you avoid violence and you're a great teacher. After Cliff, I learn most from you."

Ronnie almost blubbered. "That's a mighty nice thing to say. Thanks, Mike."

"Thanks for being my friend."

Lucy asked another question.

"Don't you envy Davey just a little, going to all those exotic places?"

"I'd love to see those places someday. But envy him? Not at all. I hope he becomes world champion and I'll be his number one fan. He's my best friend. I wish him the best in everything."

Lucy smiled beatifically.

"You're all lucky to have each other for friends."

The three graces had been taking turns asking me about my progress in writing a show about them. I couldn't get angry at them because they were so sweet and caring, but it was becoming repetitive. I made a decision and invited them to dinner on my boat and had a large order of Chinese food delivered. When they got there, Zoey knocked on the hull and I went to the ladder and welcomed them aboard. I gave them a quick tour and they oohed and aahed, then I pledged them to secrecy and they swore never to reveal where I lived. As we ate, I told them about the problem writing a show.

"It either has to be a comedy, a drama, or a documentary. I don't have any experience writing comedy or drama, and I haven't the faintest idea how to do it. As for a documentary, the only thing I can think of is how you changed from casual beach bunnies, to smart, tough, athletic doers. The change was great for you, but just because you made good choices, doesn't make it a story."

"So you're telling us our acting careers are over," Vicki pouted.

I thought quickly. "Not necessarily. If the furniture ads do well, I'll make more of them and I can use talented actresses…" Which brought a deluge of kisses and Zoey murmuring:

"You're our favorite director."

Vicki stating: "You're our favorite producer."

And Carrie adding: "Our favorite writer."

"You girls are in for more work. I'm hoping for other video projects and in a few months I'll make videos for the surfing tournament and I'll cast you in them."

This brought another round of hugs and kisses. Suddenly Vicki was kissing me passionately and running her hands down my body. I tried to pull away, but Zoey and Carrie held me and Vicki whispered:

"Carrie and I chose to see who gets you next. I won."

Zoey held my mouth, as Carrie slowly removed Vicki's clothes. I got an erection that Vicki touched, as Zoey stripped off my shirt and unbuckled my pants. This was the most exciting sex act I ever had and my resistance crumbled. Zoey and Carrie caressed me, as Vicki rubbed against me, touching herself until she came. Then Zoey put a condom on me, Vicki lay down and Zoey guided me inside her. When we finished, Vicki got dressed and said:

"We'll have to find the right way for Carrie," and they left, three incredibly beautiful girls, who I no longer had a choice to refuse.

Chapter 78

I went a little wild with Christmas shopping, getting extravagant presents for Cliff, Lucy, Ronnie and the three graces. At the last minute I got something small for Donna, so she wouldn't feel neglected. On an impulse, I sent a card and $100 to my mother, but I didn't put my address on the envelope. Everyone gave me presents, so it was a fun time. Cliff and Lucy decided to go to San Francisco for a week, so I ran the shop with Ronnie and Donna while they were gone. It wasn't very busy, so Donna and I were able to give our own lessons, staggering the schedule, so one of us was always with Ronnie. It was fun being with Ronnie and Donna, but I always missed Cliff, especially when we surfed.

Lucy insisted that Ronnie and I spend New Years' Eve with them. Ronnie was reluctant to intrude on them, until Lucy warned:

"Don't make me use karate on you," and he laughingly gave in.

We drank champagne, counted out the old year, and I got a little tipsy. Lucy refused to let me drive my motorcycle and called a cab for me and Ronnie. I wasn't used to drinking and actually had a headache in the morning, as well as my legs were rubbery during the morning run. I cut the run short for myself and had to take Ronnie's teasing. My head finally cleared when I was on the water and I concluded I just wasn't meant to be a drinker.

I was glad when school started, despite not being at the shop all day. Although we lost two more students in Chinese, Ms. Yi continued to concentrate on conversation and I was making real progress. Mr. Corliss was pleased with my progress in Perl, Lisp and C++ and planned to start me on new languages in a few months. He also delivered a message from Charlie Orsini, who said Nicky and Holly demanded I visit again soon. Since Charlie was my route to a scholarship, I couldn't refuse, but I had to admit to myself it would be fun to see them. I phoned Charlie and promised to visit in early March. Charlie urged me to write some open source code and confer with Mr. Corliss about it. Then he said they were looking forward to seeing me.

It was fortunate that the three graces weren't in any of my classes, because they spent every moment they could with me. Jimmy Longboard teased them about mothering me, but Vicki retorted:

"You 'll see in a while what Mike did for us."

The surfers questioned, demanded, made crude or funny guesses, but the graces refused to explain. Zoey stated smugly:

"Just wait and see."

The guys started asking me, but I replied:

"Talk to them."

Curiosity died down after a few days, but the three graces were proprietorial If a girl tried to talk to me, she was shooed off.

Then, on an overcast February 10th, the bad news that I had been dreading hit me like a tsunami. Big Bill was waiting for me when I left for the beach in the morning. I could tell from his expression what was coming.

"I'm sorry, Mike. The boat was sold yesterday." I nodded sadly, with no idea what to say.

"They haven't decided whether to let me do the refitting, or move her elsewhere. They know she's in good condition and they won't be using her until summer, so you'll probably have two or three more months. You've been a great tenant and I'll miss you around here, unless you want a job."

"I'm pretty busy with school and the shop. But thanks, Bill. You've been a great landlord."

"I'll talk to some owners again and see if I can find another boat. But don't count on it."

"I won't . Thanks again, Bill, for all you've done."

"I wish I could do more."

It was hard to stay positive that day. Nobody seemed to notice I wasn't my usual cheerful self, until I got to the shop. Cliff came out to meet me and said:

"I spoke to Big Bill. He told me the boat was sold. When it's time to leave, you're moving in with me and Lucy."

"I can get a room near the beach, or move in with the surfers."

"Forget it, Mike. You can have the front upstairs bedroom that looks out on the ocean. Lucy's only here a couple of times a month and holidays, so you'll have plenty of privacy."

"Are you sure, Cliff? I don't want to impose."

"I'd love having you here."

"Thanks, Cliff. I want to pay rent."

"Don't be silly. You can help with the groceries."

"I don't know anything about shopping."

Cliff laughed. "Neither do I. We can grill a lot and get plenty of take out."

The ache at losing the boat wouldn't go away quickly, but the thought of living with Cliff made it easier to accept. I had no idea what it would be like living in his house, but I knew he wanted me there. That was reassuring. I'd obviously have to make other arrangements to entertain the three graces, or other girls, but I wasn't going to worry about that now.

Chapter 79

Now that it was certain I'd be losing the boat, I invited my friends as often as I could. I had Ronnie come to visit twice a week, which he enjoyed. He always knew I lived on the boat, but never said anything to anyone about it. The three graces came to dinner at least twice a week and they insisted on bringing take out every time. I told them I'd be moving in with Cliff, and Vicki said triumphantly:

"We knew he was your father."

"He's not," I insisted.

"We heard you call him 'Dad'," Carrie declared.

"It was just a joke," I explained.

"You look alike," Zoey stated. "You even walk the same way."

It didn't matter what I said, they were convinced that Cliff was my father. When they found out that I'd only be on the boat for two or three more months, Vicki decided that they'd visit me one at a time, starting with Carrie.

"After all," she said, "we won't to be able to do some things once you move in with your Dad."

"Please don't call him that to anyone else," I pleaded. "Especially the surfers."

"We know you have your secrets," Zoey whispered. "We won't tell anyone."

What could I do? They had become irresistible. They didn't seem to have any problem sharing me, which was weird, but I wasn't complaining.

Three weeks later the tv ad starring Vicki aired, night after night for two weeks. The news spread through school and the beach like wildfire, and Vicki was a celebrity. When she told the surfers how Mike made the ad, some of them teasingly asked for her autograph. Two weeks later the second ad, with the three graces, aired, and they were the talk of the school and beach. A lot of guys and some men started coming on to them. They were smart enough to realize that it was because of their sudden fame and they only went to social events at the country club, or toney parties. I was impressed that they didn't let all the attention go to their heads. They were exactly the same with me, whether at school, the beach, or the boat.

Carl phoned me and raved about the response to the ads. The third one had just started airing and business was picking up noticeably. He was also getting calls from high priced decorators, eager to shop for their clients.

"We're going to rotate these ads for another two or three months, but I want some new ones for the summer and fall. Why don't you come to dinner at the country club Saturday

evening and we'll talk business."

"Sounds good. Casual or formal?"

"Jacket and slacks is fine. 7:30?"

"See you then."

I borrowed some clothes from Cliff, that fit surprisingly well and asked the graces not to be at the club Saturday night. Of course they demanded to know why. When I explained I wanted to keep them a bit mysterious for our sponsor, they were satisfied.

"Does that mean we'll be in the new ads," Vicki asked.

"If I can make a deal, you'll be in them."

"We'll bring dinner tonight," Zoey said "and we can discuss our roles."

"You're welcome. But we won't talk about the ads until I've got a deal. Agreed?"

"Oh, yes," Vicki whispered. "Whatever our favorite director says."

The maitre'd escorted me to Carl's table and he expected me to be impressed with the place, and he asked:

"What do you think of the club?"

"It's very nice."

"It's the most exclusive club from here to Los Angeles."

I just nodded casually. It may have been exclusive, but it wasn't anything that appealed to me. The food wasn't much better than Wally's, but the waiters were far more attentive and respectful, which was alright if you like that. Carl kept offering me cocktails, wine, or brandy, and was reluctant to believe I didn't drink.

"Is it because of your age? That doesn't matter here. You can have whatever you want."

"Thanks, Carl. I'm a surfer and I train everyday, so I don't drink."

"What do you think of the food? I know you eat at Wally's. How does it compare?"

"It's very good. I'm basically a steak and lobster guy, so this is a nice change."

He gave up trying to dazzle me and said:

"Well let's talk about the ads. They went over real big. I'm happy with them. The media analysts tell me the two ads with the girls are great teasers, but shouldn't be used again. They say the art gallery ad can be used over and over, between new ads. They recommended an agency, but I want you to do it. How about two ads for the summer and two for the fall?"

"Sure. They'll take a lot more work and be much more expensive."

"How much are we talking About?"

I thought for a minute.

"This is off the top of my head, but $7,500 each for the summer, $15,000 each for the fall."

He smiled. "The agency wanted $30,000 each for the summer. $50,000 each for the fall."

I shrugged. "I'm not an agency. Do you want me to make rough cuts first?"

"How about one. Just to be sure."

"It'll be $2,500."

"That's okay. I'll have my lawyer draw up a contract and send it to you. The summer ads to be ready by May 15th. The fall by August 1st."

"That's fine. I'll have the rough cut in two or three weeks. Have the lawyer send a check for $2,500 with the contract."

"Agreed. Some dessert?"

"No thanks. Carl. I'll be going."

He escorted me out and when we got to the manager's desk, he stopped.

"Antoine. This is Mr. Sanchez. Add him to my guest member's list. If he dines here, put it on my account."

"Certainly, Mr. Weatherstone. I'll make out a guest membership card for him."

We waited for a minutc and he handed me an embossed plastic card.

“Just show that at the desk and you’ll have full dining room privileges.”

“Thanks, Antoine.”

“My pleasure, Mr. Weatherstone.”

“Thanks, Carl, “I said.

“Make me some more winners and I’ll give you a membership.”

“The dining room’s enough.”

He walked me to my motorcycle and watched while I put on my leather jacket and helmet.

“I never rode one of those. Is it dangerous?”

“Not if you drive carefully.”

“Make sure you do. I’m counting on you for those ads.”

“Goodnight, Carl.”

Chapter 80

I was busy for the next few weeks. The weather got warmer and business picked up at the shop, with more and more lessons that I divided with Ronnie and Donna. At school, Mr. Corliss, urged on by Charlie Orsini, kept pushing me to write more open-source code. I wrote scripts for two 30 second rough cut ads for Carl, let them sit for a few days, then rehearsed one of them with the graces. It was set in the furniture store, where Vicki cellphoned her Dad. 'You were right, Dad. All the furniture we need for our dorm suite is here at Weatherstone's. Thanks for the charge card. They'll take care of everything else. The girls want to thank you'. Zoey and Carrie said: 'Thank you,' Mister G.' The last cut faded on the girls looking at easy chairs, with Zoey saying: 'nice chair'.

The other ad was reminiscent of the art gallery type. A voice over a slow montage of fine art; Picasso, Warhol, Vlaminck, Utrillo, decorative abstracts and still lifes: 'Your taste shows on your walls. Your furniture reflects that taste. Weatherstone understands taste'. After looking at the ads carefully I decided they were up to the quality of the first ads. I paid Vicki $200, and Zoey and Carrie $150 each, which pleased them almost as much as performing.

I met Carl, showed him the rough cuts and he loved them. Then he wrote a check for $15,000 for the final versions. I didn't tell him that I'd already planned the edit of the finished ads, and also came up with an elegant script for Weatherstone that could serve as a logo. I didn't need to shoot any new footage with my actresses, but I invited them to dinner on the boat and paid them $500 each for their work, which delighted them. I also reminded them we'd be making another ad together, and a video for the surfing tournament, so they were temporarily career happy.

Charlie sneakily got Nicky and Holly to phone me and invite me for a weekend. I figured to go soon, rather then wait until I got busier and I discussed it with Cliff. He understood that this was an investment in my San Diego U. scholarship, and told me to leave Friday afternoon. I left at 4:00 p.m. so I'd get there in time to do karate with the kids, then surf. I enjoyed the ride and was a little surprised at the enthusiastic greeting I got from the whole family. Nicky and Holly had joined a dojo and already tested for their yellow belts. They wanted to wear their Gi's on the beach, but I suggested that they might not like some of the attention it would attract, and they were sensible enough to listen.

After karate, which they did well, we surfed and their progress was obvious. They cavorted confidently and didn't get upset when they fell. I complimented them, and on an impulse mentioned they might want to enter the novice section of the Imperial Beach Surfing Tournament. They were eager and it was now up to Charlie and Sandy to deal with that. They wanted to know what their chances were and Holly asked:

"Can you help us win?"

"Of course not. You have to compete fair and square, like everyone else, or don't do it."

"Are you competing?" Nicky asked.

"No. I'm running the tournament."

"Why don't you compete?" he asked, and they all looked at me curiously.

"I only compete with myself to do better at whatever I commit to."

I don't think they understood, but they nodded and dropped the subject. After dinner, we sat on the porch watching the last of another spectacular California sunset and Sandy asked what I'd been doing lately. I jokingly growled:

"Writing open-source code at someone's instigation," and mock-glared at Charlie, which gave them a laugh. "We've been getting busy at the shop and I've been giving more lessons. I made some tv ads for a client."

"Real television ads?" Holly said.

"Yes. For a furniture chain."

"You made those Weatherstone ads?" Charlie gasped.

"Yes."

"The ones with those hot girls?" Nicky yelled.

"Yes."

"Wow," Nicky gushed. "You know actresses?"

"Yes. They're good friends of mine. We actually run and surf together. They'll be in my next commercial, airing in June."

"Wow," Nicky repeated.

"If you come to the surfing tournament, I'll introduce you to them."

"We're going, right, Dad?" Nicky demanded.

"I guess so," Charlie said.

"Yay," Nicky and Holly echoed.

The rest of the weekend was really pleasant. We ran, surfed, did karate, and had a relaxed, fun time. They urged me to come back soon when I left Sunday afternoon, but I said:

"If I can. If not, I'll see you at the tournament and you can do karate, run and surf with my friends."

After hugs and kisses, I waved as I rode off, feeling good about seeing them. But part of me was aware that this wasn't a casual get-together. I needed Charlie for my scholarship and I made myself very likeable to him and his family. I wondered for a minute if I was using or exploiting them. Then I decided I hadn't been pretending to like them and they sure liked me, so there was nothing wrong with my being with them. I enjoyed the ride back to Imperial Beach and got there in time for karate and surfing with Cliff.

Chapter 81

Saturday night, before I left the boat forever, I had a blow out party and not only invited my close friends, but all my surfer buddies. Ronnie and Grizzly kept an eye on everyone to insure they didn't do drugs, or serious damage to the boat. The graces appointed themselves hostesses, which was fine with me. They dispensed food and drink as if they owned the vessel. Lucy, not overly fond of surfers, made a friend of Grizzly'a wife, Megan, a tiny, but formidable woman, also not fond of surfers. She ran a small art gallery that had regular group shows of local artists, but made her living working with decorators.

A sudden commotion on deck caught my attention and I went topside to see what was happening. Donna was in full tilt punching Jimmy longboard, who looked as abashed as a surfer could look, while she was holding Tommy with her other hand.

"What's wrong with you, Jimmy?" she demanded. "He's a ten year old kid and you let him have a beer."

"I'll be eleven soon, Donna," Tommy pleaded. "I just wanted to taste it."

"I understand that. I'm not mad at you. It's that big wooden head for letting you."

"Sorry, Donna," Jimmy muttered.

"You better be!" she snarled "And as for you, young man, I catch you boozing again and you're banned from the beach."

"I won't, Donna. I promise."

"Alright. Now go home."

"Yes, Donna."

Lucy and Megan were watching, amused, and Lucy said:

"I'll drive him home. I've had enough of those water on the brain types."

"I'll come with you," Megan said. "I've had enough of them too."

Just then, Grizzly swooped down on Megan, picked her up with one arm and carried her to the ladder.

"You haven't had enough of me yet, have you , babe?"

"If you don't put me down, I'll beat you black and blue, you big beast."

"Yes, babe," and he gently set her on her feet.

"You're a good beast," and she kissed him lovingly, which drew a round of applause from the nearby surfers.

The party broke up about 1:00 a.m. and Cliff, Ronnie, Donna and the three graces helped clean up. There was a lot of paper, empty bottles and food spills, but no damage to the boat that couldn't quickly be fixed. I was determined to leave the boat in pristine condition, so Big Bill would have no complaints.

It didn't take long for me to pack in the morning. Everything fit into the back seat, or the trunk of Zoey's car, since she offered to help. The exception was for my camera, computer and IPad, which I packed carefully in a padded box. I was a little surprised about how little I owned, but not disappointed. It was sort of reassuring that I didn't need much.

Cliff and Lucy helped us lug my stuff upstairs to my new room. I noticed Zoey was very cold to Lucy and when Cliff and Lucy went downstairs, I asked:

"What's with your attitude to Lucy?"

"She's so beautiful and you're going to be living under the same roof. You won't want us anymore."

I had to laugh. But her worried look quickly made me serious.

"Don't be silly. You, Vicki and Carrie are the most beautiful girls I know. Even if I wanted Lucy and she wanted me, she's Cliff's girlfriend. I'd die before I'd betray him. Besides, she's just a friend."

She put her arms around me and snuggled close.

"You're so sweet at times. That's one of the many reasons we adore you so much…" Then in a huskier voice. "Can we make love in your new home?"

Part of me was already responding to her hot body, but another part was embarrassed, because I wasn't completely comfortable with Cliff and Lucy downstairs. I reluctantly pushed her away.

"I can't with Cliff and Lucy here."

"How will we be together? We can't bring you to our houses and a motel is too sleazy."

"Maybe we could go to a nice hotel, or a beach resort. That wouldn't be sleazy."

"So you still want us," and she kissed me and ran her hand down the front of my pants, which immediately bulged appropriately. I led her to the door.

"Goodbye, temptress," and she left with a smug chuckle.

I closed the door and sat down by the window and looked at the ocean. The hypnotic flow of the waves slowly soothed me, but part of me was trying to come to terms with my new situation. It was weird being embarrassed. I hadn't felt anything like that since I was a kid, living in the trailer. It was obvious I'd have to make a lot of adjustments living here, but I already felt a sense of security knowing that Cliff really wanted me here. I decided to think about my obligations living here, then talk to Cliff about it. I laughed that I wouldn't have to change my address, since I had been using Cliff's for the last few years. I started putting my new home in order and resolved to make the most of my new circumstances.

Chapter 82

Cliff and Lucy went off somewhere, so I didn't get a chance to talk to him until late that night. Karate and surfing had eased some of my tension. Lucy had gone back to San Francisco for her Monday morning classes, but left strict instructions for dinner. She was in the midst of a vigorous campaign to get Cliff to eat more healthily. Since she knew we'd either grill or get take out she put fish, chicken and salad on the menu. I was now included. I helped Cliff grill mahi and potatoes. After we ate we sat on the porch listening to the ocean. It took me a while to bring up my new status as houseguest and I felt awkward talking about it.

"Cliff."

"Yeah?"

"I need to talk to you about something."

"What?"

"My living here. What are the rules? What can I do and not do?"

I felt him staring at me and wondered if I said something stupid.

"You're not a lodger. You're family…" A warm feeling of belonging rushed through me... "I guess we'll have to figure things our as we go. But you don't drink, or use drugs, or have wild parties, so we shouldn't have any problems. We'll learn how to do the chores together."

"Thanks, Cliff. You're making this easy. What about girls? Can I bring them here?"

"Sure. Just be cool about it when Lucy's here. Anybody I know?"

"The three graces. We're real good friends and they're working in my commercials."

"I know. I've been seeing them. They're pretty good... The graces have changed a lot in the last year or so. Are you serious about one of them?"

"I'm trying to keep things under control, but I run, surf, go to school and work with them, so I'm with these incredibly gorgeous girls all the time. Carrie told me they're starting karate this week..."

"You're really suffering," and he laughed.

"They think you're my father. You won't think it's funny when they spread the word that I'm living here."

He laughed even harder. "Just don't call me Dad all the time... I'm going to bed."

"Goodnight, Dad."

He ruffled my hair as he went by.

In the morning, as I stretched for the run, Cliff came out and stretched.

"I may as well run and surf with you before I open the shop."

No one was surprised when we showed up together, but the graces kept giving each other knowing looks. Cliff ran pretty well for an old guy, but I sensed him slowing after a mile and a half and I slowed.

"Keep going," he said. "I'll go further in a week or two. See you back at the boards."

It was a real treat to surf with him in the morning and for the first time I didn't miss Davey. Tommy's grades had been improving, so he was allowed to run and surf with us before school, and was in awe of Cliff. He kept gaping at him and running into others, until Donna smacked him on the head.

"Pay attention, squirt, or get out of the water."

I couldn't help smiling at her and she grinned back. I really liked and respected her. She was bright, sharp, athletic, and good-looking in a wholesome way. We weren't the least bit interested in each other, except as friends, and she was the first girl buddy I ever had. Though I guess in a strange way the graces were buddies. Well more than just pals. I didn't usually think about lots of things while surfing, but maybe Cliff changed the equation this morning by being with us. I looked at the group who were my closest friends and told myself how lucky I was to have them.

Chapter 83

The school term just zipped by and Mr. Corliss gave me an advanced source code project for the summer. Ms Yi told us she accepted a college teaching position in Los Angeles for the fall, and the language department wouldn't continue Chinese. Her final advice was:

"China grows stronger and richer, while America gets weaker and poorer. If there's any way you can continue your Chinese studies, it could be very valuable someday."

Well time again for the internet. I'd have to set some kind of schedule, otherwise I'd quickly lose the progress I had made in Chinese. I ended the year with a 3.8 G.P.A. I missed 4.0 because of a dispute with my history teacher, Mr. Torrington. He told us that the Mexican immigrant invasion of the Southwest was stealing the land from America. I offered an opinion:

"Is it any different when the American immigrants stole Texas from Mexico?"

He went ballistic and raved about the daring and initiative of the American settlers, who wanted land. Then he said there was no comparison to violations of an international border by uneducated illegals. I guess if I shut up it would have blown over, but I added:

"They just want jobs, Mr. Torrington."

"Is that what you think, Mr. Sanchez?" and he stretched out the pronunciation of my name in an insulting way.

"Yes, sir."

"It's obvious where your sympathies lie."

I wisely didn't answer, but I had provoked him unnecessarily and he gave me an A-, despite my doing A level work all year. I discussed it with Mr. Corliss and he assured me San Diego U. would be more interested in my computer work, which was excellent. Maybe I learned a lesson that you can't talk reasonably to someone who wouldn't be reasonable.

Carl was so happy with the new ads that he started airing them earlier then planned, so we were still in school when they first aired. Everybody showered attention on the graces and the surfers had to stop some unwelcome advances. Older guys tried to pick them up at the beach, when the surfers again shielded them. Some college guys came on to them and were ready to challenge some of the surfers, until Ronnie and Grizzly intervened. The graces got a little carried away with the attention and dated some of the older, well to do young men, who approached them at the country club.

I was torn between jealousy and relief, because they were too much for me to handle. Now I could distance myself a little, since they dated others first. Within a few weeks they tired of the men who just wanted to capture a trophy for a while. They apparently had been shocked by the pressure for sex, supplemented by offers of drink and drugs. They had skipped their beach workouts for a few days and I was getting concerned, when they showed up one morning, a little bleary-eyed, but glad to be back. Ronnie talked to them for a while and they nodded at everything he said, like little kids. When we were surfing later, I asked him:

"What did you tell the graces?"

"To keep their heads screwed on tight and not do stupid things, just because they were on tv."

Only Ronnie could talk to them that way.

"Anything else?"

He steered his board close to me.

“The surfers always kept the jocks and the slicks away from them…” the slicks were the young guys whose family’s had money and bought their kids expensive cars and gave them charge cards, which dazzled a lot of young girls… “We protect them from aggressive guys, but we can’t protect them from themselves. They thanked me.”

I was a little aloof with the graces for a while, which bothered them, but we didn’t talk about it. School ended and I went back to full-time at the shop, which I enjoyed. I decided to make the next two ads for Carl right away and I wrote a script for the graces, set in a bedroom at Weatherstone’s. The three were lolling around, while Zoey talked to her father. ‘The furniture is fine, Daddy. We have everything we need. Tell the truth’, she said confidingly, ‘neighbors envy us. But that’s their problem. We’re comfortable. Thanks, Daddy.’ ‘Thanks, Mr. H.,” the other two echoed.

I wanted something different for the second ad and wrote several scripts that I didn’t like. Then I got a brainstorm. I went to see Megan at her gallery and asked if she and Grizzly would be in an ad. I outlined an idea that she was trying to give her husband culture, which she thought was hilarious. I offered $500 each for the rough cut, $1,000 if it went to final, and she accepted for both of them. I wrote a script, gave it to them, set a shooting date and told her to wear her best business suit. The highlight of the ad was Grizzly lying on a couch and saying:

“Wow. This is really comfortable.”

And Megan replied smugly.

“You get what you pay for,” and the Weatherstone logo came on.

Carl loved the ads, wrote a check for $10,000 and urged me to finish them soon. I paid my actors and actresses $500 each, though Megan took Grizzly’s check. Then I took themto dinner at Wally’s.

Frank welcomed us, led us to a table and the graces got a round of applause from their fellow diners.

"Soon they'll be applauding you, Grizzly," I teased.

"Don't say that," Megan snapped. "If his head gets any larger it won't fit in the house."

"Don't worry, babe," Grizzly replied. "I'm cool. Let's eat."

I delivered the two completed ads a few weeks later and Carl wrote a check for $30,000. This was a lot of money for me and I had some wild fantasies about buying things and traveling. I sensibly wrote checks for my actors and actresses, for $1,000 each, which really thrilled them. Even the girls were impressed and they came from rich familys. Again Megan took Grizzly's check, which amused me.

I made the ads for the surfing tournament using the graces as individual spokespersons for each major sponsor, the Marina, the shop and Wally's. Frank, using Wally's influence, got the local station to run the ads as PSA's, and they aired them over and over. I made the ads for $2,500 each, paid the graces $250 each, and they loved the exposure more than the money. By this time almost everyone in town knew them.

Chapter 84

It felt great being in the shop and on the beach so often. It wasn't that I disliked school, but except for Computer Science and Chinese, it was boring. Now Chinese was finished. I had serious source code to write over the summer and had to set a schedule to practice Chinese. But the pace was different, just as responsible, but more relaxed. Charlie Orsini phoned me and said they were coming to the surfing tournament on both weekends. He asked me to reserve two motel rooms for both Fridays and Saturdays, which I did. We had a nice conversation, he bragging about Nicky and Holly, and me telling him I was looking forward to seeing them.

Cliff really surprised me on my birthday. This year, July 14, came on a Sunday and he hadn't said anything, so I didn't expect much. He kept me out late Saturday night, bringing us back to the shop after surfing to do an inventory. It seemed a little odd, but I worked cheerfully and we stopped around 11:00 p.m. The house was dark when we got there and I asked Cliff where Lucy was and he said she probably went to bed. When we got in and put on the lights, my friends yelled: 'Happy birthday, Mike.' Lucy, Ronnie, Donna, the graces, Grizzly and Megan, Frank and Tommy, some of the surfers, the karate class and select beach bunnies, all hugged or kissed me. Some of them gave me presents, mostly t-shirts, but the graces bought me a Rolex watch that they said was registered. When I protested I was too young to vote, they smacked me playfully.

Lucy served half a dozen bottles of wine that were quickly consumed, then she started saying good nights. Frank and Tommy left first, followed by Grizzly and Megan. Others left until only Ronnie and the graces were still there. Ronnie made a sentimental speech about what a true friend I was, always looking out for my friends. He almost seemed ready to blubber, so Lucy had the graces take him home. Just before they left I took Zoey aside.

"That's a very expensive watch, isn't it?"

She grinned. "Nothings too good for our director."

The summer seemed to go by quickly. Fortunately the surfing tournament was a great success, with minimal effort and no problems. I spent as much time as I could with the Orsinis. Lucy made dinner for the Orsinis at the house on Friday night, after karate and surfing. Saturday morning we ran, and Charlie and Nicky drooled over the graces. There wasn't time to surf, since we had to organize the first day of the tournament. I appointed Tommy as Nicky and Holly's official host and they hit it off.

Charlie was awed by Cliff. Nicky and Holly felt the same way. I took them to dinner at Wally's Saturday night and they were dazzled by the fine restaurant and even more impressed when dinner was my treat. Nicky and Holly were delighted when they got to the semi-finals the second Saturday, before being eliminated. Tommy got to the finals on Sunday, which filled Frank with pride. He thanked me again and again for what I did for Tommy and vowed to get more video jobs for me. The Orsini's left happily, after thanking me for what I did for Nicky and Holly, and made me promise to visit them in the fall.

"We'll see you all the time," Nicky said, "when you go to San Diego U."

"I'm looking forward to it."

Then, in early August, when everything seemed to be going smoothly, Ronnie told me his father was sick and he had to go back East to take care of him. This was a real blow to my little world, because after Cliff, Ronnie was the other pillar in my life.

"When are you going?"

"Tomorrow morning."

"So soon?"

"He needs me. I talked to the karate class and they want you for their teacher. They'll all pay you $10 per week. You're about black belt level and you're a good teacher, but you'll have to find a way to improve."

"It won't be the same without you."

"You're a capable guy, Mike. You'll manage… I won't do the run in the morning, so this is goodbye."

He hugged me fiercely. "We'll always be friends," and he walked away.

Chapter 85

It was very strange not to have Ronnie with us for the morning run and surfing. It was even stranger when he wasn't at the shop. I suddenly got the idea that Cliff knew about Ronnie's departure, which was why he started running and surfing in the morning.

"When did you find out Ronnie was leaving?" I asked later that day.

"Yesterday. Why?"

"Just wondering if you knew earlier and that's why you started running with us."

"I did it because we're living together and it seemed like fun."

"I'm glad… What are we going to do without Ronnie when school starts?"

"Either I'll manage until you get here, or we'll hire someone."

"How about Grizzly?" I suggested.

"Do you think he'd be interested?"

"I'll ask him."

So Davey was gone. Now Ronnie was gone. The three graces were still running and surfing with us in the morning, but they dropped out of karate and evening surfing and were dating rich college guys and we weren't as close anymore. All I had left was Cliff. I had no idea what I'd do if I lost him.

I didn't have to go very far to find Grizzly. He showed up for karate class, joining two beginners. Despite his size, his big body seemed to dance as he moved. I spoke to him afterwards and he told me that

Ronnie asked everyone if they wanted me for their teacher and they all said 'yes'. He offered to collect the fee money for me each Saturday, which I accepted gratefully. I knew that Ronnie arranged for someone to look out for me and Grizzly was a good choice. I also couldn't help wondering if that's why Cliff was there. It felt weird teaching him, but I didn't say anything and gradually got used to it.

"Would you be interested in working at the surf shop?" I asked Grizzly.

"What would I be doing?"

"At first, helping Cliff with packing and shipping. Once you got familiar with the stock, sales and helping customers. If you want to, you can give surfing lessons. The job pays $10 an hour to start and once you're there three months, you'd get inexpensive health insurance. Surfing lessons are $30 per hour, half to the teacher, half to the shop."

"Sounds great. When do I start?'"

"Don't you have to get Megan's permission?" I teased.

He casually picked up my board with one hand. Then he reached over, picked me up, carried me into the water under his arm, and dropped me. That gave everyone a laugh, including me. When he surfed with us, I found that I didn't miss Ronnie as much. Grizzly started work the next morning and was a positive presence immediately. I had him get familiar with all the boards first, because I knew he could help customers with that right away. I had learned how bright he was when I was working with him on the furniture commercial, so it was no surprise that he caught on quickly and fit right in.

By the time school started, Grizzly had made a place for himself at the shop and the beach, so I knew that Cliff could manage until I got there. Ms. Yi was gone and I still had a language requirement, so I took French. The only other choice was German. I didn't know much about Germany, except we fought some big wars with them a long time ago, and the language sounded funny. So French it was. But Computer Science was rad. Mr. Corliss loved the advanced code I wrote over the summer and sent it to Charlie, who also loved it.

"You made a big hit with Charlie and his family." Mr. Corliss told me. "He'll be sending a letter of intent and a pre-enrollment package in November. They really want you."

"That's great."

Then it dawned on me that I'd only be seeing Cliff for holidays and summers for four years. A painful feeling shot through me.

"Anything wrong, Mike? Are you alright?"

"Sure, Mr. C. I'm just getting used to the idea."

"I'm glad for you. All you have to do is maintain your average, stay out of trouble and you're in."

"Thanks, Mr. C. For all your help."

"Glad to, Mike. You're my best student."

Well college was a year away, so there was no point missing Cliff yet. Besides. It wasn't far away. I could come home for the weekends… Come home… That was a new one. I guess I was getting over the boat. It was still sitting in Big Bill's yard and no work had been done. Apparently there was some kind of dispute between buyer and sellers. But I didn't think about the boat anymore. At least not often. Cliff's house… Our house,.. Had become home. I just had to remember never to walk around naked like I did on the boat sometimes, when Lucy was home.

Now that Jimmy Longboard had graduated, and I was a senior, I was the unofficial leader of the surfers. Two or three of the bigger guys always seemed to be around. There were so many freshmen surfers who were taking lessons from me and Donna that we took over a third table in the cafeteria. Donna appointed herself in charge of behavior, which was fine with me. She was bright, cheerful, firm in her code of right and wrong and always fun to be with. It was a treat to watch her ruling the unruly surfers. As long as nothing went wrong, this would be a very good school year.

Chapter 86

I found myself attracted to a girl in my French class. She was tall, slim, athletic-looking, with long dark hair, huge brown/black eyes, a large nose and full red lips that whispered 'taste me'. She was very aloof when I talked to her and I gave up trying. A few days later she came up to me and apologized.

"I'm sorry I was rude to you. Someone told me you were very bad and I shouldn't have anything to do with you."

"Did I do anything to give you that impression?"

"No."

"Did I ask you for anything?"

"No."

"So you believed someone without bothering to find out for yourself."

"Yes."

"That's not too bright," and I walked away.

She followed me and said:

"I'm trying to apologize. I know I did something dumb. If it means anything to you, I'm new here and don't know anyone. When this guy warned me about you, I thought he was being helpful… I'll tell you who he was…"

"Don't. I don't want to know."

"Don't you care that he was insulting you?"

"The people who know me wouldn't believe him and if strangers do, that's their problem."

"Well I just want you to know I'm sorry."

I took a close look at her and those lips were definitely saying 'forgive me'.

"What's your name?"

"Anna Louise Durant."

"I'm Mike Sanchez."

"I know. Some guy in my history class told me. He also said you're a great guy."

"Once again you believe what you're told?"

"You're not a great guy?"

"You should decide that for yourself."

"How do I do that?"

"We can get to know each other. To start you can join us at the surfers table and I'll introduce you."

"Does that mean I have to learn to surf?"

"Only if you want to. You look fit. Did you ever try it?"

"No. I'm an epée fencer. I practice six days a week."

"What's an epée?"

"It's a fencing sword. There are three kinds; foil, epée, saber. Most women fence foil, which has all kinds of rules. I fence epée, which is like a real dueling sword, with only one rule, hit your opponent before he hits you."

"Sounds like fun."

"It is, if you have the killer instinct. I do. Most of the guys hate me because I'm better than they are."

"It's too bad they don't respect your abilities."

"Guys don't like losing."

I shrugged. She was right. Most guys didn't. I took her to the surfer's tables, introduced her and the graces immediately spirited her away. I assumed they'd chase her off, because she seemed interested in me, but she rejoined me, eager to get to know me. Vicki winked at me, pointed to Anna Louise and nodded approvingly. Well there had to be something special about her to get the okay from the graces. Her schedule was very different then mine, so I invited her to run with us in the morning.

"I run a mile every morning," she said smugly. "How far do you run?"

"Four or five miles, depending."

"Oh."

"Everybody in the group runs a different distance, so you're welcome to join us."

"Where do you run?"

"At the beach. 7:00 a.m. Near the surf shop. We run barefoot in bathing suits, but wear what you like."

"I'll see you in the morning."

Cliff and I got home that evening and a letter from the IRS was waiting for me. I opened it and got a shock. They demanded immediate payment of 33% of my earnings for delinquent taxes, plus a 10% daily penalty until the money was paid.

In the morning, Cliff had his accountant, Ms. Lewison, check the figures and I owed $26, 187.41, plus the daily interest. She advised me to pay, rather then hire a lawyer for an outrageous fee, to fight a case that would be lost. So I wrote a check and sent it off, worried that I lost so much money so fast."

Chapter 87

I was at the bank a few days later and the officer who handled my account, Don… Something, remarked:

"The IRS took a big chunk of your money."

"That was a shocker."

"I'm sure you'll make it back. You've been steadily adding to your account for a while."

I thought about my prospects; no more web designs, no video projects and I shook my head.

"I don't have any prospects at the moment."

"If you're willing to risk your money, there's a mutual fund that's been paying 12 to 15% for the last year. They require a minimum investment of $50,000."

"That's about all I've got."

"Well maybe it's not for you."

"How does it work?"

"If you get in now, you'll be eligible for this years earnings, which they pay out in December."

"Let me think about it."

"Of course. But decide quickly if you want in."

I discussed it with Cliff and he thought it might be risky, but he understood my trying to get back some of the money I lost to the IRS. The next day I went to the bank and signed the papers putting $50,000 into the Tel-Dec Fund. Don told me they had inside information who was buying cable channels that would get them in on the ground floor for record profits. Once Dan handed me the papers and I realized the money was gone from my checking account, I got the feeling of dread that I just made a terrible mistake. Dan noticed something, because he said:

"Don't worry. This is a great investment. I've got some of my money in it."

I tried not to think about the money. Within a few days I was able to ignore my fear of loss, while I went through my daily routine. Anna Louise had been running with us each morning. The first day, when she couldn't keep pace with me and Donna, she pushed herself hard to go farther. I didn't offer her surfing lessons and she left afterwards without a word when we hit the water. She sat with us at the surfer's tables and became friendly with the graces, but was distant with me. It turned out her family was rich and they lived in Jamil, not too far from the graces. They accepted her as one of their own and she started dating rich college guys with them. Oh, well. Maybe the next girl wouldn't be rich.

I spent a lot more time with Cliff now that I was living with him. We didn't always talk a lot, but we were comfortable together. I began to feel very secure living there. When Lucy was home, she cooked healthy meals, lots of pasta, vegetables and salads. She was very into organic food and spent a lot of time and money shopping and preparing chicken and fish dinners that were pretty good. I didn't say it, but the organic chicken didn't taste any better then the rotisserie chicken Cliff and I got during the week. She tried so hard to get us to eat healthily that all I could do was praise her efforts.

In early November I got an official letter of intent from San Diego U., offering me a full, four-year scholarship. I showed it to Cliff, who urged me to sign and return it. Before I did, I showed it to Mr. Corliss and thanked him for making it possible. He confessed that he told Charlie

Orsini that several other schools were interested in recruiting me, so he had to act fast.

"I really wanted you to go to a great school."

Then I signed the letter and put it in the mail. It was a strange feeling for someone who generally only looked a short distance ahead, to commit to four years. But I was excited about the prospects of going to college without worrying about money.

Chapter 88

Cliff invited Grizzly and Megan for Thanksgiving dinner and the table didn't seem so empty without Ronnie and Davey. I recently got a letter from Davey that I read part of after dinner. 'Hey dude, we're still in the Philippines. Great place. Great girls. They just love surfers and I have to beat them off with my board. Ha. Ha. I won a few events. Lost some too. Some of these guys are good. Not as good as you and me. You ought to join the tour. We'll be here for a while. All the girls speak Spanish. I guess they learn in school. The place is made for you. Your friend. Davey.'

Lucy smiled. "He hasn't changed."

"Yes he has," I defended. "He didn't talk about sex," which gave us a laugh.

Then, in early December, Don phoned from the bank and instead of good news about the big payoff, he informed me the mutual fund declared bankruptcy and my investment was lost.

"Sorry, Mike. No one saw this coming. I lost my money too."

I didn't bother asking how much he lost, because I didn't care. Cliff was very supportive, and pointed out it wasn't a setback, just the loss of some money.

"You have your salary from the shop, fees from surfing lessons and the karate class fees. You still have money coming in, and you'll make a lot more on your next video project."

It took a few days for me to accept that he was right. Then my usual good spirits asserted themselves. Except for occasional twinges about how much I lost, I didn't think about the money anymore. Well not often. Cliff and Lucy went away for Christmas vacation and I ran the shop with Donna and Grizzly. We were surprisingly busy for the holiday season, with a lot of people buying surfer and swim gifts, especially through our website, requiring packing and shipping.

The karate class had grown, despite the loss of the three graces, who no longer attended. Now there were 12 paying participants. Parents kept asking me to give a class for children on Saturday. I finally agreed to do it, if they got 10 children, at $15 each for the hour. Enough parents obviously wanted it, because they told me we could start the second week in January. Cliff and Lucy didn't come back for New Year's Eve and I spent it alone. I idly thought about going to the country club, or Wally's, but realized I didn't feel like being cheerful. I could have hung out with the surfers, but decided I'd rather be alone. I didn't even bother watching the countdown of the old year and went to bed early.

Cliff came back a few days later without Lucy, who had gone on to San Francisco. He thanked me, Donna and Grizzly for our efforts while he was gone and gave each of us a Christmas bonus. I got $500, for which I thanked him. When we surfed that evening, I realized how much I had missed him. I didn't seem to be making new friends, just losing old ones, so Cliff had become the anchor that kept me focused and positive. He always reinforced my belief in myself. Maybe I lost money and friends, but I was healthy, smart, capable and good things were ahead. So I wouldn't feel sorry for myself, no matter what.

Now that Cliff was back I visited the Orsini's, at Mr. Corliss' suggestion, to thank Charlie in person for arranging the scholarship. I left Friday afternoon and got to their house in time to do karate with Nicky and Holly. They had made real progress and were getting ready to test for their green belts. They seemed a little arrogant towards some of the kids on the beach who joined us, so I sat down with them when we finished.

"You're both doing real well. Your progress is proof of your talent. I think you're ready for other levels of training, but it's up to you."

"Tell us what you mean," Nicky demanded.

"You don't want to show off your skills. You should develop a modest attitude and be more respectful to the people you're training with. You want to develop self-control and self-confidence, not cockiness. Be supportive of the kids who want to train with you. And never forget there's always someone better."

"Don't you want to be the best at what you do?" Holly asked.

"I want to be the best that I can be. I don't care if someone's better than me, as long as I do my best… I'll tell you a story that I never told anyone…" They drew closer. "When Cliff was first teaching me to surf. I asked him how good I could be. He told me: 'you could be in the top 100, maybe the top 50, but I don't know if you could be number 1'. He thought I'd be disappointed, but I was thrilled. This great surfer thought I could be in the top 50. What a rush."

"So why aren't you trying to be in the top 50?" Nicky asked.

"I don't have the need to compete with others, just myself, to always try my best at what I do. Cliff taught me not to flaunt my accomplishments and not envy others."

"He sounds cool," Nicky said.

"He is. He's the best."

"What about our Dad?" Holly asked. "He's special."

"Sure he is. But Cliff's like my Dad."

Mollified, Holly said:

"So you're telling us not to be show-offs, because we're getting good?"

"That's right. Believe in yourselves, so you don't compare yourselves to anyone else, or worry about what they think of you."

“Do you do that?” Nicky asked.

“I work at it every day.”

Charlie had been waiting to surf and finally joined us.

“I was just telling the kids how impressed I was with their progress,” I said.

“Wait’ll you see them surf,” Charlie proclaimed.

And he was right. They had taken to the waves like seals and we had fun. It was a very pleasant weekend that deepened the bond between me and the Orsinis. When I left Sunday morning they made me promise to visit again soon. It was easy to say yes. They were a fine family that really made me feel welcome.

Chapter 89

When I got back to the house, Cliff was under the kitchen sink, mumbling away about the leaky old pipes.

"It sounds like someone needs a plumber's assistant."

"We need new pipes. I've been patching these for years. Hand me that wrench."

I handed him the tool, took off my watch, put it on the counter and got down next to him. He wrestled with the elbow joint for a minute, then said:

"Put on the hot water."

I reached up, turned the knob and heard a click that I assumed was the pilot light of the water heater starting the system. Suddenly there was a loud, deafening boom, the floor blew up under us, driving Cliff's head into the bottom of the sink. I flew up, then fell back, shaken. Except for a big splinter in my leg and a ringing in my ears, I didn't seem badly hurt. Flames rushed up from the basement and covered Cliff, who was just lying there. I pulled him away from the gaping hole in the floor and fell down from the effort when my leg wouldn't support my weight. I beat out most of the flames on him and yelled:

"Cliff! Cliff! Get up! We've got to get out of here."

He didn't respond and I looked at him more closely. His head was covered in blood flowing from a deep gash. The flames were getting closer, so I got to my knees and crawled towards the door to the backyard, dragging him with me. The floor was burning under us and I could feel my flesh cooking as I kept pulling Cliff's unresponsive body. I got us to the door and watched the skin peel off my hand as I turned the knob. I got the door open, pulled Cliff down the steps and away from the house. I tried to put out the flames that were still burning on his clothes and that's the last thing I remembered.

I woke up in the hospital, groggy, achy, covered in bandages. Grizzly and the three graces were sitting by my bed.

"Cliff." I croaked. "How's Cliff?"

"Not good," Grizzly whispered. "He has a serious head injury, a collapsed lung and third degree burns."

"I've got to see him," and I tried to get up, but Zoey pushed me down gently.

"You're not going anywhere. You've got second degree burns all over your body, a leg wound and you inhaled a lot of smoke. Take it easy until the doctor says you can get up."

"What happened?" Grizzly asked.

"We were under the sink, fixing a water pipe. Cliff told me to put on the hot water… There was an explosion that knocked us down… He wasn't moving and the fire was all around us, so I dragged him outside… Is he going to make it?"

Grizzly shook his head. "I don't think so."

Tears poured out of my eyes. I started coughing, couldn't catch my breath and passed out. When I woke up, Lucy was sitting next to me, eyes red, face so pale she looked like a ghost.

"He's dead, Mike. Cliff is dead."

"No. No. I'm sorry. I tried to save him."

"I know. He hit his head so hard he was probably brain dead instantly. You're a hero for trying to save him."

"Don't say that! If I saved him I'd be a hero."

"Nobody could have saved him," and she sobbed brokenly and I cried with her.

The next few days were torture mentally and physically. I kept thinking it was my fault that I couldn't save him. The three graces stayed with me day and night. They made sure I kept drinking water and wouldn't let me scratch when the cream they put on my burns itched constantly. Visitors came to my room, friends, surfers, Mr. Corliss. I was sullen and unresponsive to everyone. Zoey appointed herself my guardian, with Vicki and Carrie's help and shooed people out after a few minutes.

"He's too exhausted to talk," she told everyone.

The day of the funeral, Grizzly brought a wheelchair to my room. The graces helped me put on a robe and slippers. I asked if we could stop at the house so I could get some clothes.

"The house is gone." Grizzly replied. "It burned down completely."

"Oh."

"The Fire Marshal said the fire was probably caused by a leaking propane cylinder," he told me. "The vapor must have drifted across the floor to the pilot light of the water heater and exploded. That old house went up like a torch."

I sat in the wheelchair in a daze during the funeral service at the chapel, then at the cemetery. Hundreds of surfers had shown up and some of them ritually burned a surfboard. I couldn't decide if it was a fitting tribute to a great surfer, but it made me cry. Lots of them consoled me, but I didn't feel any better. The ceremony was finally over and only a few of us lingered by the grave site. Lucy kissed me goodbye.

"I couldn't stay here anymore. I'm going to San Francisco. If you ever get there, come see me," and she was gone.

Grizzly and the graces took me back to the hospital and I thanked them. I curled into a fetal ball, desperate to shut out the world. A few minutes later an insistent finger kept poking me in the back and Zoey said firmly:

"Come back to life, Mike. You'll be out of here in a few days and you'll have to figure out where to go. We'll help you."

I didn't want to deal with anything. I just wanted to escape from all decision making, but part of me realized I was lucky to be alive. I knew from now on I'd have to get along without Cliff somehow.

The next day, Grizzly and the graces put me in a wheelchair and took me to the beach. Hundreds of surfers had gathered to say farewell to Cliff. Lots of his friends and former competitors were flown in by the tour, including Davey. My head wasn't clear yet, so it barely registered that Davey was here.

Grizzly put me in a small boat and we went out to where a group of former world champions were going to do the memorial paddle out ceremony. They formed a circle, clasped hands, praised Cliff, then yelled and hooted. They were quiet for a minute, then pointed their surfboards to the sky, then paddled ashore. They waved to me as we went in and ignored the crowd onshore.

Friends and strangers kept coming to me expressing their regrets. The graces and Grizzly shielded me, so all I had to do was nod. The surfer's elaborate ceremony in the water was media news, with local and network tv cameras taping every minute. When they tried to interview me the graces wouldn't let them get close. I was too weak and exhausted to appreciate the tribute from so many to a former champion. Davey understood I was out of it and told the graces he'd be in touch. When they took me back to the hospital it was finally sinking in. Cliff was gone. Davey had to fly back to the Philippines in the morning, so I didn't get to see him. I felt badly about that. One more guilt trip.

Chapter 90

The day I was discharged from the hospital, Grizzly took me outside in a wheelchair where the graces were waiting and asked:

"Do you want to stay with me and Megan for a while?"

"No, thanks, Grizzly."

"How about crashing with the surfers?"

"No. I need a place of my own, so I can figure out what to do. I still have a little money so I'd like to rent an apartment on the beach. Do you know anyplace?"

Before he could answer, Zoey said:

"We're going to help you find a place," and she helped me into her car.

They took me to see a few places and one of them, a furnished three room apartment that looked out at the ocean, for $550 a month, was acceptable. The landlady, an older, grumpy woman, Mrs. Paladino, wanted two months security and one month rent in advance. Vicki talked her into one month's security. I said I'd pay her after I went to the bank and got new checks. Zoey briefly explained what happened to me and when she heard about the fire she became much friendlier.

I started making a list of what I'd need, clothes, a cellphone, a replacement motorcycle license, a laptop, an IPad, other items. I realized it would cost a lot and I had less then $3,000 in the bank, so I needed to earn money.

I borrowed Zoey's cellphone and called Grizzly.

"We'll open the shop tomorrow and try to run it without…" My voice choked and I couldn't say his name.

"No can do." he replied. "The sheriff sealed the shop, because Cliff died without a will. He called it intestate. The place'll go to his nearest relative, a cousin somewhere up north."

"So I'll talk to him and see if he'll let us run the shop."

"The cousin just wants the inventory sold and nothing more to do with it."

"It's worth a try. Maybe we can buy the inventory and keep the place going."

"It'll take $10,000 or $12,000 to buy the stock. Besides, Cliff didn't own the building. It's a rental. The landlord said he doesn't want a surf shop. He plans to rent to some kind of fancy boutique."

"So that's the end of Wave Length," and I felt the last piece of security fly out of my life.

"I want to get my surfboards," I stated.

"I'll ask the sheriff to let us get them in the morning. Some other bad news," he said softly. "The parents cancelled the Saturday karate class and some of the surfing lessons cancelled. Donna's teaching the rest. The evening karate class is waiting for you to come back, so you'll have that money."

"Thanks, Grizzly. You've been great."

"De nada, amigo… Oh. Big Bill said he's got a job for you, if you're interested."

"I'll go see him as soon as I get some clothes and settle into the apartment."

"Just let me know if you need anything," and he disconnected.

Zoey drove me to the bank, where I got temporary checks and a credit card. My account was down to $2,839.61, and $1,100 would go to my new landlady, so I had to deal with money right away. The graces took me shopping and helped me buy some basic clothes, jeans, t shirts, underwear, socks, sneakers a bathing suit and a light jacket. They drove me to the Motor Vehicle Bureau and I got a temporary license. Then we did some food shopping, mostly canned and frozen stuff, that we dropped off at my new home. Then they took me to see Big Bill and left me there. I could get back to the apartment by myself. I thanked them for all they did for me and they hugged me, careful not to touch my still unhealed burns.

Although I knew it wasn't his fault that I had to leave the boat, I guess part of me unfairly blamed him, I had been avoiding him, which wasn't right, because he had always been good to me.

"I can't tell you how sorry I am about Cliff," he murmured, which brought tears to my eyes.

I took a deep breath and resolved to work harder at self-control.

"Thanks, Bill. I know how close you were."

"Not as close as you, but we were good friends… Now that the shop is closed, would you like to work in the yard after school? I can pay you $10 an hour."

I though it over and it seemed like a good deal, at least until I decided what to do with my messed-up life.

"Sure, Bill. Sounds good."

"One other thing. A couple of nights a week would you make a quick check of some of the big boats to be sure no one's living aboard illegally?"

"I can do that."

"When do you want to start?"

"How about next Monday? That'll give me a few more days for my burns to heal."

"Glad to have you here, Mike. You can take time in the afternoon for your surfing lessons."

"Thanks, Bill."

Chapter 91

Ten days after getting out of the hospital, my burns were healed, except for a few spots on my left hand, I returned to school. It was a very strange experience. It felt like I had been gone for a long time and somehow it didn't seem to matter as much. Some of the kids wouldn't meet my eyes, others were too solicitous, wanting to know what I was going through. Only the surfers treated me the same, ready to talk or leave me alone, but always looking out for me. I sort of functioned on automatic pilot, until I got to Mr. Corliss' class. He didn't say anything, but I knew he was watching me. He took me aside after class.

"I know you suffered a tremendous loss and are hurting, but you've got to start rebuilding your life."

I nodded because it was easier to agree than talk. What did he know about what I lost? But as if he was reading my mind, he said:

"Cliff and I talked about you several times. I didn't know him well, but I know how much he loved you…"

I burst out crying and he patted my shoulder comfortingly.

"…At the moment, everything that was stable seems to be gone, but this can make you stronger. You're the same capable person before all this happened. You still have friends who look out for you. All you have to do is hold on for six or seven months and you can start a new life at San Diego U. The Orsinis invited you to spend the summer with them, before school starts."

Although I was still racked with guilt at not saving Cliff and I didn't want to hear anything positive, what Mr. Corliss said forced me to accept that I wasn't alone. I wiped my eyes, repeated my vow for self-control and replied to Mr. Corliss:

"Thanks for telling me that… I've been real down on myself and forgot there were still good things happening."

"Charlie assured me you're in, no matter how the rest of the term goes."

That was reassuring, because I wasn't sure how I felt about my other classes now. Then he gave me a laptop, but I didn't cry.

"I know you lost everything in the fire, so this'll let you keep working."

"Thanks, Mr. C. You're a good friend."

"Glad to do it, Mike."

After school I went to the marina and was glad to see Big Bill. We walked through the yard and talked about what boats needed what kind of work and set some priorities.

"There's nothing urgent, so you don't have to knock yourself out. I'll let you know if anything changes so we have to reschedule. I really want you here because you're a positive presence and I feel better when you're in the yard."

"Thanks, Bill… What's happening with the ketch?"

"The new owner is taking it north next week on the auxiliary motor. That is if she doesn't sink when we put her in the water. I told him she needed some work, but he inspected her and he knows best."

"If she sinks and I haul her out, do I get salvage rights?"

He grinned evilly. "Only if the owner goes down with the ship."

I laughed for the first time since… And began to accept that I could go on.

I spoke to the cousin about running the shop, but he refused. When I asked if I could take one of Cliff's boards as a memento he instantly agreed. It was a terrible feeling going into the shop, not seeing Cliff and knowing I wouldn't come in here again. Under the watchful eyes of a deputy sheriff I took my two boards and Cliff's favorite, a sleek blue and yellow hybrid that he used all the time. Then I said goodbye to Wave Length, the place and the man that changed my life.

I went to the beach for the karate class and everyone swarmed me, hugging, patting, insisting on inspecting raw body parts. Greetings finally over, I started the class and it was the first normal thing I did, since… Later I kept looking for Cliff as I surfed. Not seeing him made me finally accept that he was gone. Grizzly and Donna stayed close to me. Were they worried I'd commit suicide by surfboard? When the next big wave came in, I rode it backwards, grinning like a maniac, until I fell off. They gaped at me as if I had two heads.

"It's alright, guys. I'm going forward now," and they grinned, relieved that I wasn't going nuts. Just before we said goodnight, Donna told me about our surfing lessons.

"More then half quit after the shop closed. You still have three regulars and I have two. Grizzly and I passed the word that we want more lessons. So will the surfers. You can have mine if you want them. I live at home and don't need the money as much as you do now."

"Keep them, Donna. Who knows. Maybe we'll rebuild the lesson business. I'm making enough money to manage. See you in the morning."

Chapter 92

Over the next few weeks, I got used to the changes in my life. I submerged into the surfer's group at school and the kids gradually ignored me. I only stood out in Computer Science, where Mr. Corliss always pushed me to do more and better. Work at the marina was usually painting and minor repairs and Big Bill was always easy going. There was one unpleasant incident when I checked a big boat that was not supposed to be occupied. I took the old rowboat out and when I got there, two men came to the ladder and demanded to know what I wanted. I briefly considered going aboard and kicking their asses, then decided It wasn't worth the effort. Instead I went back to the marina. On the way I called the sheriff and reported a boat burglary in progress, with the exact location. Then I called Bill and told him what happened. He rushed to the marina and got there in time to watch the show. Twenty minutes later, half a dozen law enforcement boats, and a helicopter, raced up, sirens blaring, and arrested the men. They hauled the men, who were handcuffed behind their backs and cursing the cops, not too gently to police cars, where sheriff and local police argued who would get them. Bill and I were entertained and I patted myself on the back for avoiding unnecessary trouble.

I had settled into the apartment. Though it would never be home, it wasn't uncomfortable and the front room looked out at the ocean. That was the best thing about the place. One bonus was that Mrs. Paladino was hard of hearing, and I had a private entrance, if I ever wanted to bring a girl there. My money situation had stabilized. Between Big Bill paying me $150 a week, getting $90 a week for surfing lessons and $110 a week for karate class, I paid my bills and expenses and was able to buy an IPad. I wouldn't bother with a camera, unless I got a video production job.

I took Grizzly and Donna to dinner at Wally's, a little thank you for their support and caring. Frank was happy to see me and complained that I didn't come in often enough. He raved about Tommy's improvement in school and thanked me for motivating him. Just before we left I spoke to Frank.

"I'd like to ask a favor."

"Anything."

"I lost all my videos in the fire. Can you ask Carl for copies of all the ads I made for him."

"Sure. I'll ask my friend at the tv station for copies of the Wally ads and the surfing tournament ads."

I couldn't believe how easy it might be to get the videos back. I could make a reel, in case I had a prospective video job.

"Thanks, Frank. That'll really help."

"Glad to do it. I'm still working on some people to make ads. I'll talk to Carl the next time he's in and find out if he wants more ads. I'll keep you posted."

This was a good reminder that I may have lost a lot, but I still had friends who cared about me and wanted to help.

My good spirits finally began to reemerge and it showed in everything I did. When we finished karate one evening, Donna leaned over and whispered:

"Glad to have you back."

I kissed her on the cheek and Tommy teased:

"Mike's got a girlfriend."

I rubbed my knuckles in his head and said:

"She's not my girlfriend, squirt."

"Why not? Don't you like her?"

"Of course I do. She's a great girl. But she doesn't like guys."

"What do you mean?"

"She likes girls."

"Ooh. What's wrong with her?"

I grabbed him, which scared him.

"Nothing's wrong with her. And don't you forget that. She's my friend and she's been good to you. Always respect her."

He was shaken up by my abrupt anger, but said softly:

"Sorry, Mike. I was stupid."

I put my arm around him, then I put my other arm around Donna, and said:

"Let's surf."

The surf shop was finally gone and it would take time to get used to not seeing it every time we ran, surfed, did karate. I briefly considered moving our activities further down the beach, but it wasn't practical if we wanted to maintain our surfing lessons and possibly get new ones, or old one's back. The new owner of the ketch finally moved the boat and I was in the marina that day and helped put her in the water. I watched her chug off and a lot of my memories went with her. She was my first home. Big Bill and I stood there for a few minutes and watched her move out of sight.

"How far is she going?" I asked.

He shook his head. "Some small town north of San Diego. If she makes it." I had to laugh at his cynical tone. "It's not my responsibility anymore." We walked back to the office and he said: "By the way. Can you check one of the big boats tonight. The Salty Sally. I saw a light last night and no one's supposed to be on board."

"Sure. I'll do it once it's dark."

Chapter 93

It was a dark, moonless Southern California night, perfect for me to make my cautious approach to the large yacht moored in the outer area of the Imperial Beach marina, to check out the Salty Sally, as Big Bill had asked. My battered old rowboat, propelled by an electric trolling motor, silently cut through the calm water. An inexpensive fishing rod with a cheap reel dangled a line over the side, a standard precaution I adopted after the recent confrontation with two men, to allay suspicion that I was checking on anyone illegally living on a boat. Some people knew that the night watchman, old Tom, rarely walked around so the odds of discovery were remote. The only possibility of them getting caught was the farfetched coincidence of a county sheriff's boat prowling at night, instead of chasing jet-skiers, or ticketing noisy drunks in power boats.

I pulled alongside the 'Salty Sally', which was at least 100' long, careful not to bump the side and put out a well-worn rubber fender in case the current moved the rowboat. I already confirmed there were no lights showing and I listened intently for any sounds of movement. When I was satisfied that all was still, I loosely secured the rowboat to the rail, went up the ladder and stood there quietly to verify I was alone.

I slowly moved to the pilothouse, attuned to any sounds, picked the simple lock and noticed pilferables; binoculars, sunglasses, small electronics, anything of value, that hadn't been stolen. The obvious luxury of the state of the art pilothouse confirmed the good judgment of the suspected squatter. I picked the even simpler lock to the richly appointed salon, checked it for valuables and picked up a lady Rolex watch, then put it in a drawer. I went below, straight to the master stateroom, listened at the door, then picked the simplest lock so far. I slowly pushed the door open, stepped in and a light went on. I stood frozen in place and I saw a beautiful young woman sitting up in bed, with a gun pointing at me. I put on a dumb, sincere expression.

“I’m sorry to have startled you, Ma’am. I’m from the marina. I was checking if there were any intruders on the boat.”

“Sit down,” she ordered, pointing to a seat opposite the bed, “and put your hands on your knees.”

“No need to be alarmed. I’m sorry I disturbed you. I’ll just be going.”

“If you don’t sit, I’ll shoot you somewhere that’s painful, but not crippling.”

My mind raced through options, but there didn’t seem to be any, since my dumb act failed. It was obvious I could try to dash out the door, but the shaky hand that held the automatic pistol with a very large muzzle, warned me that was a poor choice. I sat.

The woman and the pistol stared at me and I tried not to show how frightened I was. Her voice was surprisingly gentle.

“Get in the closet.”

This didn’t sound good so I tried to stall, hoping she might let me go if I didn’t move.

She said pleasantly:

“I can kill you and call the police. I can wound you and call the police. I may decide to let you go… Or I might have a job for you.”

“What kind of job?” I asked, thinking she might talk to me and give me a chance to get away.

“I’ll tell you if that’s what I decide. Now don’t make me tell you again. Get in the closet.”

She pointed with the pistol and gestured to the closet. I stared at her and read the nervousness in her face. I couldn't take a chance on getting a bullet, so I got up and went into the closet.

"Shut it so it clicks," which I did.

I waited tensely until I heard her lock the door, then I moved some clothing out ot the way and sat on the floor.

"Can you breathe?"

I quickly considered faking, but rejected it.

"Yes."

"Good. Make yourself comfortable and be quiet. I'll let you know when I decide what to do with you."

"I prefer not to be shot, please."

She laughed. "We'll see."

I silently cursed myself for getting caught like this. I hoped she was a legitimate tenant, otherwise I was in trouble. I thought about how my life had turned out recently and how I got into this ridiculous situation. The more I thought about it, the angrier I got. I decided to confront her if she didn't let me out soon.

I hadn't lost my temper in a long time, but I was really beginning to simmer and I said in a stressed but controlled voice:

"Miss. Either let me out and we'll talk, or I'm coming through the door and you can shoot me."

"Give me a minute to decide."

"Decide quick."

Chapter 94

I was about to kick the door open when I heard footsteps. The lock clicked and she opened the door. The gun was no longer pointing at me, but was at her side. I could have easily taken it away from her, but I looked her over instead. She was wearing white silk pajamas that clung to her body. It was a very shapely body. She wasn't very tall, maybe 5'2" or 5'3", slim, curvaceous, with dark hair, green eyes, a beautiful face that looked scared.

"Are you going to hurt me?"

"No," I said gently, reining in my anger. "Why don't you put the gun down."

"I'm sorry that I threatened you. I've been afraid to leave the boat and scared to stay here. All I've had to eat for the last few days was minute rice."

"Well you showed a light last night. Do you have any clothes?"

"Clothes?"

"You know. The things you cover your body with when you go outside."

"Oh. Yes."

"Get dressed. I'll wait for you topside and take you to dinner."

"Dinner?"

"Yes. A meal where people eat food."

I was beginning to wonder if she was crazy, or retarded, then gave her the benefit of the doubt. Maybe she really was scared.

"You'll bring me back here?"

"If that's what you want."

"I'll get dressed."

She came up a few minutes later wearing jeans, a sweater and sneakers. I suggested she bring a jacket. She went below and came up a minute later with a windbreaker. I led her to the ladder, helped her into the rowboat and we went ashore. I brought her to my motorcycle, handed her a helmet, got on and started the motor. She got on behind me and the heat of her body raced through me like turning on the oven. I could feel every part of her pressed against me and it felt incredibly sexy.

I rode to Wally's, parked, led her inside, where Frank greeted me happily.

"Hi, Mike. Great to see you. I've got something for you before you leave."

"Thanks, Frank. Is it too late to get a steak for this young lady?"

"Not for you."

He looked at her quizzically and she said:

"I'm Brin," and she stuck out her hand, which he took.

"Any friend of Mike's is welcome." He signaled Paul, "Have the chef put on a steak for Mike's guest. How about you, Mike?"

"Sure."

Frank led us to a table, while Paul went to the kitchen. Luis brought water and bread and we chatted for a minute in Spanish. Paul came back and I asked him to bring a glass of red wine for Brin. Paul brought the wine and water for me.

"Aren't you having wine?"

“I don’t drink.”

“Are you a Mormon?”

I had to smile. “No. I’m in training.”

“For what?”

“I run, do karate and surf.”

“Are you any good?”

“Not bad.”

Luis had been hovering nearby and blurted:

“He’s a great surfer. He could win it all if he wanted to.”

I asked him in Spanish not to brag about me, but he added:

“He’s a great teacher. He kept my kid brother out of the gang life,” and he rushed off to the kitchen.

“You’re very popular here.”

“They’re good friends.”

“Does your father own this place?” She asked sarcastically.

For a moment a flash of rage went through me and I wanted to hit her. She saw that I was angry, and muttered:

“Sorry.”

I was beginning to wonder if I made a mistake taking her off the boat, but just then she

reached out and put a hand on my arm.

“I didn’t mean to annoy you,” and I let it go.

She devoured a basket of bread, drank her wine and I asked Paul for another, ate more bread, a big salad, then gobbled her steak like a famished predator. She actually ate two desserts. On the way out, Frank handed me a small box, grinned and said:

"Surprise."

On the way to the parking lot, Brin asked:

"Are you guys drug dealers?"

I really had to wonder about her.

"These are copies of videos I made for clients. I lost everything in a fire not too long ago."

"You make videos?"

"Among other things. Now I can take you back to the boat, or you can sleep on the couch at my place. Your choice."

She suddenly looked very young. "I'm afraid to go back to the boat. I haven't slept in three days."

I handed her a helmet. "Get on."

Chapter 95

Now that Brin was stuffed with meat, on the ride back to my apartment her body felt even hotter against me then earlier. I had to figure out whether my body temperature changed from the fire, or if I had been away from girls too long.

"You live on the beach. How nice."

There was something in her tone I didn't like, but I wasn't about to apologize for not having a luxury beach house. I was beginning to wonder if I made a mistake bringing her here. I had no idea why I did it, but I was too tired to worry about it now. I pulled out a t-shirt and sweat pants for her, a sheet and blanket for the couch, and said:

"I have to be up early. You're welcome to spend the day here and I'll bring Chinese food for dinner. Help yourself to anything in the kitchen. If anybody comes by, say you're a friend of mine, staying here for a while."

"Who's going to come here?" she asked in a nervous voice.

"I'm not expecting anyone, but some of my surfer buddies might stop by. It's just in case. If you decide to leave, don't go back to the boat in daylight, or you might get arrested. Unless you're up at 6:30, I'll see you tomorrow night."

"What do you do that early?"

"I go to the beach and run, surf, go to school, go to work at the marina, teach karate, surf, then come home."

"You go to college?"

"High school."

"How old are you?"

"Seventeen."

"You're so sure of yourself. I thought you were older. You're just a kid."

"I haven't been a kid for years," I said bitterly.

I had trouble tearing my eyes away from her body. She seemed to pose provocatively no matter what position she was in. The memory of the heat of her body against me sent a rush of desire through me. Part of me knew I just had to reach out for her and she'd come to me. Another part warned me she was a battered bird and not to get involved. I just said:

"Please don't use my toothbrush. Goodnight."

I went to my room and closed the door. I got undressed, put on a pair of warm-up pants and lay there listening to the ocean. Somehow it wasn't the usual reassuring sound that soothed my troubled spirit. It was more ominous, as if it would roll up the beach and wash me away. I suppressed an impulse to go to the kitchen for a drink of water, a pretext to get another look at Brin, and fell asleep.

Brin was snoring away when I left in the morning, looking sweet, innocent, beautiful and vulnerable. 'Don't get involved', I cautioned myself. I had to lug my surfboard to where we started and finished the run, then surfed, one more change to get used to now that the shop was gone. Then I had to bring the board back to the apartment, grab my books and go to school. I kept my other board at the marina, so I didn't have to go home for it after work.

The day would have passed uneventfully, except for the gossip mongering that started during the morning run with Tommy.

"My Dad said you brought a beautiful girl to the restaurant last night. Who is she? A new girlfriend?"

I didn't want to talk about Brin, so I said: "Button it, squirt," but it was too late. The three graces heard him and they wanted to know who she was. Donna and the surfers wanted to know also. Fortunately, Big Bill wouldn't have been interested, except if he knew where I found her. But he wasn't in the rumor network. Even Grizzly wanted to know who she was when we surfed that evening. By the time I headed home, with a big order of Chinese food, I hoped she would be gone, which I already knew would save me a lot of trouble.

Chapter 96

I resisted a silly urge to say 'I'm home', when I unlocked the door. I didn't see Brin. I had a momentary pang of regret that I wouldn't get to explore that tempting body, but it was a relief to know that I had one less problem. I went into the kitchen, started to unpack the food when I heard the bathroom door open. It was Brin.

"I didn't know who it was, so I hid in the bathroom."

"If someone was looking for you, they'd find you there."

"I didn't know what else to do. I had my pistol."

"Did you ever fire it?"

"No."

"Do you know how to fire it?"

"No."

"Then what's the point of having it?"

"It scared you."

I couldn't argue with that and feebly said:

"I'm not experienced with guns… Who's looking for you?"

"I'm not sure."

"What were you doing on the boat?"

"Hiding."

"From who?"

"I'm not sure."

"What do you know?"

"I found my boss dead in the hotel suite where we were staying. I panicked when I saw his body with blood all over the place and took a bus to Chula Vista and went to the boat. It was supposed to be part of my employment deal that I would live on the boat, which our company owned. He was supposed to stock it with food and stuff, but I guess he didn't get a chance…" and she broke down crying.

At least I understood why she was so freaked out. I gave her a minute to pull herself together, then said:

"No one knows you're here. You don't have to worry tonight. Let's eat, then you'll tell me what happened and we'll try to figure out what you should do."

She wiped her eyes, then said in a child-like voice:

"You're really very nice."

I nodded. I heard that before… It was funny. I never wanted to be a bad boy, or a tough guy. I had to fight to survive the trailer and to earn the money to get out of there, but I avoided violence when I could. I reminded myself regularly never to lose my temper. I came close on the boat with Brin. I didn't bother with plates for the food, just opened the cartons and we helped ourselves. Again she ate like there was no tomorrow. When she consumed enough for three surfers, she reached for the fortune cookies and tossed me one.

"Check out your fortune," she said.

"I'll pass. Did you have enough to eat?"

"Yes," and she burped, then giggled.

"Why don't you tell me about you and what you're involved in."

She took a deep breath, then slowly began to talk:

"I graduated from the University of Florida last May and I majored in Computer Science. I got a job in Fort Lauderdale writing software for a travel agency. I lived on a houseboat on the Intercoastal Waterway, which I loved. I met a man at a party, Andy Paulson, who told me he had a franchise for the West Coast, to develop a gaming circuit…"

"What's that?"

"Professional gaming players tour cities and compete for prize money. They play in small arenas and auditoriums and take challenges from local gamers…" I nodded I understood and she continued: "He wanted me to write software programs that would run the circuit and develop Apps that would attract gamers. He offered me 15% of the company, but I didn't jump at it. He upped the offer to 20% and added that I could live on the company yacht, anchored in Chula Vista, California. He promised big money and it was exciting to think of living on a yacht, so I said 'yes'."

"Did you check his references? Check out the company? Ask enough questions to find out what you were getting into?"

She glared at me for a moment, indignant that I asked the obvious questions that she should have asked. Then she got a pathetic look, and whispered:

"I was in a dead end job, with no idea what to do and the man was giving me a way out. It's easy to see that I should have dealt with it a lot differently, not taken the job, but I did. Do you want to hear the rest?"

"Sure. Go on."

"Andy told me to give notice to my job and he'd send me an airline ticket to Los Angeles, where we'd stay in a hotel suite until the yacht was ready. A car service met me at the airport and took me to a posh hotel. The suite was big and luxurious. I never stayed in a place like that before. I was eager to start work on the gaming circuit app, but Andy kept putting it off. Finally he told me he was a gambler and owed a lot of money. The only way he could pay his debts and get to work on the gaming circuit was if I created a gambling app that could be used for an online gambling site that would cheat the players of their money. This wasn't what I was supposed to do and it really disturbed me. I told him I had to think about it and went for a walk. After a while I decided to tell him I wouldn't do it. When I got back to the hotel I found him… Dead on the floor. I grabbed my things and got out of there. I took a bus here, got some old fisherman to take me out to the yacht and hid there. That was five days ago. I found the gun in a drawer and I felt a little better knowing it could scare people…"

"It wouldn't have scared the people who killed your boss. Do they know who you are?"

"I don't think so."

"Did you register at the hotel?"

"No. I just stayed there for a few days."

"Did you order room service and sign your name?"

"No. Andy took care of it."

"Did you sign any kind of corporate papers, or documents?"

"No. Andy said they were being prepared. What's with all the questions? You sound like a detective."

"I'm trying to find out if the police, or Andy's not so friendly friends, know who you are."

"I don't think so."

"Does anyone besides me know you were on the boat?"

"No. But I guess the police could find out because the corporation owns it."

"Your corporation doesn't own it. It was rented for three months that would have been up a few weeks ago. It was paid for with a check made out to cash from a Canadian bank, and the check bounced. There was no name on it, so it probably can't be traced."

"Is that important?"

"If the police or gangsters are looking for you, and you're traceable, they might find me. I wouldn't like that."

"Do you want me to leave?"

"Maybe. We'll talk about it tomorrow night."

I got my computer and did an online search for killings in a Los Angeles hotel five days ago. I found a short article about a former gambler who was shot to death in his hotel suite. The police were looking for a woman who lived with him. The description was so vague that it could have been anyone. I showed it to her, then said:

"That's the guy you lived with, right?"

"I didn't live with him. We shared the suite. I never slept with him."

"Whatever. But that's him?"

"Yes."

"Unless you're not telling me something, I don't think they know who you are."

"I told you everything… You don't think I'm very bright, do you?"

"How old are you?"

"Twenty-two."

"I don't know you well enough to know how smart or stupid you are, but you're naïve and inexperienced. I'm going to bed. I'll see you tomorrow night, unless you leave during the day… By the way. I got you a toothbrush."

I heard her murmur 'thanks', as I went to my room. I got undressed, put on warm up pants, got into bed and lay there listening to the ocean. I wasn't sure if Brin was in trouble, or was bringing trouble, but I guess I was involved. I fell asleep, uncertain if I wanted her gone when I came home tomorrow night.

Chapter 97

Just before I left in the morning, I remembered that when I told Big Bill no one was on the boat, I mentioned I'd do an inventory. He gave me the list and the pistol was on it, but the lady Rolex wasn't. I decided to give the watch to Brin as some compensation for her trouble, but not tell her yet. I went to the couch, called her, said her name, but when she didn't wake up I shook her gently.

"Brin. Wake up."

"What? What is it?" She mumbled groggily.

"I have to do an inventory of the Salty Sally and I need the pistol."

"Alright. Here," and she took it out of her handbag and handed it to me. "Do you know how to use it?"

"No," I replied. "If I had to, I would have Googled it and learned how."

"I didn't have a computer."

"Then you should have looked at it carefully and figured out how to use it."

"You're infuriating," and she pulled a pillow over her head.

Before I ran, I went to the marina and put the pistol in a secure place. I tried to put Brin out of my mind, but I kept seeing her very appealing body. I guess I was a little distracted all day, because the graces kept asking me what was wrong, both at the beach and at school. I just said I had things on my mind and let it go at that. After school I went to the Salty Sally, put the pistol in a drawer, did the inventory, then took the rolex. After the evening surfing I didn't bother getting food, since there was plenty of Chinese food from the night before.

Brin was still there when I got home and I was surprised that I was glad to see her. She had combed her hair, put on lipstick and was wearing a light blue dress that clung to her body. Maybe it wasn't a surprise that I was glad to see her. When she heard me at the door she heated soup and served it a minute later, while the rest of the food was heating on the stove, or in the microwave. At least she was making herself useful. We were just sitting down to talk after dinner, when there was a knock on the door.

Brin almost panicked. "Who is it?" she whispered.

I shrugged, went to answer and she ran for the bathroom. It was the three graces. They each kissed me hello, in a weird, formal way, considering I saw them in the morning and at school.

"We were afraid you were feeling depressed," Zoey said.

"Thanks for caring," I replied. "I'm fine. I've just got a lot on my mind."

"We know that," Vicki stated. "Some of that is our fault for pressuring you to write a show for us."

I shook my head. "It's not a pressure, just a problem I haven't solved yet."

"Well we have," Carrie announced triumphantly. "Let's do a reality beach show."

I looked at them blankly for a moment, then said slowly:

"I don't want to disappoint you, but it would still have to be a drama, comedy or documentary, otherwise what would be interesting after the first day?"

"Oh, poo," Vicki muttered. "You're right. And we thought we had a great idea."

"It could be, if there was an interesting story," I consoled.

"Do you think so?" Zoey asked hopefully.

"Maybe. We'll have to have a story conference."

I guess Brin had been listening from the bathroom, for just then she came out and three pairs of eyes clicked on her.

"Who's that?" Zoey asked.

"This is Brin," and I pointed one at a time. "This is Zoey, Vicki and Carrie."

"Are you living with Mike?" Zoey demanded.

The hostility was obvious and Brin smiled sweetly.

"Yes. Is that a problem?"

The graces looked at each other and didn't know how to respond. We had just been exceptionally good friends lately and even though they were desirable and took good care of me, they were dating other guys. Vicki chose not to let an argument break out, and said:

"We'll have the story conference another time. See you in the morning," and she went out the door, followed by Zoey and Carrie.

"Friends of yours?" Brin asked coolly.

"Very special friends."

"Do you want to tell me about it?"

"No."

"What did what's her name mean by a story conference?"

"Vicki. Among other things, they've been actresses in my videos and tv commercials."

"They are beautiful," she admitted. "Which one was your girlfriend?"

"Let's not talk about them now. We've got other things to settle. Do you want to stay here until you decide what to do?"

"Can I go back to the boat?"

"No."

"Well I have no money, so I'd like to stay for awhile, if it's alright with you."

"Alright. I'll ask Mrs. Paladino if you can stay here. I may have to pay some extra rent."

"Can you afford it?"

"Yes. If you stay in Chula Vista you'll have to get a job. I have some friends who might help."

"What if Mrs. Paladino says no?"

"Then if you want to stay together, we'll find another place, or I'll pay for a room for you, until you get a job."

"You'd do that for me?"

"As long as you don't get me killed."

She laughed. "That's funny."

I hoped it was.

"Something else. I understand you're afraid. But if the police or gangsters trace you here, hiding in the bathroom won't save you." She nodded and I added: "You're welcome to run with us, learn to surf, learn karate, but you have to start doing something."

"Can I use your computer?"

"Sure… I'll come back after school and talk to Mrs. Paladino."

"Do you want me to stay?"

I looked at her and accepted that I wanted her.

"Yes. Goodnight."

Chapter 98

I was having an incredibly erotic dream. A beautiful, sexy woman was pressed tight against me, her thighs gripping my thighs as she rubbed against me, building herself to orgasm, while squeezing my cock hard. I woke up with Brin mounting me and sliding my cock inside her. She was wet, taut and moved up and down, faster and faster, moaning like an animal. Suddenly she opened with a loud cry, shuddered and came in a rush. I swelled and came, shooting into her and she came again with a yell, then collapsed on top of me. We lay there panting and sweaty and I fell asleep.

I was alone when I woke up and it took a minute for me to be certain that our wild joining really happened. I took a quiet shower, grabbed an energy bar, then headed for the door, serenaded by her snoring. I really enjoyed the run, particularly with the three graces, who looked both confused and annoyed at my cheerful smile, but they didn't say anything. I felt so good while surfing that I did some silly tricks, like a handstand and a back flip, which startled my buddies, who usually saw me finding serenity with the wave. Vicki said:

"You've been acting like a doofus all morning. I bet someone fucked your brains out last night."

"I'm just enjoying myself," I replied innocently.

They watched me walk off, trying to figure out what was going on. They looked at me in the same way at school, but I avoided being alone with them, so there wouldn't be any kind of discussion. Mr. Corliss remarked that it was the first time in a while that I didn't look woeful and gave me some .Net exercises. Instead of going to the marina after school, I went home and asked Mrs. Paladino if it was alright for a friend to stay with me for a while. She was very agreeable, for another $100 a month, which I thought was a bargain to get Brin.

Brin was very happy that she was a legitimate tenant and didn't have to hide from the landlady. She kissed me passionately, then led me to the bedroom where we had gentle, but exciting sex. I took a quick shower, dried and I had to resist pouncing on her as she lay in bed, with the sheet clinging to her body.

"Here," I said and gave her the lady rolex.

"What's this for?"

"So you don't have to have sex with me."

She grinned like a wicked imp, slowly pulled the sheet down until her breasts were showing and whispered:

"It's nice to be given a rolex…"

Before I could reply, she reached up and pulled me to her…" I haven't been with a man for more than two years. I wanted you from the first night you took me off the boat, but I was too scared to admit it."

I ran my hand over her sleek side.

"That's nice to know. The watch will give you some security if you decide to take off."

"I'd like to stay, if you want me."

"I'll tell you later. Now I have to go to work." I handed her my key. "Here's some money. Go to the avenue and get a key made for yourself, then do some food shopping. If you want to come to the karate class later, or get a surfing lesson, wear a bathing suit."

"I don't have one."

I gave her more money. “Get something practical. You’ll be working out in it.”

“Would your other friends be envious if I wore a string bikini?”

“They don’t have to envy anybody. See you later,” and I left before this could go any further.

Chapter 99

Brin showed up for karate in a t-shirt and shorts, but slipped them off and was wearing a modest two-piece bikini. She had a dynamite body and it was an effort to tear my eyes away from her succulent flesh. I assigned Tommy to give her the introductory lesson. He was immediately besotted with her and Donna smacked him across the head.

"Get to work, squirt."

Abashed, he showed her the beginner's white belt form. I watched her for a minute and she caught on quickly and seemed to be enjoying herself. I had Tommy give Brin the introductory surfing lesson, and once again she caught on quickly. Tommy had her in the water in fifteen minutes and she actually got a ride on the third try, a very good accomplishment. Afterwards, we walked home, arms around each other, and I remarked:

"You did well on land and sea," which made her laugh. "I was pleasantly surprised at your confidence."

"It was the first time in a week that I wasn't scared out of my wits. I had a great time. Can I do it again?"

"Sure. You can run with us in the morning if you want to get up early."

"And you surf after that?"

"Yes."

"I'd love to."

"Did you ever run before?"

"I jogged a couple of times a week."

"This is a little faster. It's very important that you don't overdo it the first few times out and injure yourself. You don't have to compete with anybody, or impress anyone."

"Not even you?" She joked.

"You're surprising me with your attitude. Everybody runs a different distance, so start with an easy pace and stop if you feel strained or tired. The three graces may tease you…"

"Is that what you call them?"

"…Yes. Because they're smart, athletic, talented and beautiful."

"I don't think they like me."

"They're my good friends, so please get along with them."

"I've been trying to figure out which one you slept with."

I ignored that and said:

"I suggest you take it easy for a few days, just exercise and get your head ready for a new phase of your life."

"I'm confused right now. I could go back to school and get a graduate degree."

"Maybe. If that's what you want. But it seems you have no obligations and are free to decide what you want to do."

"I owe you for helping me."

"There's no bill for my services. You can leave whenever you want. No strings attached."

"Do you want me to stay?"

I had been gently caressing her sleek hips as we walked and she had been stroking my back.

"I want you so much if there weren't people on the beach I'd throw you down and fuck you right here."

"Then let's hurry home," she whispered in a husky voice.

Just as we got to the house, she said:

"I'm having trouble keeping my hands off you."

"Me too," and we rushed inside.

Chapter 100

We made love four times during the night, each time different, from almost rough coupling, to tender consideration. We didn't get much sleep and we quickly made love when we awoke, but I was exhilarated and eager to run and surf, and Brin looked pretty perky. The three graces saw us approaching from a distance, arms around each other, carrying surfboards, happy and bouncy. They gaped at me, glared at Brin, but didn't say anything. This was the second time they were speechless about seeing us together, a rare occurrence for them.

Tommy took charge of Brin and monitored her closely during the run, stopped her a little short of a mile and praised her efforts. He told her to walk back slowly to where we left the surfboards, then continued his run. I had been watching her whenever the graces weren't staring at me and I was impressed with her first outing. The graces were only up to a mile and a half and they'd been running for a while.

If the graces were startled by Brin's arrival for the run, they were shocked when she hit the water with the rest of us. Zoey paddled to me and asked:

"Is she going to be with us regularly?"

"Yes. Brin did karate yesterday."

Zoey blushed and stammered:

"I know we've been neglecting some things lately…"

"You don't owe me any explanation. I'll never forget how you took care of me when…"

"You know how we feel about you."

"I hope you know how I feel about the three of you… We should have that story conference soon."

"You still want to work with us?"

"Of course. I always want to work with you."

Zoey talked intently to Vicki and Carrie and by the time we got to shore they thawed considerably towards Brin. They weren't welcoming her with open arms, but they were not unpleasant. Brin and I walked back to the house and we quickly made love. I told her to rest if she planned on karate and surfing later. She grinned mischievously, licked her lips suggestively and I left for school before I was tempted to play hooky. Mr. Corliss remarked that I was looking cheerful for the first time in a while. I couldn't help wondering if I was betraying the memory of Cliff by feeling good, then dismissed the thought. I knew Cliff was permanently welded in my heart.

Tommy came up to me before karate started and said:

"My Dad has to speak to you. Either come to the restaurant for dinner tonight, or phone him."

Just before we surfed, Brin asked who Tommy's Dad was. I told her it was Frank, part owner/manager of Wally's, who she met a few nights ago.

"You have a network. I didn't realize that. You're lucky. I never had one."

"It's gotten smaller lately," I replied bitterly.

She wanted to know what I meant, but I told her I'd tell her another time. When we got to Wally's, Frank hugged me, then demanded:

"Why didn't you give me your new cell number? Carl was trying to reach you and called me frantically. Call him tonight."

"Sorry, Frank. I've been a bit out of it lately."

He smiled gently. “I understand. You know I worry about you. Now call him.”

Brin wanted to know what Frank was referring to, but I said I’d tell her later and I phoned Carl.

“I’ve been trying to reach you for a week. Frank told me what happened to you and I’m sorry for your loss and injuries.”

“Thanks, Carl.”

“I need two new ads. The agency wants to do them for $100,000 each and I don’t like their ideas. Can you do them?”

“I’m sure I could do them for you. We should get together and talk about it.”

“Good. Join me for dinner at the club tomorrow night. 7:30?”

“Sure. See you then.”

Carl had been talking loudly and Brin heard every word.

“Can I go with you to the club?” she asked.

“Another time. This is business.”

“Is it a nice club?”

“It’s the poshest country club between here and Los Angeles. I have a dining room membership. I’ll take you there for dinner soon.”

“I don’t have anything to wear.”

“If I take the job, I’ll buy you a new dress.”

“And if you don’t get it?”

“Then go naked, but wear your rolex.”

She slid her hand on my leg under the table and I got an instant erection.

“I’ll model it for you later,” she murmured.

Chapter 101

Carl was still trying to impress me with the country club, but he was more concerned that I might not do the ads, and he'd have to go with the agency. He babbled away about business in general while we ate, and finally asked me outright:

"Will you do the ads?"

"Sure. We'll go through the usual process, two rough cuts at $5,000 each. Then the final version at $25,000 each. If that's agreeable, have your lawyer do a contract with $10,000 for the rough cuts in advance…"

"How come?"

"I lost some of my equipment in a fire and I have to replace it, so I can get to work. When the rough cuts are approved, $25,000 in advance, the balance on delivery."

"Agreed."

"When do you want them?"

"As soon as possible."

"How about the rough cuts in three weeks, say March 10th, and the final versions by April 10th?"

"Great. The agency would have taken four months. I'll have a check for you tomorrow and I'll send you the contract in a few days."

"Let me give you my new address."

"I heard what happened to you," he said hesitantly. "I'm sorry for your loss."

"Thanks, Carl."

He sounded sincere and I appreciated that. Then, just as I was rethinking my opinion of him, he said, as if the momentary sympathy was over:

"How do you like the club?"

"Is the food better than Wally's?"

I guess I expected a little more sensitivity, or something, and I just said:

"I've got to go."

"Alright. Stop by my office tomorrow."

"See you then."

"Did you enjoy dinner? He asked hopefully, as I was leaving.

"It was fine."

I knew he wanted me to rave about the club and it would have pleased him, but I wasn't the raving type.

I rode home feeling a little bitter about things, hopeful that the recent series of disasters might be over. It looked like I was going to get a big chunk of money soon. That would at least give me a cushion when the next setback happened, which I assumed was inevitable. And there was Brin.

I was already more deeply involved with Brin then any girl before. It was a major effort not to think about her all the time and I had no idea where our relationship was going. I had to smile when I imagined I'd get home and she'd be gone. The only involvement she had here was me and I didn't know how real it was. Now that she thought the threat from the police or gangsters was over, she was as free as a bird and could go anywhere. Well, I could live without her… But I'd sure miss the wild sex we'd been having.

When I opened the door and didn't see her, I felt a pang of loss. Then I shrugged mentally and reminded myself that after losing Cliff I could get along without anyone. I went into the bedroom to change and Brin was lying in bed, posed with the sheet carefully placed to reveal her tantalizing flesh. It was the sexiest pose I ever saw. She moved sensuously and I got an erection. She pointed to it.

"Bring that here."

I walked to her, she unzipped my pants, took out my penis and licked it, watching my reaction. I stood there and she squeezed me hard, then sucked me until I came. I knelt down, slid the sheet off her, licked her breasts, then worked my way down her body, probing with my tongue between her legs, licking or sucking, depending on her moans, until she came with a shudder of pleasure, yelling my name: "Mike. Mike." She pulled me by the hair next to her and we fell asleep in each others arms, me still dressed, she naked.

In the morning I got undressed, shaved and slipped on a bathing suit. Brin was ready to go, so we grabbed our surfboards and headed for the beach in what was already becoming a familiar routine of going with her. Later, the day seemed to drag as I was impatient for school to end so I could go get Carl's check. I asked Mr. Corliss if he minded if I did a quick personal search in Computer Lab and he said it was alright. I looked up professional video cameras and made a list of five models I would be happy with.

I stopped by the marina, told Bill I'd be by later, then went to Carl's office and picked up the check. It was too late to go to the bank and deposit it. Besides. I had decided to change banks. I wasn't sure who to blame for losing all my money, but the bank should have at least been concerned, since their executive recommended the investment.

I went to the camera store and they had some good cameras, but all were more than $5,000, which was a little pricey right now. The salesman showed me a 'slightly used' Sony PXW FS7 4k, that he swore was in perfect condition. I tried it in the store and outside and it seemed to be in excellent working order. He asked $2,500, but settled for $2,000, which I put on my charge card. He promised to take it back for a full refund it it didn't work properly. I had done business with the store for the last two years and I knew they were reasonably honest.

I rode to the marina and did some work for a while. Just before I left, I spoke to Big Bill:

"I need to adjust how much you pay me. I've been working closer to 10 hours a week, rather than 15. My pay should be $100."

"What about the evenings you check on the boats?"

"It's just a couple of hours."

"Leave is as it is for now."

"Thanks, Bill… I need to get insurance for my camera and laptop. How do I do it?"

"Call my agent and ask him. Here's his number."

I called from the office and they gave the call to someone who handled home insurance. They had a policy for home coverage of $25,000 that was pretty cheap and I requested it, saying I'd put a check in the mail in the morning. I had learned a little lesson when all my possessions went up in smoke. Brin was mildly curious about the camera and we made love, then went to the beach for karate and surfing.

Chapter 102

I didn't say anything about the new video project in the morning. At lunchtime, I ducked out of school and opened a checking account at a new bank. They gave me temporary checks and a Visa card, so I was ready for business. When I got back to school the graces were just leaving the cafeteria and I was tempted to tell them they'd be working as actresses again. They were escorted, as usual, by several surfers, so I decided to wait until morning. Later I asked Grizzly if he and Megan wanted to do another commercial and he responded 'yes' eagerly.

That evening I told Brin about the new ad project, but for some reason I didn't mention money. I asked her if she wanted to work as a production assistant, for which she'd be paid.

"You don't have to pay me," she said. "You've done so much for me already."

"This is a professional job. Everyone gets paid."

"Alright, boss. Just tell me what to do."

"Right now it's time for some cheap sex."

"I can do that."

In the morning, the three graces were stretching as they got ready for the run. They greeted me warmly and Brin politely, so they were at least getting used to her. I took them aside and said in a mock-solemn voice:

"We'll have to postpone our story conference for a while."

"Why?" Vicki demanded. "Have you lost interest in us?"

"Never. But I have a priority project and I'll be busy auditioning actresses."

Zoey let out a squeal and jumped on me.

"You're doing a new video."

Vicki and Carrie jumped on me, knocking me to the sand and Vicki said:

"We're ready to audition. What do you want us to do? Sing? Dance? Recite Shakespeare?.. Be sexy?"

All the while they were sitting on me, pulling and pushing my arms and legs, and Carrie kept asking:

"When do we start? When do we start?"

"You can start by getting off your director, or I'll really have open auditions."

They pulled me to my feet, dusted the sand off, smacking me extra hard on the butt. Then Vicki said coyly:

"How's that, Mister Director? We really took a cue."

I looked at Grizzly and shrugged mock-weakly. "Actresses."

"You're an awful tease," Zoey chided. "Do we have a schedule?"

"I have some writing to do, but I guess early next week."

They surrounded me, petted and kissed me and Vicki crooned:

"You're our favorite director. We'll do anything to please you," and she stressed 'anything'.

I couldn't help grinning at these irrepressible beauties.

"Then let's run," I said, and off they went, scampering and frolicking like playful children.

Brin had only seen them acting cold and haughty, but couldn't help smiling at their exuberant spirit.

The graces were even more amusing at school. They fussed over me a lunchtime, bringing my tray, feeding me and wiping my lips with a napkin. The surfers thought it was hilarious. One of them, Billy 'Chromo', nicknamed for all the chrome on his jeep, wanted to know what was going on.

"I hypnotized them last night," I replied, "and now they have to do my bidding."

"Yes, master," Zoey said in a mechanical voice. "We are your slaves."

"Then let us go to class."

"Yes, master," they all murmured.

On the way out, Billy asked urgently:

"Mike. Can you teach me to hypnotize girls?"

"Sorry, Billy. It's a family secret."

"Aw, shit. I could really use it."

I just shook my head and walked away.

Grizzly confirmed that Megan wanted to do the commercial, so I had a cast, a crew and money. Things were definitely improving. That night I talked to Brin about what I'd be doing.

"I'm going to be busy writing scripts for the next few days, but I'd like to sit down with you on Sunday and discuss what you'd like to do in the near future."

"Are you getting tired of me already?" she asked huskily, and that led to lovemaking. Later I told her:

"You'll have to make some decisions what you want to do, otherwise you'll just hang out and get frustrated and unhappy."

“Well you’ve made sure I’m not frustrated.”

“I’m serious,” I said with a little annoyance. “You don’t want to drift.”

“Sorry. I didn’t mean to irritate you. I have been thinking about what I want to do. I’ve been doing a lot of research during the day. We can talk about it Sunday… Now it’s time for my favorite director”, and she imitated Zoey, which made me smile, “to get some sleep.”

Chapter 103

On Sunday, the only day we didn't run, do karate, or surf the usual time, I slept late, then surfed with Brin on the beach in front of our house. She had made real progress and was enjoying herself. I gave her an informal lesson, mostly little adjustments that let her ride better. She caught some big waves and was absolutely fearless. She was definitely growing on me.

We came out of the water and sat in the sand, relaxing. I had been working non-stop, so this was a pleasant change. I lay there, content to bask in the sun, with Brin at my side.

"Do you want me to tell you what I'd like to do?" she asked.

"Sure."

"I thought about what I trained for and I don't want to work for Microsoft or Apple. I don't seem the type to come up with a brilliant start-up and I'm not much of a networker. I decided I'd really like to try building a gaming circuit business. There are a lot of questions to be resolved, but I think it could be fun and make money." She waited for my reaction and when I just nodded, she went on. "There seems to be an enormous market for gamers and there have been some successful circuits on the East coast."

"Do you want to go back East?"

"No. I like California, now. And I want to stay with you."

I ran my hand over her body. "That'll be nice."

"Don't do that, or I'll jump your bones right here on the beach," and she kissed me passionately.

I pulled her away. “Alright. I didn’t mean to distract you. Go on.”

She took a deep breath. “There are lots of things I need to learn, but the basics are; I’ll need to raise enough money to operate the business, recruit professional gamers to work the circuit, identify small arenas and large auditoriums to rent…”

“There’s a theater and other spaces in Chula Vista that we can look at.”

“You mean you’ll help me?”

“Sure. It sounds like fun.”

“There are a million details I have to learn about. I don’t know how much anything costs, rentals, equipment, all the other expenses… I’ll have to get a job and start putting money away…”

“We should do a test event to see how everything works. Just to be sure it’s practical.”

“That makes sense. Once I get a job, I’ll make an event budget, so we’ll see how much it costs.”

“I’ll be coming into some money soon, I’ll finance your test.”

“It could cost thousands of dollars.”

“I can manage that.”

“Then we’ll be partners. Fifty-fifty. We’ll set up a corporation and make it official... I have a feeling we’ll have a great future together.”

“There’s something I have to tell you.”

“Just don’t say you’re planning a sex-change operation.”

“No. Nothing like that. I’ll be going to San Diego University in September. I’ve got a four year scholarship to study Computer Science.”

“So we’ll move to San Diego.” she replied sweetly.

I had to smile at her cheerful attitude.

"I'm not sure about living arrangements. I assume I'll be assigned a dorm room, but I don't know if they'll pay for an off campus apartment. I don't think they'll let you live in the dorm with me."

"As long as you want me, we'll work something out."

"I'll only have time in the evenings and on the weekends to work with you."

"That's fine with me."

"Then you've got yourself a partner."

"I know good things will happen for us."

"I hope so. I know you've had some rough times lately. So have I."

"Then we'll make up for them together."

Printed in the USA
CPSIA information can be obtained
at www.ICGtesting.com
CBHW021556041124
16902CB00024B/99

9 789390 202287